Consensus
Organizing

This book is dedicated to Pat Libby

Consensus Organizing

Building Communities
of Mutual Self-Interest

Mike Eichler
San Diego State University

SAGE Publications
Thousand Oaks ■ London ■ New Delhi

For information:

Sage Publications, Inc.
2455 Teller Road
Thousand Oaks, California 91320
E-mail: order@sagepub.com

Sage Publications Ltd.
1 Oliver's Yard
55 City Road
London EC1Y 1SP
United Kingdom

Sage Publications India Pvt. Ltd.
B-42, Panchsheel Enclave
Post Box 4109
New Delhi 110 017 India

Printed in the United States of America

Library of Congress Cataloging-in-Publication Data

Eichler, Mike.
Consensus organizing : building communities of mutual self-interest / Mike Eichler.
    p. cm.
Includes bibliographical references and index.
ISBN 1-4129-2659-9 or 978-1-4129-2659-1 (pbk.)
   1. Community organization—United States. 2. Social action—United States.
3. Consensus (Social sciences)—United States. 4. Community development—United States.
I. Title.

HM766.E53 2007
322.4′40973—dc22

                          2006023878

This book is printed on acid-free paper.

06 07 08 09 10   10 9 8 7 6 5 4 3 2 1

Acquisitions Editor:	Kassie Graves
Editorial Assistant:	Veronica Novak
Marketing Manager:	Carmel Withers
Production Editor:	Catherine M. Chilton
Copy Editor:	Taryn L. Bigelow
Typesetter:	C&M Digitals (P) Ltd.
Proofreader:	Gillian Dickens
Indexer:	D. Teddy Diggs
Cover Designer:	Candice Harman

CONTENTS

INTRODUCTION

Do you see things around you that just do not seem fair? Are you upset when you see poverty in the midst of great wealth? Are you frustrated when some of our schools provide inferior education to poor children? Do you hurt inside when you realize that people in our country go to sleep at night hungry? Many of us are feeling upset, frustrated, and hurt. We want to do something to change these terrible circumstances, but we do not know how. We do not even know where to begin. If this is the way you feel, this book is for you. We must help people. Trying is not enough. We must be strategic. We must be effective. No person is born with the ability to create solutions that work on a grand scale. We must learn how to help others, one step at a time. We must practice. Please know that you are not alone in your feelings. You are not alone in your intentions. I want to build on your feelings and intentions so that by combining them with analysis and strategy you will start to become effective. Change is exciting when you have confidence and newly acquired abilities. Change is daunting when you feel overwhelmed.

To build your confidence, this book is written in a style you may never have experienced before. I have tried to make it jargon-free. That's right, no more reading stuff like, "assessment personalization skills" or "facilitate conditions" or (one of my all-time personal favorites) "limitations of cognitive restructuring." The use of jargon can have the tendency to develop an exclusive club of members who understand it while keeping out the rest of us who do not. Instead, I want all of you to understand and participate. I want you to read each chapter and learn some new things and never say to yourself "Whaaat?" I have always found that people who communicate clearly sometimes feel guilty. They say, maybe subconsciously, I have to add to this, make it more complicated, harder, or else people will think I do not know much. Well, I think more highly of you than that. I think you will want to learn more when you realize you can learn it and do it and like it. I think I will increase my chances that you feel this way if I keep it simple.

I will try to show you that you can help people and their communities through learning simple concepts. I will try to engage you by telling you stories, because I think that is a great way to learn. I will try to talk about real people and situations because when it's real it just means more, and sticks with you longer. I will try to make the learning process relevant to you. Like all good lasting relationships, we will need to build on our mutual self-interest. My goal is that this book inspires you to never feel overwhelmed again when you see social problems around you. Instead, you will see these same problems and say, "I can do something about this." "I can get these people together, and with their determination, create change." My goal is for you to take what you have learned here and use it. So do we have a deal?

I will be talking a lot about trying to change things. Community organizing is a method to create change. Consensus organizing is one particular method of community organizing. Think of it like you think of therapy or clinical practice. Therapy tries to create change in individuals, one at a time. Community organizing tries to create change to benefit an entire group of people or an entire neighborhood. If done effectively, community organizing can have a big effect on a lot of people. If done ineffectively, you will start to find yourself becoming frustrated and overwhelmed. You will lose your own confidence and the confidence of others. You will begin to think no matter how hard you work your efforts will make little or no difference.

So what is consensus organizing and how was it started? Consensus organizing is a way of thinking. Once you understand and choose to use it, you may never stop. It will affect your personal and professional life. It will affect those around you, and change the way they think of you. Consensus organizing will have a big impact on the way you think and behave. You may find yourself less self-centered while, at the same time, feel more balanced, well-adjusted, and satisfied. You will find yourself listening more carefully to others, while they, in turn, become more genuinely interested in you. You may find yourself thinking about yesterday, today, and tomorrow all at the same time and not even getting mixed up. You will find strange, hidden similarities among people or situations that no one else sees. Your life will be much more interesting.

Consensus organizing was stumbled upon. It was not part of a grand scheme, grand plan, or grand design. It was a last-ditch, desperate effort to solve a serious problem. It was attempted after everything I was taught didn't work. It was not dreamed up in an ivory tower, think tank, or mountain retreat. It was born out of practicality. It has continued to be used for primarily one reason and one reason only: It works. In countless sets of circumstances, it seems to help people in lasting ways. It was tried out in desperation. It now is chosen strategically. Some efforts using consensus organizing have continued to help people long after flashier, headline-grabbing mobilization efforts have fizzled and dried up.

BOOK FORMAT

This book contains 13 chapters. I have tried my best to keep the tone of the writing friendly and accessible. You should be able to grasp the overall theme with a fairly quick and easy read. This book is arranged in a very unusual way. Each chapter will begin by talking about a particular aspect of consensus organizing and conclude by taking you on a road trip with real-life examples from different cities. The road trip will involve stories and tales that I hope will stick with you throughout your career. I think you will find these examples to be memorable and easy to retain. These stories should clarify and anchor the theme in your mind forever. Each story really happened. I tried to serve up the most illustrative examples.

I want you to feel like you are in the passenger seat on our trip. If we get lost, it's my fault. If we run out of gas, it's on me. If we drive too much in one day, just speak up and we can rest for a while. At times, when things are going smoothly, just enjoy the trip. At the conclusion, I want you to take over the wheel. I want you to have some fun (that's right, fun!) and learn some things down the road. I hope that you can reflect on your experiences from reading this book and tie them into your hopes, dreams, and careers. When we pull back in front of your place and you are home again, I hope you will want to keep consensus organizing in your personal and professional life.

So what kind of trip are we taking? Pack carefully, because the climate will change. I would suggest you utilize the concept of layering. We are starting out in Buffalo, New York. From there, it is south to Pittsburgh and the Mon Valley, in Pennsylvania, and Houston, Texas. We will come back up to New York City, then down again to Atlanta, Georgia; West Palm Beach, Florida; and New Orleans, Louisiana (I know there will be no complaints on that particular stop except maybe the 10 pounds we gain from the gumbo and étouffée—more about that later). We will be out west in Las Vegas, Nevada, and San Diego, California. You should update your passport, because I'd like to fly to Belfast, Northern Ireland, as well. Everything along the way will be real. You will know because I will be talking about things that no one could just make up. I have lived this life in the hope that one day you would be interested in taking this trip with me. I have even sprung for satellite radio because no one should travel cross-country having to listen to the same five songs. Buckle up that seatbelt, sip that large coffee, and leave the radio dial alone. Learn how to become a consensus organizer and the next time you drive, you get to pick the tunes.

My goal is for you to see that consensus organizing can be practiced not only by me but also by you. My hope is that you can begin to see yourself using consensus organizing and someday substituting your stories for mine. Your stories will be even richer, more enjoyable, and more interesting. Think of it as baking an even better chocolate chip cookie with more morsels, more flavor, more taste. Others will not be able to wait to begin to taste all that you have to offer.

At the conclusion of each chapter, I have included a small number of straightforward questions to help you think and reflect on what you have read. Most of these questions are serious, with a couple thrown in that you will enjoy only if you read the chapter. This book is designed to make you want to talk to others, listen to others, and tell others about what you have read. It should make you want to go out into a real community and do something. If the book is really good, it will pass the toughest test of all. It should make you not want to sell it. (I know, I know, it will be tough to pass up the $1.25 the book buyers will cough up.) I really hope you will want to keep it and, maybe in a few years, read it again.

ACKNOWLEDGMENTS

Influence is a funny thing. You look at life and wonder how you got to where you are. You are there because of the influence of others. I want to say thank you to the teachers who have influenced me—Mrs. Patricia Watt of Holy Name of Jesus School; Mr. Paul Westmiller, Mr. Joseph Conley, Father Donald Joyce, and Father James McGee of Bishop Fallon High School; Dr. Thomas Weinburg of Buffalo State College; and Dr. James Cunningham and Dr. Morton Coleman of the University of Pittsburgh.

Thank you to the sweetest aunts and uncles—Rose, Mike, Grace, and Andy.

I want to tip my hat to friends in Pittsburgh who couldn't care less what I do to make a living—Bob Metcalfe, Dick Ditmore, Don Walko, Skip Schwab, Matt Hawkins, Robert Pearlman, and Bob Holmes.

Thanks to all those I had the pleasure of working with around the country—George and Jo Debolt, Reverend Bill Thomas, Paul Brophy, Jim Capraro, Richard Manson, Tom Lenz, Ben Butler, Bob Pease, Karen Demasi, Jerry Altman, Tom Murphy, Rob Fossi, Mary Ohmer, Reggie Harley, Richard Barrera, Manuel Jones, Dale Smith, Ronelle Neperud, Jeff Baloutine, Kathy Tyler, Peter Goldberg, Barbara Buckley, Hans Dekker, Pat McElligott, Dave Bergholz, Harold Richman, Anita Harbert, Bill Murrah, and Steve Weber.

Thanks also to all those who have supported consensus organizing, in particular, Diana Lewis, Hank Bukema, Mike Watson, Jan Kraemer, Dr. Bob Ross, Pat Jenny, Herman Davenport, Peter Goldmark, Rebecca Riley, Julia Lopez, Ruth Goins, Olga Cañon, Ruth Riedel, Tom Beech, Lady Jean Mayhew, Bill Schambra, Mike Sviridoff, and John Gardner. Most especially, my thanks go out to Craig McGarvey for his help, encouragement, support, and friendship. Without him, there would be no book to enjoy.

I would like to express my gratitude to those who have written about consensus organizing—Mark Gerzon, Bob Fisher, Elizabeth Beck, Ross Gittell, Avis Vidal, Herb Rubin, and especially Shep Barbash.

Thank you to all the students at the Consensus Organizing Center, in particular Jessica Robinson, Day Rice, Paula Anderson, Karin Amiling, Madelyn Ochoa, Jorge Nunez, Angelica Garcia, and the flying fingers of Henok Negash and Sarah Minas.

I would like to express special recognition for the skills and caring of Dr. Becky Ziner and Dr. Jeffrey Gaines.

And a very special mention is extended to Anne Teachworth for putting the pieces of me back together and for making New Orleans my spiritual home.

This book is also dedicated to the memories of the warmest, kindest father and father-in-law—Victor Eichler and Harris Libby.

Last, to Pat Libby, thanks for making every day a true gift.

1

COMMUNITY ORGANIZING

Conflict and Consensus

In this chapter, you will learn:

◆ There are many different community organizing approaches and methods.

◆ Saul Alinsky is the most famous community organizer of all time.

◆ Definitions of conflict organizing and consensus organizing.

◆ Your own personality shapes the method of community organizing you will like.

I f you have any image at all of a community organizer, you probably picture a person (male, I bet) with an angry look, firing up a crowd of people to march on down somewhere to get somebody to take notice and start treating some group better. The organizer looks a little disheveled. The organizer talks fast. The organizer is pretty upset. If this were your image of a community organizer, I would equate it to the image of a therapist with a notepad gazing over a client stretched across a leather couch, saying with concerned reflection "hmmmm." The therapist is pondering. The therapist is detached. The therapist is analytical. In other words, your image would be stereotypical. Therapists come in all shapes, sizes, sexes, and sexual orientations and use approaches that are not only varied and complex, but also are sometimes contradictory. Community organizing has the same mixes and matches. There are a variety of approaches. Community organizers come in a variety of packages and styles. They sometimes contradict one another. So you can already see, you might have a little learning to do. You do not want to look at community organizing in one narrow, stereotypical way.

Robert Fisher (1994), in his book *Let the People Decide,* takes you through the history of community organizing. He shows you in detail how economics, politics, and world events shape and influence different community organizing approaches. Many other writers have tried to categorize these approaches by model, type, and definition. Many of these writers are academics trying to fit people's works into boxes and diagrams. In the real world of community organizing, nothing fits neatly into a box on a page. Many organizers think much more flexibly. They approach each day willing to do almost anything that might help a community. So let's start from a different spot. Let's look at why those who practice community organizing enter it, and try to see if you would fit into it. Later, we'll examine some of the different methods and approaches.

As Fisher (1994) says, no matter what historical era you choose, there seem to be some of the same things that drive people to want to be community organizers or at least gain some community organizing skills. Try to imagine the hilarious blue-collar comedian, Jeff Foxworthy, taking his trademark routine "then you just might be a redneck," but applying it instead to community organizing. If you aren't familiar with Foxworthy, he sets up his jokes (available on his website), many with an activity or tendency followed by "then you just might be a redneck." For example, "If you list 'staring' as one of your hobbies, you just might be a redneck" and "If you put ammo on your Christmas list, you just might be a redneck." So let's try it with the community organizer. "If you ever looked into our public school system and saw that it was unequal, writing off millions of low-income students, saying they can't learn, then you just might be a community organizer." "If you ever fumed over our two-tiered health system and saw poor and working-class people avoiding medical treatment because they can't afford health insurance, then you just might be a community organizer." "If you ever felt that it is unfair to have a federal minimum wage that keeps full-time workers and their families in poverty, then you just might be a community organizer." In each case, you see something grossly unfair and want to work with those suffering these injustices. That desire makes you a prime candidate to become a community organizer. If you have a sense of outrage at the unfairness in our society, you are already halfway across the water, swimming toward the goals and aspirations of community organizers throughout history. You now just need to gain some skills and techniques and focus on an approach or approaches you are comfortable with.

If you have a desire to create change that leads to fairness and equity, you have many different choices and paths to get you there. Sure, some organizers really do get people angry at large rallies, but that is just one of the methods you can choose. Let's look at four approaches among many. (Hey, now's the time for that neat little chart with the bullet points.) Throughout the evolution of community organizing, people have tried to explain it in different ways. My attempt is simple. Don't get lost in the terminology. Instead, try to imagine each approach and how you would do if you selected one or another.

Four Approaches to Community Organizing

Saul Alinsky and Conflict Organizing

The practice of community organizing is associated with one person more than any other: Saul Alinsky. A good parallel in the practice of therapy would be a person you may have heard of at one time or another: Sigmund Freud. Alinsky was born in Chicago in 1909. He was the son of immigrants, yet he managed to get through college studying archeology and criminology. His professional goal became the empowerment of everyday people. His work began to attract attention when he zeroed in on the famous Chicago neighborhood, Back of the Yards, and organized the Back of the Yards Council. This neighborhood acquired its unusual name because cows were sent by railroad from farms to be slaughtered and processed into meat at stockyards right in the middle of the community. Alinsky was interested in this particular Chicago neighborhood partly because it was the very same area that Upton Sinclair (1906) wrote about at the turn of the century in the book *The Jungle*. Most of the wretched conditions that Sinclair described still existed more than 50 years later. People felt trapped in either joblessness or in jobs that paid low wages with dangerous working conditions. Workers lost fingers and hands using unsafe equipment. They were fired and replaced by new immigrants. They lived in unheated buildings without indoor plumbing.

Alinsky came into the neighborhood as an outsider using one of his most important skills—listening. He listened to the complaints and frustrations of the people there. He saw a pattern that prevented change. Each person felt isolated and alone, that only he or she was stuck in these miserable circumstances. He knew he needed to be trusted by the residents. So he made a special effort to befriend the Catholic parish priests who could legitimize his organizing effort. The "father" could say it was not only right for the members to participate, but he could also prescribe or even require participation. Alinsky also painstakingly contacted other neighborhood institutions and organizations.

Alinsky distinguished between grassroots efforts and the efforts of various social service programs, which he felt were under the control of wealthy donors or unsympathetic government officials who would never choose the side of the oppressed when conflict occurred. He felt that social workers were do-gooders who were strong on rhetoric but nowhere around when things got hot. He knew that the residents were suffering from despair, apathy, and helplessness. He knew he had to confront these barriers or the neighborhood would remain powerless and continue to suffer.

He attacked feelings of "there is nothing we can do about it" head on. He first explained that residents needed power and that power comes in two different forms—money and people. Of course, the people had very little money but, on the other hand, there were certainly plenty of people. In this set of awful circumstances, he was able to point out that there was great potential for change that could come from collective action.

Alinsky used tactics he became famous for—boycotts, strikes, and pickets. He disrupted meetings. He brought community people to places they were uninvited and unwanted. He organized the "have-nots" against the "haves." He would use anger as a motivator. He turned politicians against one another. He polarized situations as a strategy. He personalized his attacks. Instead of going after the bank, he went after the particular bank president, naming him and blaming him. He worried his targets by unification. After pressuring and pressuring his targets, concessions would begin to be granted. Rents were reduced. Municipal improvements were initiated. More equitable mortgages and bank loans were made. Fairer wages and benefits were paid. His successes made him famous and in demand. This style of organizing that puts pressure on personalized targets to create improvements is referred to as conflict organizing. It is still practiced today all across the country.

Conflict Organizing—Using anger and blaming a selected, targeted individual by putting pressure on the target to create a concession and cause change

Women Centered Organizing

Alinsky talked about power as something others had. Often, those in power did not treat the poor, women, or minorities fairly. He believed power should be removed from those who abused it and transferred to the oppressed. Feminists and women centered organizers, on the other hand, believe in a different principle: power sharing. They are committed to creating balanced power relationships through democratic practices of shared leadership, decision making, authority, and responsibility. Many women centered organizers believe that, without this approach, they would mirror more traditional, hierarchical institutions. They would become part of the problem instead of a part of a solution and a shining example. They believe in equality and inclusion. One Canadian-centered group, the Advisory Council on the Status of Women in *Feminism: Our Basis for Unity*, succinctly summarizes its view of power sharing:

> Through the healthy practice of power sharing, we nurture an environment that is peaceful, empowering and respectful. We share power through inclusion, consensus building and skills development. Other practices include validating women's experiences, anticipating challenge and conflict, including diverse voices, creating safe places, evaluating our work and sharing roles and responsibilities. Respect is at the root of successful power sharing, as is a genuine commitment to the principles, practices and processes of feminism. To foster healthy and equitable power relationships among staff, board members and volunteers we must demonstrate our commitment to feminist leadership rather than simply assume authority. (Advisory Council on the Status of Women: Newfoundland & Labrador, n.d.)

It would be fun to bring back Saul Alinsky and have him compare approaches with members of this advisory council. They have distinctly different ideas about power. Some observers, such as Kristina Smock (2004) in *Democracy in Action,* have commented on some of the trade-offs of what she calls the women centered model. She says there can be tension between process and product.

The emphasis on internal relationship building and inclusive decision making can hinder the achievement of tangible action oriented outcomes. Providing participants with the personal support while helping them to discover the connection between their own problems and public issues can be an extremely time consuming process, one that frequently slows down the organization's ability to move toward broader action. Similarly, the insistence on including all voices and reaching genuine consensus can make it difficult for women centered organizations to move effectively from deliberation to action. (p. 253)

The women centered model emphasizes that relationships should not be built on self-interest but rather on understanding and responsibility. It puts a high priority on personal development as well as community development.

Community Building Approach

Community Building—Forming collaborative partnerships among a neighborhood's stakeholders to strengthen their internal capacity to solve their problems

---

Community builders believe that the internal social and economic fabric of a neighborhood needs to be strengthened. They believe that the biggest challenge that people in neighborhoods face is the lack of capacity to address their own needs. Because many low-income communities are isolated and cut off by the traditional power structure, the rebuilding must come from within. Because people in these communities have been systematically isolated, they need to "learn to trust one other, establish roles, and improve from within." This represents a new form of community organizing. Organizers are faced with the challenge of developing the residents' assets and skills. They must not only harness and expand the skill base, but also then build collaborations throughout the community. These collaborations must be built among various stakeholders in the neighborhood. This approach sometimes tilts heavily toward staff. It includes some residents, but often those already in leadership positions, such as block club presidents, civic association chairpersons, and so on. It may shy away from other residents not affiliated with existing efforts. Also, the complexity of comprehensive, neighborhood-wide efforts may overwhelm the "average" citizen, let alone the nonnative, non-English speaker or someone with very little formal education. Organizers may have to overvalue those with degrees and expertise and existing positions of power and, by default, leave out others. There is also some concern that the community building approach requires multiple trade-offs and compromises to get everyone on the same page. Many problems are not challenged or addressed.

The community building approach has been supported heavily by regional and national philanthropies. They find comfort in the comprehensiveness, logic, and order of entire-community efforts. One community group steps forward and presents the philanthropy with an opportunity to play an investment or grant-making role that feels comfortable and appropriate. Some of these philanthropies might not have supported conflict organizing (too disruptive) or women centered organizing (too process oriented).

Consensus Organizing

Consensus Organizing—Tying the self-interest of the community to the self-interest of others to achieve a common goal

---

This has nothing but pluses, no shortcomings, and the guy connected with it is nothing short of a genius! Meanwhile, back on the planet earth, I will try my best to make this an objective introduction to a community organizing approach I happen to like. Consensus organizing requires you, the organizer, to do two parallel, simultaneous jobs. I can hear you now, "Hey, I already don't like this one. It's twice as much work!" Come on, where's that sense of dedication and commitment?

Some community building efforts are heavily reliant on government funding. They can become dependent on this support for their continued existence. Saul Alinsky would call this "sleeping with the enemy" and feel that such efforts would be in serious jeopardy of being co-opted and never building power.

A consensus organizer brings together interests within a neighborhood in a way that is similar to the community builder approach, while at the same time bringing together the political, economic, and social power structure from outside the neighborhood. We see both the internal and external players as equal participants loaded with dedicated, honest, fair participants. After both groups are organized, articulate, and focused on their self-interest, you bring them together. This approach runs very contrary to the conflict organizing ideas of Saul Alinsky and his disciples, and has something in common with the other two approaches. Alinsky would never see the power structure as a potential ally. In his mind, elites were the cause of problems and never part of a solution. They were only valuable when they did what the community group demanded. On the other hand, power sharing is talked about in the other models. The major difference is that nobody else looks at the external forces affecting the community in quite the way a consensus organizer does.

The consensus organizer recognizes the value and power of mobilizing honest and dedicated people from both groups—the community and the power structure. Of course, there will also be prejudiced, self-serving, and arrogant individuals from both groups. The idea is to work around them.

Those who embrace consensus organizing see it as the most logical, natural, and sensible way to proceed. It resonates with how they think, choose their friends, and lead their lives. Others see it as a sellout, a public relations–driven, superficial effort that doesn't begin to address the root causes of problems. There! I told you I'd be fair. Is the world composed of a variety of people who need to be skillfully brought together? Is it something you'd like to know more about?

I've always been fascinated by the personalities of community organizers and how their personalities might match some approaches better than others. I bet in your case, right here in Chapter 1, you feel you match up better to one more than the other three. In my experience, most of those who are attracted to Alinsky and the conflict approach have a drive to correct unfairness by putting the blame where it belongs. You know the personality, "I'm right, you're wrong, and I'll prove it!" They see women centered groups as not serious about taking action because they won't take power away from those who "don't deserve it." Community builders see the need to create order and harmony from within. You know the personality type, "Here we are, we've met, gotten to know one another, and we agree." A consensus organizer has the kind of personality that sees the actual and potential good in everyone. Think of pop icon Madonna. Some see her as a manipulative, media-conscious chameleon that changes her image over and over to maximize her earning power, never really believing in anything. A consensus organizer could see her instead as a fascinating woman who started with nothing, came to New York from Detroit at 17, refused to be packaged and manipulated into someone's idea of who she should be, and has evolved into, among other things, a caring mother and a writer of children's books.

YOUR PERSONALITY AND COMMUNITY ORGANIZING

Some students in the helping professions end up working in agency or institutional settings. There, they tend to have the expertise and control, and the parent, resident, or child is the "client" who benefits from their expertise and goodwill. The "helpers" see no connection to the messy business of community organizing. They see no need to gain community organizing skills. They believe their personality suits the more structured, set approach of building a one-on-one relationship. Well, I'd like you to look a little deeper into this with me. Let's talk about the power relationship in more "clinical" settings. Sure, you have read ad nauseam, and have been taught time and time again that you and the client are equals, but, the last time I checked, that's not how the client sees it. In fact, I would venture to say that no matter how hard you try and no matter how sincere you might be, the client will never believe it. The client sees *you* with the expertise, *you* with the insights, *you* with the answers (also *you* with the paycheck, *you* with the degree, and, most times, *you* with a house or apartment in a different neighborhood). Most important, when there are only two of you in a room, there is no ability for the client to help someone else. It is hard and sometimes downright impossible to create reciprocity. All you have done is to create a one-way street—you give, the client receives. In all forms of community organizing, however, the resident gets help and gives help. There are no one-way streets. Ideas come up as a group of people think together. Everyone feeds off of one another, which enhances creative thought. There can be a sense of belonging to the group and there is a sense of helping to work toward the greater good. Your role as an organizer can change from moment to moment. This fluidity can increase effectiveness at moving along strategies for community improvement. One person might need your help in thinking ahead. Another might need your praise. Another might need you to be firm and consistent.

So I now ask you to imagine using one or more of the organizing approaches mentioned. Do you have the type of personality that can thrive by getting in people's faces and pushing them to do what is needed? Do you have the type of personality that is comfortable with finding similarities and commonalities to minimize conflict? Do you feel equally comfortable with both? What types of life experiences have shaped your view of fairness and justice? Try to go back in your life and remember some sets of circumstances when you were justifiably upset. Try to remember the times you most wanted to change something that was bothering you. These are the times when you have seen your true organizing personality come out. It was when you felt the need to change something that you chose strategies. It was when you were upset and frustrated yet determined to "fix it" that your own organizing style began to emerge. Did you try to appeal to someone else's sense of fairness? Did you force someone into doing the "right" thing even though they didn't want to? Did you get other people involved rather than trying to change things all by yourself? You will see that you already might have done some community organizing even though you didn't know that was what it was called. You might have tried to organize your brother and sister, an eighth-grade class, a high school coaching staff, or fellow church members. These are all examples of organizing and you were the organizer. If you think and reflect, you may find that you already have begun doing some of the work we are going to talk about. Some of you even may have practiced consensus organizing. You even may have had some success. You may have done it naturally and never even known it by its name.

So let's take a deep breath. Let's go back to a time long ago and far away to my hometown. Let's hear a few stories about what it was like before the turn of the 21st century. What happened back in those dark days and how did it affect the shaping of a different theory of community organizing? So put on your boots. Put on your scarf. Put on your gloves. Button up that parka or you'll catch your death of cold, because you're heading for Buffalo, New York.

That's a Shame

It snows a lot in Buffalo. It's pretty windy, too. Some would describe it as terribly bleak. Summer is nice, the whole 6 weeks. The other 46 are a little rough. One old Buffalo joke goes, "What color do kids from Buffalo prefer the most? Gray. It's the only color they have ever seen." I get to tell such jokes because Buffalo is my hometown. My family's neighborhood for the first 21 years of my life was the Eastside of Buffalo. Holy Name of Jesus Parish was our parish. Schiller Park was our park. We had stability on the Eastside. We did not have a lot of upward mobility. We never expected to move, let alone move up. Most families were big families, four, five, six kids. Almost all of these kids had Polish names—mine the German exception. I had to learn enough conversational Polish to drop a phrase here and there to fit in with my friends' families. Almost all these kids went to Holy Name School. I did and I remember it. What I remember most is that life on the Eastside of Buffalo had a series of absolutes. There was good and bad, right and wrong—nothing in the middle. There were the golden gates of Heaven and the chance of rotting everlasting in Hell. On a typical school day, I walked 6 blocks to school, 6 blocks back home for lunch, and then repeated the trip each afternoon. I estimate that on the walks I would meet 10 to 15 adults. Everyone knew my name. Every one of them had authority over me. If I were up to anything, and I mean anything, every adult would feel obligated to discipline me and then to tell my mom and dad, who would repeat the procedure. Adults would never tell other adults that it was none of their business. They all believed it *was* their business.

My neighborhood had everything. I could walk or bike to Schiller Park, two movie theaters, two bowling alleys, three candy stores, a used comic book store, a model train store, "the woods" (trees and open land to play in), railroad tracks with real trains and real hoboes, a public library, two pizza shops, four delis that sold baseball cards, and an ice cream parlor. I mean, what else do you need? I can honestly say that as a 12-year-old boy, I couldn't imagine a better place to live. That is, until one day when I went to the dentist.

Our family dentist had his office in another neighborhood. My parents did not own a car so we had to get to the dentist by catching two buses. I went with my mom on each trip until I turned 12. At that time, she announced conclusively one evening without debate at dinner that I was old enough to go by myself. I had a mixed reaction to this pronouncement. I liked the recognition that I had reached this rite of passage, but the dentist's office was in a different neighborhood. My mother gave me bus fare, wrote out the bus route numbers, and pushed me out the door. I felt like I was going to Siberia. (Hey, no more Buffalo jokes.) It seemed so far away. Years later, out of curiosity, I checked a street map. It was a journey Marco Polo would have admired—6 miles. I arrived on time with no mishaps, but the block walk from the bus to the dentist's office was strange. Not one adult recognized me. I did not like that. I went up to the receptionist, just past the tropical fish tank, and gave her my name. She, of course, wanted to know where my mother was. Parking the car? "No, she had sent me by myself." The receptionist then, matter-of-factly, just making conversation, asked where I lived. I, equally matter-of-factly, told her. She looked up from the appointment book, dropped her pen, and made a distinctive strange sort of clucking noise with her tongue against her teeth. She slowly rotated her head from side to side and said pointedly from deep inside her throat, "Oooh, that's a shame!" It was odd. I remember feeling neither happy nor sad. I was completely puzzled. The only time I remembered a reaction like this was when my friend's dog died and he told my mom. Only now, there wasn't a dead dog. All I did was tell someone in a dentist's office where I lived.

All the way home on the bus, I replayed what had happened. Slowly, I put this puzzle together. The lady felt sorry for me. This made me mad. I did not want her pity. She hadn't been mean, but she might as well have been. If my dad had been there, he might have said she "meant well." But I did not feel that she did. Why was I getting so upset? I got off the second bus and carefully looked around. My neighborhood looked even better than I had remembered. It felt wonderful to be back. Then, something even stranger happened to me. It was a new feeling, starting from within my stomach, moving up my chest, and eventually spilling into my head. I felt resentment. I fought it at first because she was an adult, she was to be respected, and she even worked in an office. She was clean when she came home from work. She didn't need to wash up. I was supposed to look up to her. If I had had a sister, she would have hoped to be successful like her. Despite all the thinking and analyzing, this deepening feeling of resentment could not be stopped. I couldn't stop it because it felt so justified. She started it, not me. I did nothing to provoke this. I did not bring it upon myself. I resented her and her neighborhood. There was no way that she was better than my friends, my family, my school, or my street. The fact that she thought she was better proved she wasn't. I didn't need to discuss this with anyone. I assumed everyone older than me already had figured this out. I had sorted it out and come to an adult conclusion. I resented her and my whole neighborhood would have resented her. That I felt this, I suppose, was just a shame.

When it was time to choose a high school, I chose a Catholic one. It was located way over on the other side of town. It advertised and promised that every kid who graduated would go on to college. I took that to mean even kids from the Eastside. Most of the students would be Italian from the Westside of Buffalo. I surmised that I had little to worry about. My theory was that the receptionist would have put these kids down, too. I was pretty sure that because I felt I was equal to them, they would feel the same toward me. I was right. It was easy to be friends with them. It was a long trip back and forth, though. The bus trip required me to remain very, very alert. After all, I was required to wear a suit coat and a tie every day and carry Latin books while all the other Eastside kids got off at a public school along my bus route. This public school was not just any public school. It happened to be the public school you went to when you were thrown out of all the other public schools. After a few weeks of taunts, stares, and dirty looks from most of the other kids on the bus, I started to develop additional theories. Because I had done nothing to merit the negative treatment I was receiving, maybe I was a sort of representative of all the other kids who were forced to dress like me. Maybe other kids who went to private schools thought they were superior to my fellow travelers. I certainly didn't. Slowly, it started to sink in. They thought that I looked at them the way the receptionist had looked at me! Now, it all made sense. I guessed that this kind of stuff never ended.

My high school years were 1964 through 1968. I rode that bus route all 4 years. Through riots, burnings, shootings, and curfews, I went to school. Bishop Fallon High School met its end of the bargain. I applied to and was accepted at three colleges. The cheapest by far was Buffalo State College so, of course, that's where I went. I had a conversation with my parents about my preferred choice, Syracuse University. I talked for at least 20 minutes about why it was the best school for me. Syracuse had an excellent faculty, great facilities, solid academic programs, and so on. I was into my presentation. I did everything I could to convince my parents. At about the 15-minute mark, I noticed something. They had stopped listening. The last part must have sounded to them like blah, blah, blah, blah. I finally came up for air. My mother said just eight words and with that it was all over. Those eight words were "How are you going to pay for it?" Man, Buffalo State never looked so good. We had never discussed college in my family. It was always understood that if I wanted to go to college, it was up to me to figure out how to do it. If I did not want to go, it would also be fine. Steel mills, the rubber plant, and the auto plant were all hiring. You could find work if that's what you wanted. I saw another life that I wanted instead. I wanted people to stop resenting me and to start respecting me. I wanted people from my neighborhood to know that I was not better than they were. I wanted people from outside the neighborhood to know that I was not inferior. I did not think it was too much to ask. I wanted to find something within my new giant college that would become my balance beam. I felt my future would always be filled with judges and competitors. I needed to be a gymnast on a beam. I wanted every judge to see me differently by finding something they admired. I wanted something that made each of them score my performance most positively. No matter how distinctive the particular judge, I wanted to give each of them something they appreciated and respected. I was going to find my way to do it in this college.

THE OUTSIDE AGITATOR

I started college in 1968. If I graduated on time, I would finish in the year 1972. Many historians now rank those 4 years as some of the most, if not *the* most, turbulent in United States history. There was anything but apathy on campus. During 2 of the 4 years, we had final exams canceled because of antiwar protests and violence that ensued. The administration considered it too dangerous to continue teaching. In my 4 years, I was teargassed, chased, and interviewed by the FBI. It is still hard for me to relate college to anything but politics and foreign policy.

Buffalo State evolved from what was originally a teacher's college. By the time I entered, it had developed into a full-blown college with more than 40 majors to choose from. People in my neighborhood, however, when hearing about my acceptance, invariably showed their enthusiasm by shouting, "Mike's going to State Teacher's!" Whereas some of the students were local commuters like me, many took the New York State Thruway to Buffalo from other parts of the state, usually from New York City. It only took the first hour of orientation to discover that the New York City kids were different. First, they seemed to think that Buffalo, the second-largest city in the state, was a farming community. I learned this because they said so, loudly and frequently. When they made a point, they would use references that almost always escaped me. Every 18-year-old from New York City seemed 35 years old to me. They had so much experience and so much attitude. How could they all have done so much, seen so much, felt so much at such a young age? The point was, I found them fascinating. I never let their attitude build a wall around me and stop me from befriending them. One of my favorite ways to bond was to invite them to my family's home and show them my neighborhood. My gritty community was suddenly an asset. It worked pretty much every time. They then treated me as an equal. I learned a lot about politics from them. Many of them were very active in the civil rights, women's rights, and antiwar movements. They read a lot and would loan me their books. I joined the Student Convocation Committee, in which I helped select the speakers who would be invited to campus. The committee was almost entirely composed of New York City activists. You can imagine how the members leaned politically when they selected their speakers. They leaned decidedly left (very liberal).

Committee members had responsibilities for each speech. Some wrote press releases, some put up posters, some distributed tickets, and some did the grunt work. Once a year, however, when you were selected to organize the entire convocation, the duties became even more intense. The responsibilities were more complex. You negotiated the contract, did the introduction, fielded inquires, and assigned all the other committee members to the various tasks—excellent experience for a 19-year-old. If you had to take on all this responsibility, you certainly wanted it to be directed toward a famous person that you wanted to meet. You wanted *your* speaker. You were prepared to lobby and twist the arms of other committee members to get your first choice.

In one of my sociology classes, Analyzing Social Problems, we read a book called *Crisis in Black and White* (Silberman, 1966). We read about a community organizer named Saul Alinsky from Chicago. He caught my attention. He motivated people to have much higher expectations, an idea that thrilled me. Every page seemed like free gas flowing into an empty tank. I must have been like the young actor, musician, or athlete who screams excitedly one day, "You mean, I can get paid to do this?" What he was doing resonated with me. Here I was reading about this guy who went into neighborhoods like mine, got all the residents together, and fought and won improvements from government, corporations, and landlords. I was mesmerized. Not only was he able to do this, he was also alive *and* he made speeches.

At our selection meeting, committee members chose Bernadette Devlin, Father James Groppi, Jonathan Kozol, and Cesar Chavez. If we successfully negotiated with their agents, we would then be promoting them, meeting them at the airport, eating dinner with them, introducing them, and getting to know them. I couldn't believe my good fortune. I was on the committee because the members thought I brought some perspective, ability, and good work habits. Timidly at first, I dropped the name of Saul Alinsky. After all, I had read that he was the guy who helped train Cesar Chavez, the successful leader of immigrant farmworkers. It was Chavez who organized an effective national grape boycott, forcing the growers to improve workers' wages and living conditions. As luck would have it, the more I dug up about Alinsky, the more excited I became, and the more excited committee members became. It turned out that his organization, the Industrial Areas Foundation, had trained and sent organizers to Rochester, New York, just 70 miles away. That information paled in comparison to his reported exploration of expansion into Buffalo, New York. Actually, the Industrial Areas Foundation saw great possibilities in one particular Buffalo neighborhood, the Eastside! That meant that Alinsky himself would be coming to work in my neighborhood. He would be flying in from Chicago, landing at the airport in Buffalo, and be driven into my own neighborhood to cause trouble. He would be legitimately referred to as an outside agitator. I was more determined than ever. He had to speak at my campus and I had to organize it. It was in the cards, it was fate, it was destiny.

The committee unanimously approved my recommendation and I was put in charge of the operation. By this time, I was completely engrossed in the idea of community organizing. I befriended a faculty member who introduced me to the local Industrial Areas Foundation staff member assigned to build the Buffalo program. I felt that with some experience,

I could do what he was doing. I could motivate, engage, and I could strategize. Organizing strategy, staying ahead of everyone else became my main interest. I attended every meeting I could. I met and admired paid professional organizers. I thought all of this would help prepare me for the night of my life when I would meet and introduce the most famous community organizer in the entire world, Saul Alinsky.

Without my knowledge, however, another group of New York State taxpayers had their own take on the situation. They had organized to express their distress about their taxes being used to pay people who "hated America" to come to our campus and poison students' minds. They targeted a group on the Buffalo State campus that had taken the lead in the poisoning. It was my committee. The last straw, apparently, was the decision to bring in Saul Alinsky, identified by them as a communist. Unlike other potential speakers, he wanted to stir up trouble right in Buffalo. These New Yorkers wrote letters to the newspapers, appeared on television, and demanded to meet the campus president and the New York State University Trustees. They also intended to show up, in force, to protest Alinsky's speech. Ironically, they were going to protest the protester. Alinsky, upon hearing this from his staff, was ecstatic. With no small ego, *he* was now the center of controversy, a place he found warm and comforting. I realized I had fallen into a wonderful situation myself. Reporters constantly called my house for quotes. The protesters wanted me to cancel the appearance. The entire swirl was rapidly leading to my first opportunity to meet Alinsky. What a great set of circumstances in which to be introduced. I got to do my favorite thing—strategize. How could I use this once-in-a-lifetime opportunity to show him my organizing ability? What would he do if he were in my shoes? I remember how clearheaded I felt when a light bulb slowly floated into the air and paused above me.

I called the media and announced that because of massive pressure from citizens groups, I would reluctantly be making an announcement about a major change in committee policy on bringing in speakers. The announcement would be made immediately prior to Mr. Alinsky's address. I suggested that all the concerned taxpayers attend. Then, I also called all the activist groups on campus and told them the same thing. This meant we were guaranteed an overflow crowd, some who were there in hopes of hearing about a future ban on people like Alinsky, and some who were there to put pressure on making sure that there was no change. I hoped this would impress him. The committee designed posters with Alinsky's quote, "When I die I'm going to Hell and organize." There was a huge buzz all over campus. Even people who a month earlier had never heard of Alinsky were now keenly interested in him. I felt like a boxing promoter. My job was to fire up both sides, so they would all show up.

> Controversy can create interest. Interested people get involved. I felt that the more controversial his visit became, the more successful it would be.

I invited my parents to the speech and some of our neighbors as well. The activists from campus showed up in full force. The taxpayer activists also showed up in droves. All the chairs were filled 30 minutes before the scheduled start. The aisles filled up as well. I prayed the fire marshals wouldn't show up. The television stations, radio stations, and newspapers were all there and all set up. I had organized it. Alinsky barreled into a room behind the stage with a few of his staff members, right on time. He wore a dark suit and a narrow tie. I remember that he looked huge and I felt very small. I spoke aggressively about the circumstances surrounding his speech and said I was going to make a major announcement. I was trying to make him nervous. He wasn't. He listened very well. He said very little. I brought my parents backstage to meet him. My dad told him I wanted to be a community organizer.

It was time. I walked onto the stage and faked nervousness. I was in front of the largest crowd I had ever spoken to. I cleared my throat. The audience was markedly and physically divided. The activists on both sides had their own signs and posters. Pockets of people with pointed opinions clung to one another in clumps woven like a giant quilt patched together. I spoke very slowly. Alinsky was staring at me from behind the curtain at the side of the stage. "As you know, me and our student committee have been under tremendous pressure these last few weeks." I wanted each word to mean something to both sides of the audience. Now this was fun. I spoke about how we as students were obligated to listen to criticism with respect and reflection. As students, we were bound to the wishes of our financial supporters, the taxpayers. I pushed it so far; all the activists were on the edge of their seats, ready to explode in fury, as I appeared to be caving in. There they sat and stood, watching me apparently sell out. Then, with the rest of the audience drawing the same conclusion, I put the hammer down with my final remark. "So, with very careful thought and consideration, I stand before you all tonight to announce that the convocation committee of Buffalo State College will no longer be bringing young, radical, left-wing, liberal speakers onto our campus. (Pause.) We are instead going to bring in *old, left-wing, radical speakers!* Ladies and gentleman, Saul Alinsky!" The whole room erupted; it was like a courtroom hearing the verdict for an accused murderer, "Not guilty." I felt like I was 10 feet in the air, as if time was standing still. Alinsky came charging out from behind the curtain, leaned down, grabbed my shoulder hard, and yelled in my ear "That was the worst [expletive]ing introduction I have received in my entire life." His smile, however, told me all I needed to know. I had impressed him. I was going to be a community organizer. I felt that I had a "feel" for moving large groups of people to where they needed to go. I felt that maybe I had found the "gift" that all of us seem to have: a gift for something. Some have an athletic gift, some an artistic gift, or some a gift for sales or law or medicine. I felt my gift was in organizing, to get justice for those who deserved it. I felt an obligation to use my gift. What if a gifted artist could please Vincent Van Gogh or the gifted basketball player could please Larry Bird? Wouldn't they, then, want to paint or play ball? I had just successfully performed in front of the greatest community organizer in the world and he had recognized my gift.

The world we live in is full of injustice. There are things you see every day that need to be changed. Change can be achieved through many different approaches. We all see the world we share through different eyes. I wanted to create change. I had begun to choose a path to get there.

Now, I want you to start to think about yourself. We are at a spot at which you get a chance to reflect. Please do not skip ahead. Take some time and ponder the following questions. Some of them will be fun; but some will take some time. Share your thoughts with others and be curious about how they answer the same questions. Check in the back of the book in the "Answers" to Reflection Questions section for some input from yours truly. This is important because it should make you think even more. Look under the "answers" for Chapter 1. Then, and only then, move on to the next chapter.

Reflection Questions

1. If Saul Alinsky were alive today, what would he be doing? What issues would he be addressing?

2. Which speakers would you bring into your school if you were in charge of the convocations committee?

3. What has happened in your life that makes you want to help people?

4. What style of organizing matches your personality?

5. How did the community you grew up in affect you as an adult?

6. Would you ever want to visit Buffalo?

References

Advisory Council on the Status of Women: Newfoundland & Labrador. (N.d.). *Feminism: Our basis for unity.* Retrieved March 3, 2004, from http://pacsw.com

Fisher, R. (1994). *Let the people decide: Neighborhood organizing in America* (Updated ed.). Boston: Twayne.

Silberman, C. E. (1966). *Crisis in black and white.* New York: Random House.

Sinclair, U. (1906). *The jungle.* New York: Doubleday.

Smock, K. (2004). *Democracy in action: Community organizing and urban change.* New York: Columbia University Press.

2

EVOLUTION OF CONSENSUS ORGANIZING

In this chapter, you will learn:

◆ The importance and power of negative stereotyping.

◆ The pitfalls of overgeneralizing.

◆ The definition of myth and anti-myth.

◆ The process and negative effects of blockbusting.

It takes all kinds of people to make the world go around—some good, some bad. Sometimes bad people do bad things. Many people are motivated to make as much money as possible and will stop at almost nothing to reach their goal. Some people have so much anger and resentment inside them that they can rationalize hurting the poor because they "deserve" it. Some people are just so filled with rage and hate that it pours out of them through prejudice and discrimination toward others. The reasons that people develop these attitudes would require writing a different book. Let's just say, many smart people do bad things for reasons that aren't fair. But you could figure it out if you had the time or interest. In the minds of community organizers, bad people doing bad things must be stopped. We zero in on those subjected to this venom and we go back to the cause and we want to stop it, change it, and fix it. When we see an individual, a for-profit business, or a major corporation go after maximum profit, we know people will be hurt. When people seek to maximize profit no matter what the social cost, they can justify anything, and I mean anything. This includes poverty wages, substandard housing, inadequate health care, environmental destruction, and even war.

Community organizers see this and become one-dimensional. They see everything from one perspective only: their own. When they see something is unfair they label it as such and try to rectify the injustice. They develop the perspective of the people they are trying to help. They don't see things from the point of view of those causing the problems, or those tolerating the problems. They don't even attempt to broaden their perspective. They believe in narrowing it to only those who are oppressed, held back, or discriminated against. They never walk in the shoes of those causing the problems. They don't understand their perspective because they claim they already know it. Think of the flip side. Bosses seldom understand the lives of their minimum-wage employees. Why? Because they feel they already understand. They know their low-paid underlings are lazy, unmotivated, and looking to do anything to get out of working. See what I mean? Organizers do the same thing. They overgeneralize and are often comfortable doing it.

I had exactly this attitude when I began my organizing career. I knew that the world was unfair. I was going to do all I could to correct it. I wanted those who were held back to be set free. I wanted the have-nots to get what they deserved. I knew what it felt like to have others look at you as inferior before they even knew you. I thought that everyone richer or more powerful than me wanted to hold me back. I generalized. I didn't even know anybody who was rich and powerful. I felt I didn't need to. I just had all the confidence in the world that I was right. Depending on our background and life experiences, I think we develop this attitude and this confidence in its correctness when we are quite young. We develop negative stereotypes in our society quite easily. We then find proof to justify our feelings. We filter out any information that might force us to change those stereotypes. Politicians, authors, talk show hosts, even some religious leaders are adept at the simple process of pandering to our negative stereotypes. Books written by conservative authors paint liberals as godless, elite, latte-drinking, Volvo drivers, whereas liberal authors portray conservatives as gun toting, illiterate, beer drinking, pickup truck drivers. They become popular by badmouthing others that we would like to badmouth. Sometimes I wonder if they even agree with their own statements; instead they will say anything they feel will resonate with the public. They help to narrow our already narrow perspectives. They use a technique that is the opposite of real learning. They tell us what they think we want to hear. Learning is a different process. Learning widens our perspective. Learning has us change, enrich, and expand our points of view. When I became an organizer, I was not a learner—I was telling people what they wanted to hear.

Coming from a working-class background, it seemed simple and logical to me that all rich and powerful people were motivated to pursue the almighty dollar and if that meant stepping on me and my family and my neighbors, so be it. I believed that their goals stopped me from succeeding in my own life. If they got what they wanted, I believed, I would be prevented from getting what I wanted. It was easy for me to relate to people from minority groups because most felt the same way I did. They were ripped off even more by the same people. I was sold the bad meat, the car with the hidden engine trouble, the insurance policy that never paid off when it was supposed to. Those things would happen to people like me throughout my whole life and it was done to us on purpose, to benefit the store owner, automobile chain, and the insurance company. It was our destiny to be taken advantage of by the rich and powerful. That is, unless we did something about it. When you are born poor or working class, you are socialized to shut up. Just shut up and do your job. You are not encouraged to challenge, question, or object. To do so would be to make trouble and, after all, your boss and the people in charge know more and are smarter than you are. Why? Because they are the people in charge. To be poor or working class means that you lower your expectations. You take what is given to you. You don't push yourself to try to obtain something that is unattainable. Usually, we don't try things that we are in effect told not to try. I was lucky enough to go to college. I was lucky enough to be exposed to books about social problems, and lucky enough to find out that I could get paid to do something called community organizing.

Community organizing seemed to me to be a true chance to prove how right I was about those rich and powerful oppressors. In the conflict approach of community organizing, I found a potential avenue that would do for me what everyone wants out of a career—prove that I was smart, correct, justified, and superior all at the same time. Community organizers not only said the rich and powerful ripped us off, they also developed skills to go after them and beat them! What was better than that? Nothing.

It is possible to get a point across through community organizing. The point can then be understood by lots of people who would then want to create change.

The idea that low-income tenants could beat a landlord, or low-income residents could beat a mayor, or a working-class community could stop a polluting company seemed like a dream. This wouldn't be happening in a play or a movie or a novel. It would be real. This was majestic—the chance to make things fair and not just for me but for hundreds or thousands of others as well. I could help people who deserved help. I could help them become respected. Even better, I wouldn't be giving them something like food or clothing or providing a service like counseling. I wouldn't be saving anyone. That idea would have turned me off. I didn't like the idea of being a savior. These people did not need to be saved. They needed to fight and win. I loved the idea that others, through their own joint efforts, would gain confidence, respect, and power.

At the same time I was reaching these conclusions, many who were rich and powerful were making decisions about their own lives and the people around them. They had been told, more than once, that poor and working class people were mostly lazy, uneducated, and shifty. They heard that the rich earned their money by being smart, entrepreneurial, and hardworking. They deserved to be rich. The poor deserved to be poor. Government officials, or at least the liberals in government, were "do-gooders," hell bent on redistributing the wealth. The liberals were seeking to take hard-earned money away from those who earned it and give it to those who put little or no effort into bettering their own lives. This trend of punishing the successful was assaulting the social fabric of the nation. A whole generation of working class and poor people were growing up believing that wealthier people owed them a better life. After all, everyone knows that the bottom line in America is that anyone can be successful if they try. Aren't there examples of people who came from nothing to achieve great success throughout our history? The United States is even called the "land of opportunity!" Thank goodness we lived in a country like this so the wealthy could feel justified in the advantages they were being given. Because, even if they were born into a poor family, they believed they still would have a wonderful chance to be successful.

It was easy for these people to stereotype my neighbors. It was easy for them to have the supreme confidence that they were right. David Shipler (2004) in *The Working Poor* writes about what he calls the "American myth" and the "anti-myth."

Myth—Hard work will always lead to success.

Anti-myth—No matter what you do, you won't succeed.

The myth states that any individual from the humblest of origins can climb the ladder. People who work hard and make the right decisions in life can achieve anything in our country. It is only our own actions that hold us back. There are no other limits. This American myth provides a justification for blame. As Shipler (2004) writes,

> In the puritan legacy, hard work is not merely practical but moral. Its absence suggests an ethical lapse. A harsh logic dictates a hard judgment. If a person's diligent work leads to prosperity, if work is a moral virtue, and if anyone in the society can attain prosperity through work, then the failure to do so is a fall from righteousness. The marketplace is the fair and final judge: a low wage is somehow the worker's fault. For it simply reflects the low value of his labor. In the American atmosphere, poverty has always carried a whiff of sinfulness. (p. 95)

At the opposite extreme sat all my buddies and me. We aligned ourselves with the comfortable American anti-myth. (Isn't it interesting how people seek comfort above all else when we develop our philosophies?) We held that society and its inherent unfairness are responsible for poverty. My neighbors were victims of forces beyond our control. The rich and powerful made sure our schools, housing, and health care were inferior to theirs. We were being pushed into delinquency and dead-end jobs. We believed the "system" squashed us at every turn and it did so intentionally. We were never allowed to compete fairly with the rich. Most of their wealth was inherited for crying out loud. Talk about not working for it! There were always more people than jobs. That kept the wages low; it kept us in our place.

So there you have it—two myths dividing us up and keeping us apart. Because both groups of believers have very little interaction, it was simple to just cling to our stereotypes of one another. I began to see community organizing as my chance to "get even" and try to change what I saw in my view of the world. I saw my father come home at night, exhausted with his hands bleeding from overtime at the factory. Let someone just try to say the reason we didn't live in a better neighborhood was because he was lazy! Were the wealthy there to see my mother on her hands and knees keeping our kitchen immaculate after going to their houses and washing their floors as a low-paid domestic? I saw the world as I thought it was. I wanted to work for people and alongside people whose history was similar to mine. I found it natural and justifiable to follow all the steps in conflict organizing. I had no problem identifying who the enemy was. I found it even easier to personalize the targets and blame living human beings. They deserved to be attacked and blamed. I didn't even give it a second thought.

Community organizers use the conflict model because they are predisposed to distrust the rich and powerful.

Community organizers using the conflict model are predisposed, just like I was, to distrust the rich and powerful. A significant assumption is made from the very beginning. They feel that the system is set up to treat poor and working-class people unfairly. I subscribed to this assumption for the first part of my organizing career. When organizers make this assumption, the organizers, too, can be stereotyped. We are seen through the eyes of the believers of the American myth as wanting something for nothing. We feel we are owed. We feel that resources should be forcibly turned over to the poor. We are seen as people who rationalize that the poor are without any blame or responsibility, and we romanticize them as pure and noble. In point of fact, I knew some lazy, corrupt, nutty people in my community, but I wasn't going to admit it because that's what everyone outside the community thought.

Was it remotely possible that some of the rich, deep down, knew that their success wasn't always earned through sweat and intelligence? Was it possible, deep down, that some of them didn't even fit the stereotype I constructed? Well, I didn't even want to consider that because it took away from my argument. Was it possible that people could finally start getting past the stereotypes and begin a really fair and unbiased analysis of the mess we find ourselves in? Would it be possible to admit that the world we share is complicated with half-truths, nuances, exceptions, and contradictions?

As I plugged along, quite successfully I felt, in my organizing career, I came to a startling conclusion. It forced me to take a look into something I really didn't want to. It forced me to throw out a lot of what I had learned. So what is "it" exactly? "It" requires a trip south from Buffalo. We are going to Pittsburgh, Pennsylvania, the steel city. We are going to stay for a while.

We have a lot of work to do. So be ready to be surprised. Be ready to be shaken up. Be ready to read about the very beginning of understanding linking the self-interest of others. Be ready to read about the beginning of consensus organizing.

Once the Neighborhood Changes

Starting at about age 12, I got a treat each summer. My brother would take me to Pittsburgh. I would pack my suitcase and we would drive for 5 hours due south. We went to watch the Pittsburgh Pirates play at Forbes Field. I love baseball and I love the Pirates. They were my favorite team because when I was 10 years old they beat the New York Yankees in the World Series. They were huge underdogs. No one gave them a chance, but they played very hard and refused to quit.

We would drive down Route 19 through the hills and small towns of western Pennsylvania, and I would get more and more excited until I could see a distinctive orange glow in the sky. That meant we were getting close to steel mill pollution and the greatest right fielder the game of baseball has ever known, Roberto Clemente. Pittsburgh was gritty, cobblestoned, raw, and exhilarating. It felt like muscles and fists surrounded you. The people were reserved, quiet, and down-to-earth. The people seemed friendly and somewhat distant, all at the same time.

Forbes Field, the home of the Pirates, was like a dream—beautiful wooden seats, an ivy-covered left field wall with a city park behind it, and all its greenery in the distance. Instead of a giant concrete parking lot, a living, breathing neighborhood surrounded the stadium. You could live in that neighborhood and actually walk to a game. You could see the University of Pittsburgh all around the field. These wonderful boyhood memories made me want to move there. I had read stories about the Pittsburgh neighborhoods at the Buffalo Public Library. I just felt in my heart that it would be the place that I could become an organizer. I decided to move to Pittsburgh. I rented a room from a very nice older woman. It was as nice as could be expected when all I could afford was $40 a month in rent. I could walk to Forbes Field from that room, but by 1972 Forbes Field had been demolished. Only a small section of the left field wall and the ivy remained. One night after massive rainstorms, a leak developed right at the foot of my bed. I got up in the middle of the night, and I had to put a bowl over the blanket to catch the drops from the roof. When the radio alarm went off at 7:00 a.m., the news came on. Halfway through the news report, the announcer said that a famous community organizer named Saul Alinsky was dead due to an apparent heart attack while walking in Carmel, California. A song came on, and the water kept dripping. He was dead.

I heard about a community group called Perry Hilltop Citizens Council on the north side of Pittsburgh that wanted to hire someone as an organizer through the federal antipoverty program VISTA. I was interested. I applied and had an interview scheduled with the executive director, Tom Murphy. Murphy looked like a big, mop-haired kid—wide-eyed, fidgety, and unable to sit still. I admired his vision, energy, and his commitment to the organization. It would not have been surprising to find out that he had political ambitions. (He later served in the state legislature and became mayor of Pittsburgh.) He saw something in me and hired me immediately, placing me in the northern part of the working-class integrated neighborhood. I would have access to Tom for advice, but he left it up to me to identify an issue, mobilize the people, and secure a victory. The victory would lead to a stronger Perry Hilltop Citizens Council. This was the type of non-detailed, fly-by-the-seat-of-your-pants opportunity I had been praying for.

I hung out on the streets, at the shops, churches, and parks. I introduced myself to everyone. I listened carefully. It was not hard to find the issue that could galvanize the community. I had my boss to bounce things off of and I had access to the entire board of directors. Frank Simon, who ran the family business Simon's Funeral Home, chaired the all-volunteer board. It had to be important if you wanted some of Frank's time. He was a busy man. On a particularly pressing day, I sought out Frank's wisdom. He was on his way out the door and told me if I wanted to talk I had to "come along in the van." So you're thinking jump in, tag along, what's the big deal? That might be easy for you to say. Tagging along was a funeral euphemism for picking up a dead body. You really had to want his opinion. You had to zip up and carry.

It turned out that the neighborhood was being blockbusted. Blockbusting is a practice in which real estate agents use pressure and racial fear to create panic selling on the part of homeowners.

Blockbusting—A practice in which real estate agents use pressure and racial fear to create panic, causing large numbers of homes to be put up for sale at the same time

---

After creating panic, the real estate agents steer only minority buyers into the neighborhood to create an even larger turnover and bigger profits.

Neighborhoods can create fortunes for the real estate industry when this practice is successful. On a given Saturday, a neighborhood resident might be washing a car in the driveway. As Mr. Smith (homeowner) wipes away, an unannounced real estate agent approaches. He tells Mr. Smith that as a professional, he feels obligated to inform Mr. Smith that a change has begun to occur that will significantly lower his property value. A different "type" of buyer has now begun to target the neighborhood. If Mr. Smith decides to sell now, there are still buyers willing to pay top dollar. If he holds on to his property, no one will want to buy it in a few years and he will lose almost all of the equity he has built up. No more money for retirement, kids' college funds, or hospital bills. If Mr. Smith agrees to sell, the same agent shows up at both of the immediate neighbors' homes and says "Hundreds of families like the Smiths have decided to get out now." This is why it's called blockbusting. The block is actually being busted. This slimy use of people's racial anxiety was disgusting. I felt it was my job to design a strategy to help stop it. This is considered to be a tough issue to tackle in the organizing profession. If you are not careful, you can be perceived as a racist yourself, trying to deny access to minorities. It can divide neighbors rather than unite them. The most difficult aspect is that it can fail when people stick to themselves, refuse to participate, and quietly move away until everyone is gone.

Murphy thought it was a great issue and he gave me a lot of rope and trusted my strategic ability. You know what they say about rope, it also can be used in hangings. The neighborhood was already integrated and I knew I had to have a unified front of both black and white homeowners fighting the blockbusting or we would fail. So I remembered Alinsky and how he talked about uniting against a common enemy. The common enemy here had to be identified as the blockbusting real estate broker. I wanted to have both black and white homeowners "feel" this anger and hatred of the offending broker simultaneously. I did not want the whites to blame the blacks or vice versa.

I had to make sure whites and blacks would be angry at the same target and not at one another.

I recruited homeowners and matched them racially into pairs—one pair black and one pair white. I then trained each pair to go visit the blockbusting real estate company. Each pair would then give the agent a story in which each had the same income, savings, credit rating, family size, and housing desires. The only difference would be their race. Supposedly, if two people had the same income, savings, credit rating, and wanted the same features in a house, they would be shown the exact same homes. I knew that this would not happen. I needed the homeowners to see it firsthand. So at 10:00 a.m. on a Saturday, our white volunteer would present herself and her housing goals to the real estate agency. Real estate agents steered her to various suburbs that were virtually all white. Our volunteer (concealing that she was a satisfied Perry Hilltop resident) then requested to see homes in Perry Hilltop because she thought it would be a good choice. The agent said, "I don't think you would be comfortable there. It's a changing neighborhood and once the neighborhood changes you will never get your investment back. I would never show you a neighborhood that I wouldn't be comfortable having my own family live in." The irony and arrogance of this was that he was saying this to a person who lived in Perry Hilltop and loved the neighborhood.

An hour later, the black volunteer would have an appointment with the same agent from the same real estate company. She had the same income and savings as the white buyer. That same agent said, "I have some lovely homes to show you in a neighborhood called Perry Hilltop. It's safe, convenient, friendly, and a great place for your family." Our volunteer then asked to see homes in the same suburbs that the agency had recommended an hour earlier to the white buyer. The agent looked her right in the eye and told her unwaveringly, "Unfortunately, there is nothing that you can afford there." For a community organizer, you have just reached nirvana. You now have the anger and hatred focused right where you want it, a laser-beam shot at the real estate agent. My professional goal was to get the volunteers to reach this point. I had climbed to the top of the mountain. I did this exercise with pair after pair of residents until I had enough experienced volunteers to fill an entire room with this channeled anger and hatred. We rallied together at the Catholic church. Everybody was seething as the volunteers described how they felt as they were being manipulated. They now understood the severity of the problem and the enemy had been clearly identified.

We now had to choose tactics. I felt that the media had to be involved. It seemed they would be allies. This issue had everything the media lust for. It had conflict, greed, racism, and manipulation—everything except sex. If only I could have found the real estate broker sleeping with the real estate commissioner. Then, it would have been perfect. That would have made it seem like the pilot episode for a popular TV show. It was still close enough. As the organizer, I wanted the residents to go after the offending real estate agent's boss, the real estate broker. Jointly, we devised tactics to put pressure on him at his home, his place of business, even his house of worship. Our volunteers told the media about what his agents were doing daily to our neighborhood while he tried to appear like a God-fearing family man. The media covered all of our "actions" and were very sympathetic to our cause. We also took legal action, filing formal complaints with the real estate commission. Eventually, the broker surrendered. He stopped practicing blockbusting in Perry Hilltop.

I was trained to show the volunteers how they "won." We declared victory. We had a celebration. We felt the power of our collective action. We basked in the glow of our success. I reflected on our effort. I was a proud and happy organizer. As an afterthought, I figured it would be even more gratifying to find out how much money the company had lost as a result of our efforts. I thought it would be an even greater satisfaction for the residents to see a statistic dramatizing lost profits. It turned out to my surprise and horror, the company profits had not decreased. They had increased. Although it was true that the broker no longer made money in Perry Hilltop, he had increased sales dramatically in many of the wealthy all-white areas surrounding the city. It turned out that many future sellers read and watched the media stories we had planted and were glad to see that there was a company steering blacks away from their communities. When it came time to sell their own property, they switched from other real estate companies to the one we had fingered. I looked at the numbers again and again. The sinking feeling would not go away. It was undeniable. The real estate agency's overall profit had increased significantly, in great part, because of us. Our success now took on a strange hollowness.

The legal action we took resulted in a slap-on-the-wrist fine. Again, even after being caught, there was no financial pain felt by the broker. Even more important, my volunteers were very tired. Where was this euphoria of power, where was the positive carryover? I just did not see it. I saw a sense of relief. The Perry Hilltop homeowners were relieved that their efforts were no longer needed. But relief is not empowerment. I had used fear and anger for motivation. Fear and anger are very draining; they deplete one's energy. It is very difficult to use these emotions and carry them over to further increase involvement. Think of it—how long do you prefer to stay mad? I had gone from what I thought was a textbook victory to something much less—a puzzling defeat.

It was time to rethink what had happened and rethink what to do next. I sat by myself in my basement apartment. On my kitchen table, with a yellow legal pad, I wrote the word power at the top of the page with a question, "Who has it?" I could not see real power transferred to members of the community. I concluded that the power must have remained within the real estate industry. The more I thought about it, the more animated I became.

If one had this power and chose not to abuse it, wouldn't everything be fine? If this was true, it meant the power was there for the asking. We didn't have to transfer it. We had to compete for it. If we had that power and did not abuse it, perhaps everything would be fine. We didn't need to fear or resent the power of the real estate industry. We needed to *have* the power of the real estate industry. For the first time, I saw the difference between stopping an action and creating a solution. If we were right where the power was, we could take the power and help our community. An idea that would be very logical in most professions seemed so revolutionary to me, the community organizer. Being a part of the system and proposing to be a part of the system was a very strange feeling. In this particular set of circumstances, the way we could actually have power was to compete within the system and sell the houses ourselves.

Taking a fresh look at the situation meant that we had other options.

I called some fellow organizers from other neighborhoods to bounce my ideas off of them in the hope of getting them excited. They were very excited. Excited to kick me in my butt. I felt a venom and hatred that actually frightened me. "You call yourself an organizer? How could you ever want people to be part of this corrupt system? How could you sell out your volunteers? Don't let those bastards off the hook." Over and over again, they blasted the idea of Perry Hilltop residents entering and benefiting from the real estate profession. My reaction to all of this was schizophrenic. I should be listening to fellow professionals whom I respected, people who dedicated themselves to correcting injustice and discrimination. At the same time, I had always felt that when you get this type of overreaction you probably have exposed some deep-seated uncertainty. Luckily, I took the idea to my board of directors. These were the volunteer leaders of the Perry Hilltop Citizens Council. Have you ever presented an idea to a group of people when you were unsure of their reaction? You keep qualifying and qualifying your idea. That's what I did. I did not want my head snapped off. "You might want to consider. . . ." or "One possible option could be. . . ." I took a deep breath and hunkered down in my imaginary foxhole waiting for the pin to be removed from the hand grenade. I opened my eyes and actually saw smiles all around the table from almost every board member. They started asking rapid-fire questions, like kids who are told that this year they get to pick their vacation. "Wow, could we actually be real estate agents? You mean we can open an office! Hey, we might actually be great at this." There was genuine enthusiasm. There was an energy I had not seen before. I had worked with these people for a year and never felt or saw anything like this.

Positive opportunities can create positive energy.

Of course, I was not prepared to answer the detailed questions they were asking. I knew nothing of how the real estate industry worked. All I needed to know previously was that it was bad. I now needed to find the answers. I could not wait for the next meeting.

HAVE I GOT A HOUSE FOR YOU

It turned out that a person could become a licensed real estate agent in Pennsylvania without having a college degree, a lot of money, or any experience. I was shocked that the profession that had caused us so many problems was so open to having us join it. This easy access was very good news to the residents of our working-class neighborhood. It meant that we could enroll in a course, take it on Saturdays for just a couple of hundred dollars, and then take a standardized test. If we passed, we could work for a sponsor, a licensed real estate broker. The good news was that the profession was open to us without the barriers I would have expected. Community activists always see systems as roadblocks full of discrimination and barriers. The bad news from my point of view was that we could not control the whole thing and start our own company from day one. Instead, we would have to work for an existing real estate broker and his or her existing company. After our agents had 3 years' experience, they could then take additional courses, pass another test, and become brokers in their own right. Then, we would finally have control.

As an organizer, I was taught that control was crucial. Much of the conflict in low-income neighborhood activism centers on the theory that without taking control away from others we would be treated unfairly. Without control, we would be stepped on and spit on. I cringed at presenting my findings to fellow organizers. As expected, they did not take the news well. They reacted predictably. One organizer said, "You mean you intend to put money from the sweat of the community into the broker's pocket?" It was the original venom I had seen, but now turned up to the third power.

It was time to make another presentation to my volunteer board. The members reacted with the same positive energy I had seen from them earlier. It proved consistent and unshakeable. Their questions centered on which existing companies we should pick to speak with. They were thinking about who would make a good partner. I was intrigued. Why was it that the organizers hated the idea but the residents loved it? All I knew was that I worked for the residents and not the organizers. We met at the same church where we had earlier planned our attacks on the real estate profession. Now we planned our strategy to enter that very same profession. I wrote two columns on a chalkboard. What did we have to offer? What did the brokers have to offer? The residents filled in the columns.

Community	Real Estate Broker
Credibility	License
Motivated agents	Money
Connections to homeowners	Experience
Relationships with key leaders, such as pastors, teachers, funeral directors	Connections within the profession

We felt the list proved that there was potential for a partnership. I saw for the first time in my organizing career the potential power of the idea of mutual self-interest. Because of past injustice, I had been shaped to believe that members of the community deserved all of the benefits. We should not have to share with anyone because we had had nothing for so long. I felt that we were owed the entire profit. The trouble with this concept was that no one besides the organizers would ever support it. Again, the residents were much more practical. Of course there had to be "something in it" for the broker in order for him or her to want to become our partner. The residents just wanted to make sure the partnership was equal and that we all benefited equally. The list showed the residents and the brokers there was potential for equality.

We needed to negotiate around everyone's self-interest.

We refined our negotiating stance and added some points. We wanted the broker to relocate his or her office within our neighborhood in a building that we would purchase and rehabilitate, making the broker a tenant and community members the landlord. Finally, we wanted the broker to make a charitable contribution to the citizens council upon the completion of each sale. This would motivate everyone in the neighborhood to list and buy with the broker, further increasing profits and sales.

We chose the largest, most financially successful broker to be our first choice as a potential partner. In the past, I would have recruited hundreds of homeowners to cram into his office to drive home our agenda. I would have thought anything less would mean we would be taken advantage of. We would be treated unfairly. This time only three residents made the formal presentation, with me present but in the background. The broker listened intently. The presentation was concise, logical, and businesslike. The broker took a deep breath and contemplated the idea the residents had presented. He said he was intrigued by it and would very much like to be our partner, but he added one more thing. He wanted to begin our partnership in 3 years. This was a company that was rapidly expanding with loads of financial resources. Why would he want to wait 3 years? He explained very casually that he felt that the block-busting that had caused our property values to plummet had not run its entire course. He felt confident that the properties would bottom out in 3 years. Then, he would use our partnership to buy up the properties, and he would sell those properties to yuppies, gentrifying the neighborhood, and turning it all white! I was devastated. The image of a gigantic Alinsky, his followers, and the sounds of their laughter and glee rang in my ears. No wonder they had advised me not to sleep with the enemy. I left the meeting like a dog with a tail between my legs. I could hardly bear to look at the volunteers. I felt I had failed them again and my organizing career was over. How could I have recommended a strategy that led us to this horrible spot?

When I finally mustered the courage to pick my head up, I couldn't believe what I saw. The homeowners' energy was still there. They did not look devastated. One volunteer spoke with conviction, "Let's go to another company, and negotiate. We'll show that son of a bitch." The other two were right behind him. It was then that I learned two of my greatest organizing lessons. Lesson one, the broker told the truth. Why? Why didn't he say that he couldn't help us yet, make some flimsy excuse, and dupe us into coming back in 3 years? I believed he told the truth because of how we dealt with him. We were straightforward, putting our own cards on the table without posturing. We told him the truth with no exaggerations. We didn't talk to him about how much he owed us or how unfair his profession had been. We did not lace our presentation with threats and recriminations. We talked to him like his pals do on the 16th hole. This apparently had made him comfortable. It increased the odds of him putting his cards on the table and talking to us honestly.

> The truth can motivate people to act. False hope can make people give up.

Lesson two, why were the residents energized? The broker's response kept them focused and increased their determination. I believe the response was a response to the truth. The truth motivates people from low-income and working-class neighborhoods. What deflates us is the "I really want to help you but. . . ." response. City government officials have perfected this response, but you can also hear it from almost anyone. You know it and you've heard it. "I stand ready to help you but according to our funding priorities, previously developed plans blah blah blah blah. . . ." This is what deflates people. So when organizers begin relationships with manipulation and posturing they get it returned tenfold. The truth increased the chance for a truthful response. Truthful conversations can lead to truthful relationships. Do we really keep close relationships with friends because of their skill at lying and manipulation, or do we keep friends because of their truthfulness? Thus, with these two stumbled-upon lessons, a new community organizing approach began. It had no name or written formula, but it was not business as usual.

The second company we approached was much smaller and modest in its goals. Our volunteers explained the proposal with increased confidence. The broker listened and jotted down notes on a yellow legal pad. They looked like dollar amounts. I leaned over and saw a plus sign at the bottom of the pad. The broker said, "I'll do it." We now had our partner.

> Could the self-interest of the neighborhood and the broker be the same?

Four agent candidates studied together. Their study efforts were documented in our little neighborhood newsletter. Their neighbors brought over snacks and baked goods while they reviewed their lessons. It became a true community effort. A large number of real estate students fail the exam on their first try and have to start over. In our case, all four candidates passed on the first try. We secured a building, a long-term lease was signed, and we were in the real estate business.

Once the office opened, it was positively dreamlike. Here was this renovated building where dedicated people worked to help our community. They were no longer just neighborhood activists. They were now knowledgeable businessmen and women. To get listings from people who wanted to sell their property, we canvassed the neighborhood and made residents aware of our new office. It worked just as we had anticipated. Key people vouched for us and steered listings our way. Crossing guards, postal workers, and funeral directors kept their ears open and whenever a family was planning to leave for "normal" reasons (not racial panic), we got their business. When people panicked and felt they were going to lose all their money, our agents advised them to stay. This dual function proved to be very powerful. In both cases, it was the agents' credibility as persons with real estate expertise that made the difference. Speaking as community activists only, their advice probably would have been dismissed because their motives would have been marginalized. Residents would have felt that they were asked to stay by people who were do-gooders and didn't know any better. Now they were asked to stay by people who knew what they were talking about.

Finding buyers, though more difficult, was also proceeding along nicely. Frequently, a potential buyer would express reluctance to purchase a property in Perry Hilltop because of the negative publicity about the neighborhood that we previously had generated. Again, the credibility of the agents won out. The agents would tell the prospective buyers that no matter what they had heard, we lived there, shopped there, worshipped there, and it was a great, great place. Their credibility carried the day and we started to see business come our way and sales contracts signed. Life was good. Our new approach was working just as we had planned. Except for the next step. That proved to be slightly more difficult. The next step was never addressed in our planning. We had to get a mortgage loan from the bank.

THEY'RE SCREWING US

In traditional Alinsky-style organizing, you consistently oversimplify. As you define your target, the target becomes the cause of all evil. To motivate people and mobilize them, you have to tell them about simple solutions.

Rarely will you hear an organizer say, "It's actually much more complicated than it seems." Instead it's "All you have to do is. . . ."

There is danger in oversimplifying a problem. There is always more to it than it seems.

Well, I'm here to tell you that this was much more complicated than it seemed. Here, we had planned out a very innovative idea to what I thought was perfection. But the idea came from an organizing issue that had woefully simplified the problem. It was not just the real estate industry that had created the problem—far from it. The real estate operators were just one spoke in the wheel. After securing the listing and finding a buyer, the buyer has to line up financing to be able to purchase the property. Rarely are sales made entirely in cash. Banks and mortgage companies are almost always essential partners. In our neighborhood, the lenders proved reluctant to lend. They believed that the future quality of life in our neighborhood was in question and so were the property values. Remember the "You haven't bottomed out" speech made by the first real estate broker? Lenders lend for long periods of time, 15, 20, 25, 30 years. If a homeowner is delinquent in his mortgage payments, the lender eventually takes back the house. If the house is worth more than the amount that was borrowed, the lender still makes a profit. But what if the house is now worth less than what was borrowed? Then, the lender has a very serious problem. Lenders do not like to take risks that can lead to losses. They frequently take a negative look into their crystal ball and if the neighborhood is undergoing ethnic or racial change, loans may not be made. Perry Hilltop was such a neighborhood. The lenders had our newspaper stories to prove it. When appraisers, professionals hired by lenders to determine property values, went out to inspect houses, they were put into a position of determining whether or not the loan would be approved. If a house sells for $100,000 but the appraiser determines the worth to be $88,000 and the buyer has only a $10,000 down payment, the loan request would be rejected. If the house were appraised at $90,000 or more, the loan would be approved. The potential abuse of power of the appraiser (by completing the appraisal) was never targeted in our old style of organizing. It was never even recognized or understood. This other profession, appraising, was protecting powerful discriminatory practices in complete obscurity.

When we received the first loan rejection we were confused. We went to see our broker. I remember going to see him filled with disgust and obligation. I did not see him as a source of a strategy or solution. I will never forget his reaction. He screamed, "They're screwing us!" Us. What a lovely sound that word had when he used it. We had an ally. This was not the same as having him be a sympathizer or supporter. A supporter never says "us"; they always say "you." All of a sudden, this outsider, interloper, and opportunist was not only one of us, but a person with some expertise and determination. His self-interest and our self-interest were perfectly matched. We were about to become a great team.

We solve problems together when we have the same problems.

The broker explained the process to our community group. He showed that it was far from an exact science. He showed how much judgment and wiggle room there was in the appraisal process. He explained the three different appraisal methods that were used and how the official forms were filled out. He showed us what the lender would eventually see. We jointly devised a plan to change how the appraiser made his determination. We used our respective strengths as a team. We even had some fun in the process. The appraiser needed a key to get into the houses, and our agents had the keys. We knew the name of the specific appraiser, the company he worked for, and the time he would do his inspection.

We had the neighbors waiting for him when his car pulled up. You should have seen the look on his face. There he is on automatic pilot, muttering to himself about how quickly he needs to get this over with, when he suddenly sees a group of people waiting for him who know his name. This time we had no media, signs, or chanting; but we still had plenty of pressure. This was a different type of pressure for sure. One volunteer said, "You must be Mr. Smith." He was stunned and afraid. What did these people want? "Let me introduce you to all the neighbors of the Johnsons, the new family moving into this lovely house, after the loan is approved." Each neighbor then recounted in detail all the recent improvements they had made on their homes. Then in a coup de grace, we presented him with a complete appraisal form with all the "facts" determined; this proved that the value of the property was well beyond the loan request. We told the appraiser how lucky the Johnsons were to get such a good deal. After all this, if he lowballed the appraisal, he would be taking an enormous risk. We felt it was a risk he would choose not to take. As suspected, the appraiser concluded that the true value of the property was above the loan amount, and the deals started to sail through.

This success fascinated me. We were still able to use some of our organizing tactics, but we did it in a new, subtler way. We never embarrassed anyone, and nothing became public. We burrowed inside the system. We understood the obstacles and the intervention that was necessary. We were doing what members of wealthy communities knew how to do. We were making the system work to *our* benefit. By bringing in our new partner, the broker, we gained strength. I felt that we were learning a great deal. I watched the confidence build among the agents and saw the profit flowing into the company, which then recycled back into the community.

Perry Hilltop today remains a stable, integrated community. The newspaper, the *Pittsburgh Post-Gazette*, did a series of articles on race relations throughout Pittsburgh, almost 20 years after this effort. It recognized Perry Hilltop as one of the best examples of how a neighborhood could develop and maintain real, deep, lasting relationships and friendships among races. It talked about how everyone respected one another and got along. Twenty years after the fact, I read this story with great pride. The residents had done much more than win a battle. They had won the war.

So there you have the very beginning of a different model of community organizing. We stumbled onto a new way of looking at a problem caused by powerlessness and the abuse caused by those in power. It seemed very different. I promised I wouldn't put a graph on every page, but maybe a little visual layout might help make sure you grasp some of the key differences in organizational methods before I move on and continue the story. Please take a look at these carefully. It would be helpful if you tried to take an issue that affects you either in your job or where you live and try to plug it into both of the outlines. Don't worry about the scale. You can pick something as basic as getting the garbage picked up or a stoplight being installed. The smaller the issue, the more the exercise will seem real to you. Try it out by first digesting two tables. Table 2.1 shows the difference in two organizing models—conflict and consensus. Table 2.2 shows how both methods were applied to the blockbusting problem. Figure 2.1 shows obstacles and how to overcome them by using consensus organizing.

Table 2.1 Conflict Organizing Versus Consensus Organizing

Topic	Conflict Organizing Strategy	Consensus Organizing Strategy
Issue Selection	Unity, community against a common enemy	Ties self-interest of the community to the self-interest of others
Emotions	Get community members angry	Get community members optimistic
Tactics	Target an individual identified as the "holder" of the power	Develop a partner who will benefit from the effort
Power	Take it away from those causing the problem	Grow power for the community and the partner
Roles	Advocate by pressuring and embarrassing the target	Engage and energize all the partners
Initial Goal	Mobilize the largest number of community members possible	Get everyone to articulate their real interests
Final Goal	Get target to "give in" to demands	Have all partners benefit
Next Steps	Find a new issue in which an injustice unifies a community against a new common enemy	Build on positive relationships among partners to find new opportunities to involve additional partners

Table 2.2 Blockbusting Problem—Conflict Organizing Versus Consensus Organizing

Topic	Blockbusting—Conflict Organizing Strategy	Blockbusting—Consensus Organizing Strategy
Issue Selection	Panic created by real estate tactics	Chance to gain control of real estate market
Emotions	Anger over being manipulated and tricked by real estate company	Hope, enthusiasm, optimism to take positive steps to control market
Tactics	Pressure real estate broker at his home, office, place of worship	Find mutual self-interest in controlling market
Power	Gain power through pressure and force	Gain power by forming partnership
Roles	Mobilize neighborhood residents (good guys) against real estate broker (bad guy)	Community gets buyers and sellers acting as agents' broker. Uses expertise, money, license as business
Initial Goal	Stop blockbusting	Sell real estate—control market
Final Goal	Drive real estate company out of the neighborhood	Stabilize racial composition, make profit, improve community
Next Steps	Prove how powerful we are	Form more partnerships

Step 1: Stop Blockbusting—Form a partnership with a real estate company.

Step 2: Get Mortgage Loans—Use broker's expertise and community power to change appraisals.

Step 3: Stabilize Neighborhood—List and sell houses for "normal" reasons, e.g., job transfer, house too big, too small, and so on. Stop people from leaving out of fear, and still make a profit for brokers, agents, and neighbors.

Figure 2.1   Obstacles Overcome by Consensus Organizing

Reflection Questions

1. Do you believe mostly in the American myth or the anti-myth? Why?

2. Did you ever wish you were Robin Hood? (Goal: Take from the rich and give to the poor.)

3. Did you ever wish you were a conservative radio talk show host? (Goal: Take from the poor and give to the rich.)

4. Do you think that blockbusting still occurs? If so, what strategies would you use to stop it?

5. Other than community organizing, what other professions try to fight for justice and equality?

6. Which is a better sandwich—beef-on-weck or chip-chopped ham?

Reference

Shipler, D. (2004). *The working poor.* New York: Random House.

3

ISSUES ANALYSIS

In this chapter, you will learn:

◆ The importance of listening.

◆ How to do individual interviews.

◆ How to determine commitment.

◆ The importance of social capital.

There is certainly no shortage of problems that need to be addressed in low-income and working-class neighborhoods. There usually is no shortage of social service providers in these same neighborhoods. Frequently, social service agencies declare which problems need to be addressed in a given community, how they are going to be addressed, and who will address them. (Surprise! Themselves!) Organizers do the opposite. They look at what community members want to change and develop their personal commitment to do so. Organizers must look at their role in a very different way. Invariably, students think the first thing to do is to hold a big meeting and ask all the people what they think. No! No! No! No! Imagine trying to get anything done in your personal life this way. For instance, suppose you were dating a number of people at the same time. You were confused about what you should do next, how to decide on only one you wanted to see more seriously, and, at the same time, stop seeing the others. Would you invite them all to a large conference room and, with all of them in the room, ask them what they thought you should do? No, I bet you wouldn't. Because if you did, they would all have different ideas, they would all disagree with one other, and they would all start looking at you with a little less of a heart flutter. In fact, the only conclusion they could come to would be what an idiot you were. That's why you wouldn't use this strategy as an organizer either. Think a little more about the "Hey, I got it; let's invite everyone to a big strategy meeting." Suppose there was a crime wave in the neighborhood. Suppose you invited people to a big meeting to discuss the problem. God help you if a lot of people showed up. (Luckily, they probably wouldn't.) If they did, the people would bitch and moan and argue with one other about who was committing the crimes and that "somebody" should do something about it. Each person's circumstances would be portrayed as worse than anyone else's. The problem is worse on *my* block, *my* side of the street, *my* sidewalk. People would play a contest of "Oh yeah, that's nothing, let me tell you about me." It would be like an open mike night in a coffeehouse: folksinger after folksinger, crooning off-key in song after song about train wrecks, coal mining disasters, and lost love suicides. It might be a bit of a downer. There would be no positive energy or group cohesion.

So, if it's not the big meeting, and it's not deciding for yourself what everyone else needs, like the social service agency, then what exactly is it? It's the totally unglamorous, repetitive process of listening to individuals one-on-one. You listen to each person very carefully. You hear what people say. You look for the emotions behind their thoughts. You look for the values that shape their thoughts. This is a skill that can be gained through practice. After all, we live in an American society that rewards talkers and undervalues listeners. When was the last time you turned on the TV or radio and watched or heard a "listen" show? There are no listen shows. There are a lot of talk shows. We see politicians and we judge their ability to give speeches, not their ability to listen intently. We study public speaking in college and never are asked about our skills in listening. Do we give citations and awards at our place of employment to great listeners? Don't let the underappreciation fool you. It is the community organizer's greatest skill. So let's go through a series of steps to lead us to taking a specific action. Organizers refer to this process as developing an "issue."

ONE-ON-ONES

One-on-Ones—Meeting with one person, listening carefully to determine his or her self-interest

---

There are several practical reasons why speaking and listening to people individually is the place to start.

1. There is a good chance of an honest exchange. When there is no one there but the two of you, there is much less tendency to posture, lecture, and overdramatize. There are no cameras rolling. There is no roomful of people to impress. Remember, you cannot build a real relationship around anything but honesty.

2. You can listen and not miss much. When you only have one person to listen to, you listen a little better. The person can catch you if you yawn. The person can tell when you drift away to that vacation in Hawaii you've always wanted to take. As you zero in to listen to that one person, you can pick up nuances, inflections, and deeper meanings. There is a big difference between someone saying positive things with an eyebrow versus someone saying those same things with a raised eyebrow.

3. You can ask pointed questions. As the person speaks, you can zero in on the really important stuff. You can get to the heart of the matter. You can drill to the core of the person's beliefs with precision. In a group or large meeting, sometimes things stay too general. Sometimes members of a group stay superficial because relationships of trust have not been built. With one person, you can follow up with questions that get to the motivations you need to recognize. There is a big difference between "Yes, I am concerned about the homeless" and "Here's how I felt when my family was homeless." Organizers need to gauge motivation and depth of commitment and individual conversations get you there quickly and accurately.

4. You can connect on a personal level. Seeing one person elevates the importance of that person to you.

When someone has been asked to meet with you as part of a large group, well, it doesn't quite sit as well with that person. If you meet with just Rachel, then Rachel feels she rates in your book. It is a powerful psychological message to send. "Rachel you are so important, that even though I could be doing millions of other things, I'd rather spend my time listening to you." Now that says a lot about what you think of Rachel who, in turn, thinks you are a really astute person. She is not some statistic at a rally; she is the key to success.

Many activists feel guilty about spending a whole hour talking to one person. They say, "Shouldn't I be doing more with my time so I have a bigger impact?" Resist this feeling of guilt suggesting you are not doing enough. You are doing exactly what you should be doing. You are building relationships through honesty and trust. There is a big difference between someone telling you what they think you want to hear and someone telling you what they really do think. In low-income communities, people will frequently fish around to see what services you or your organization might provide or the candidate or ballot issue that you support. Be very careful when this happens. This is a technique to determine your agenda so they can then tell you what they think you want to hear as a way to make you happy and get rid of you. It goes like this. You say, "Hello sir, I am with the East Side Youth Organization. Do you think loitering is a problem?" They say to you, "Don't you run those wonderful basketball leagues in the summer? Why that's the kind of wonderful thing our young people need." They do this to get their young cousin into your program and have you leave without asking a bunch of inane questions. You leave like the cat that ate the canary, thinking how respected you are and how good it is to get input from the community. See how far away this is from what people really care about and what they might be willing to do about it?

Also, beware of an almost opposite problem: the appearance of disinterest. People sometimes hide genuine interest because they are isolated and think they are the only one with a particular concern. They believe they don't have the power to change it. They think you are not interested in helping them accomplish what they want. When this reaction kicks in, instead of admitting one or more of these reasons they say, "I don't really have any interest in changing anything." A novice could easily misread this and, even worse, start blaming the residents for unwillingness to get involved. You have to push past this half-fake disinterest. Say something like "Why do you still live here?" to break the logjam. For instance, one person might say, "I'm not a member of any group in my neighborhood." Another might say, "I try to keep to myself." And another might say, "I just don't trust strangers."

Is this an apathetic bunch? Maybe; maybe not. Could it be that they all happen to live in a very high-crime neighborhood? You would really have to listen to know. Only through careful listening could you determine the reasons and causes for their statements. Once you have determined the true meaning behind the comments, you will know better which issues to focus on and which direction to take.

COMMITMENT

Commitment—People's willingness to do real work while addressing their concerns

---

As you listen to more and more people, a pattern begins to develop in what you hear. Even though the words and phrases are different, similarities surface. These similarities hold the potential to become a direction for collective action. You see ideas that could hold a larger number of people's interest. For instance, maybe all the people you talk to remember fondly a time when they were proud to be living in their community. Many talk about specific things they were proud of. They show emotion talking about what they have lost. They would love to get it back. When this happens, you can begin a second step. This second step tests people's willingness to participate in bringing back the thing they have lost (library, store, police station, etc.). If people are unwilling to participate beyond articulating their feelings, you have reached a dead end. You never have a viable issue if people are unwilling to put personal effort into addressing it.

Community organizing is not a social service approach. People cannot demonstrate a need and then have community organizers provide the program to address that need. Instead, community organizers must discipline themselves at this key stage to make sure that they do not design or propose a specific program or intervention. Instead, community organizers raise the bar and ask the residents to participate and make a commitment to be part of the solution. This is the exact spot where many professionals (government employees, school administrators, social workers, counselors) make a key mistake. They feel that as professionals, they have expertly identified a need and now must appropriately design the expert intervention that leads to the eventual solution. Stop! Do not pass "Go." Do not design a program. Do not fund-raise. Do not collect $200. Take a deep breath and in this Monopoly game, try to get a "Get-out-of jail-free" card. This is your chance to savor the real freedom that comes from a good organizing strategy. This is not a time to spoil all your efforts. You have just seen a real pattern in what people care about. You now have a chance to involve them in completely new ways. You have the opportunity to have them experience some collective and individual power. For some of them, this may be the opportunity of a lifetime. They will not be empowered through some program you design. Instead, tap their creativity, their desire for respect, their hunger to be involved with others. You must be the one who sees their abilities to play these roles.

When you grow up poor or working class in our society, you are told, indirectly, hundreds of times each day, that you are a very limited person. You are told you are only good for certain things. If you see yourself as an equal to anyone in power, you are portrayed as arrogant, pushy, ungrateful, and "too big for your britches." God forbid that a parent could know as much as a teacher, a teenager could know as much as a counselor, or a voter could know as much as an elected official. Over the years, and unfortunately now sometimes over entire generations, people learn that they must develop low expectations of themselves, their families, and their neighborhoods. You are the one who breaks the links in the chain or ties the chain tighter. You have the ability to be the first person to see the real potential that has been locked away. Look at yourself as an excellent talent scout. Try to not only recognize their abilities but also to fully count on those abilities. Organizers tell people that nothing can be accomplished without their involvement. We can only be successful if they become involved. Most professionals do the opposite. They frequently focus on what they can do for the client, resident, parent, and so on.

Issue Strategy

Issue Strategy—A detailed plan that addresses a problem in a clear, easy-to-follow, and measurable way

Strategy is key to any organizing effort. Change requires people to do things differently. Doing things differently requires thinking differently. Thinking differently comes from strategy. Think about your own family. If your younger sister always got her own way at your expense and you wanted to change this, how could you be successful? Would you just go to your parents and whine and complain? You might. If you did, it would not work. Your parents would not want to listen to your whining and complaining and would see you as the cause of the problem. If, instead, you talked separately to your mom and dad about your sister and they both in their own way started to hint that they realized your sister was behaving a bit too immaturely, voilà, you now have gotten to the spot where strategy might get you results. Strategy must always be clear, easy to follow, easy to measure and reach achievable results in a reasonable period of time. The issues can't be so entrenched that they can't be addressed in a period of time that will hold people's interest and keep them involved.

Many organizers make the mistake of feeling that they are the ones saddled with the burden of devising a strategy. Strategy instead should evolve from input from a number of participants. You can have the kernel of an idea, but others help pop the kernel. The most effective strategies evolve from a series of discussions with committed individuals. Even if you are a brilliant strategist, strategy development should never be an "individual" responsibility. Say a brilliant strategist decides to brilliantly strategize all alone. If things later get sticky, watch what happens to a plan developed by a committee of one. Because no other participants were allowed to design the strategy, they begin to blame the solo artist. Instead, when the strategy evolves from an entire committed group, members of the group meet to retool, think together, stay on their toes, keep devising and revising strategies until they formulate a solution and achieve their goal. Now, to be realistic, some organizers are excellent strategists. They have the ability to stay ahead of the pack. They may remain a little quicker and more accurate than many of the people they are working with. If you are lucky enough to count yourself in this category, you still must develop everyone else's confidence so they learn to strategize as well. If you are not the greatest strategist, take notice! There are many others who are better. See how lucky you are?

THE EXTRA WRINKLE—SOCIAL CAPITAL

Social Capital—A series of relationships that cause people to want to help one another and be helped in return

In my experience in conflict organizing, deciding on an issue followed a pretty simple formula with a series of steps that took you down the same path no matter where you worked. In one-on-one interviews, you looked for what made people mad. You helped them to focus on a target for that anger. You personalized the target. You mobilized people to put pressure on the target. You sought concessions from the target. There was time pressure to achieve these concessions or it was feared that people would get frustrated, lose confidence, and give up. As a result, the issue had to be "winnable," with the victory coming in a relatively short period of time. Once I began to believe there were limits to this approach, I wanted to move on and build additional relationships beyond just the people who were angry and suffering from the problem. I wanted to build connections with people outside the situation who might have their own self-interest in helping. I wanted to test an assumption that sometimes even those people or organizations causing the problem might be coaxed into becoming part of the solution. Robert Putnam describes this additional step of going beyond the "victims" and reaching out to others very well. Putnam is famous for writing the book *Bowling Alone* (2000). He won me over right away because the book jacket on the original hardcover edition has a picture of him and his 12-year-old pals wearing their team bowling shirts. I mean, you have to like a guy who puts that photo on the cover. He writes a great deal about the concept of social capital. Social capital is the glue that holds communities together. It is a series of relationships that lead to social networks and people helping one another and being helped in return. Your extended family, church group, college roommates, poker buddies, and neighborhood crime watch participants can all be sources of important social capital. The denser the spiderweb of social capital, the stronger the community becomes. In other words, the relationships you build are valuable and as more relationships are built, power grows.

Organizers look inside the community to build relationships among the members. Putnam (2000) also looks inside the community and sees the need to build positive, reciprocal relationships in which the residents know one another and help one another. He calls the process "bonding." Later, I came to the conclusion that there needed to be additional allies, friends, and partnerships with people outside the community. Putnam calls this effort "bridging." I believed the working-class and poor communities I worked in needed to bond to grow stronger with residents helping residents, but they also needed to bridge to make new outside contacts to become even more effective. This process of bonding and bridging became the cornerstone of what is now called consensus organizing. I started to think that issue selection still would be dependent on what the one-on-ones revealed but those one-on-ones also needed to be done on at least two parallel tracks. I had to determine what the self-interest and level of commitment was from potential reciprocal relationships stretching from inside to outside the community. What did both "sides" think? What topics were they interested in and why? What might be a way to get a commitment from them? How similar could proposed solutions become?

OK, as I said, this doubles your organizing work. But it also increases the chance that some real change can occur once an issue is pinpointed. If the issue can be framed in such a way that all involved want the same solution, we might be on to a pretty different and promising approach. For now, just try to let the idea of consensus organizing sink in a little. It helped one little neighborhood. Could it stand the test of one of the toughest, problematic, divided regions in the nation? Can you even conceive of the area we are going to on our trip? Let's really put the model to the test.

WHY DON'T THEY JUST LEAVE?

Dave Bergholz had been a musician, student activist, and community organizer. He never hesitated to give his opinion, get in your face to defend it, and always feel he was right. Dave Bergholz was an interesting guy and in 1985 he worked for an interesting organization: The Allegheny Conference on Community Development. The "Conference," as it is called in Pittsburgh, was the ultimate good-old-boy network. You served on the board based on earning the position of chief executive officer in one of Pittsburgh's major corporate headquarters. Pittsburgh, despite its rather small size, has a very high percentage of companies that choose it as their international home. The Conference did not allow any delegation to vice presidents, public relations staff, or executive aides. If you were the CEO of Westinghouse, Heinz, U.S. Steel, or Mellon Bank you were asked to serve, expected to serve, and, as a result, you served. Bergholz has a striking resemblance to a bulldog. Saying he is intense is not quite capturing his true essence. He had an interesting pre-Conference life. He was an ex-1960s hippie, guitar-playing folksinger who, because of his supreme intellect, analytical ability, and political skills, had earned his way into the position of conference assistant director. In 1985, he wanted to see me. I had met him through my earlier Perry Hilltop work. He wanted to talk about a region of small towns that lined the Monongahela River right outside Pittsburgh city limits. The area was called the Mon Valley, shortened from the name of the river that ran through all the small towns. By the mid-1980s, the economy of the region had dried up. The towns were built completely around the steel industry. Coal, mined in nearby West Virginia, was sent up the river to these towns where factories were built to make the steel. Downtown Pittsburgh housed the white-collar workers and projected the corporate presence. These steel mills, however, had enormous impact on the entire United States. The mills and the workers in them produced the steel that helped win the Second World War. They made the steel that built the Golden Gate Bridge. The region was so famous and so "state-of-the-art" that former Soviet leader Nikita Khrushchev, when planning his historic U.S. visit, wanted to see two things: Disneyland and the U.S. Steel Homestead Works in Mon Valley.

By the mid-1980s, no one famous wanted to see anything in Homestead, Pennsylvania. Steel production had peaked decades earlier. Now, one by one, the factories were closing. This was a difficult time for the region. This was different from all the other cyclical slowdowns that had occurred before it. This time the closings were permanent. Experts predicted that 120,000 jobs would simply disappear.

Steel and banking executives, sitting on the Conference board, had made these decisions to close the factories. Lives of the families of the steelworkers were changing in dramatic ways. Incomes that had allowed families to achieve middle-class status had fallen through the floor. Men went from well-paying union jobs with excellent benefits to service jobs at or near the minimum wage. Many became permanently unemployed. Back in Buffalo, New York, my pals from the Eastside, who had laughed at the absurdity of going to college when you could make good money at the factory, also were being laid off. As they received their last paychecks, I was taking an elevator to the top of the U.S. Steel building in Pittsburgh. The view was breathtaking. To the north you could see Perry Hilltop. To the south you could see the first of a string of closed steel mills. The sky had lost the orange tint I used to anticipate on trips from Buffalo to Pittsburgh with my brother. Mr. Bergholz was ready to see me now.

Dave is a very direct bulldog. He cut right to the chase. He knew I had some experience organizing a community credit union in the Mon Valley; he knew about how I worked. He and his boss, Bob Pease, and the Allegheny Conference board of CEOs had been strategizing about the Mon

Valley. There were thousands of very angry people looking for someone to blame. Who better to blame than the corporations? Bergholz wanted to know what I would recommend that they do. Have you ever had an opportunity to tell people what to do when you have no responsibility for following through? It's fun. I talked and talked. Then, after listening very carefully, he said something that almost made me slide off my chair. He said that he liked my suggestions and offered me a job. Me? My father was a warehouse worker who never went to high school, let alone college. My mother cleaned other people's houses for a living. I did go to college, but it was Buffalo State, not Harvard or Stanford. CEOs? Billionaires? I thought, come on, is this some sick joke? I knew these people might respect my strategic ability, but to hire me was to say something entirely different. Hiring me was saying that they trusted me as if I was one of them. To take the job meant that I was saying something about my roots and myself. It would be like a peon being invited to rub elbows with the upper crust. Class issues are seldom talked about but often deeply felt. I said no as politely and gently as I could.

I clenched my fists on my armchair. I looked out at the skyline. I braced myself for what I thought would be a venomous tirade. I expected a vindictive speech about how I was an ungrateful idiot who would never work in this town again. Or maybe even worse, he might make an effort to accentuate the salary and explain what the opportunity would do for my status and career. I could not have been more wrong. I knew Bergholz was brilliant, but I didn't know how brilliant. He looked into my blue-collar, Catholic, working-class eyes and taught me the supreme power of understanding another person's values. He knew yelling would backfire. He would have justified my decision if he had become vindictive. He didn't appeal to my desire for money or status because I had no such desire. Instead, he became as calm as I ever saw him and said, "Well, then we won't hire anyone else to try to help these people because we only trust you." He played the guilt card. He knew every time I watched the news and saw an aimless protest march, every time I heard about an ex-steelworker on a bridge contemplating suicide, every time I saw the line stretched around the corner at the food bank, I would think about what I might have been able to do to help. I said, "When do we start?"

Every person has different ways in which he or she can be effectively motivated. The key is to understand how to motivate each particular person.

When people heard about my new job, they were in complete shock, and so was I. A few non-organizing friends thought it was a terrific opportunity but even they couldn't believe the Allegheny Conference wanted me to work for them. I knew that my life was going to change the next day when I realized I had only one suit. I couldn't wear it Monday through Friday. So I went downtown to Kaufman's Department Store. The salesman asked if I had gotten a new job. He said that most people that buy several suits at once had gotten a new job. With only passing interest, he asked where I would be working, and when I told him, he gave frantic instructions to the tailor to make sure he got everything just right. These suits were going to be worn in the offices of the Allegheny Conference. This made me feel extremely uncomfortable. I was afraid no one would think I was no longer the same person. I was the same kid who had sat in the dentist's office years earlier. Except now, strangers were reacting to me with something other than pity. It made me feel just as confused as when I was at the dentist's office.

It was my first day in the office at the top of the U.S. Steel building and I was 15 minutes early. I stopped at Weiner World for a cup of coffee and looked straight up; I noticed how worried I was that I would spill the Weiner World coffee on my brand new suit. It was the first time I ever had worried while in Weiner World. On my first day, I saw how much independence I would be given. The entire staff was friendly and they all kept asking me enthusiastically, "What exactly are you going to be doing for us?" I had no job description, no specific tasks, and there was no orientation for me to attend. I decided to put my thoughts down on paper. I thought, reflected, and planned. Every day I got memos about what the rest of the staff was doing. It was important stuff about the mayor, the governor, and the state legislature. On the bus on the way home, a headline in the paper quoted U.S. Steel CEO, David Roderick, who had announced more layoffs. When he was asked what advice he would give to the ex-steelworkers he said, "Why don't they just move?" This was not going to be a walk in the park.

How's the Cranshaw?

I was developing a series of simple ideas and shaping them into a proposal. Although Mon Valley steelworkers were similarly affected by all the disinvestments and plant closings, I knew the residents fell into three ideological camps. Camp number one felt the closings were the result of the greed of international corporations that had figured out how to use slave labor overseas, leaving the Mon Valley raped and devastated. Camp number two felt that the greedy, self-serving, shortsighted unions had bled the company dry with outrageous, irresponsible wage and benefit demands that sapped profits and forced the closures. Camp number three felt that the poor and minorities were always discriminated against by both the company and the union, and it was only because white people were losing their jobs that the current situation was being noticed. These three views were loaded with negative stereotypes. There was an almost total absence of trust. I felt that the first step needed was to create an "atmosphere" in which reinvestment could occur. To do that, these negative stereotypes would have to be dismantled. Some stereotypes are built on partial truths. I felt the need to chip away at these by understanding an organizing technique I call "The exception to your rule." For instance, if people saw Mon Valley residents as lazy and uncreative, mired in yearning for a past that would never return, you must recruit residents that completely refute that image. You then say, "Wait until you meet this person"—he or she is the exception to your rule. If someone finds CEOs to be uncaring, fat-bottomed rich guys who never worked hard a day in their life, you find a decent, concerned, hardworking CEO to present as the exception to the rule. In either case, you would never lecture people about how unfair and incorrect their stereotypes were. People do not stop stereotyping because someone tells them to. Rather, stereotyping disappears when experience teaches people to decide for themselves that the stereotype no longer applies. In our society, we are the captains of our ships when it comes to stereotypes. We hold onto them as long as we want to. People don't badger us into throwing them overboard. They remain aboard our ships until we say otherwise.

I knew that real change was needed in the Mon Valley. Real results had to occur. We didn't have years to spend planning, thinking, and searching for order. Jobs had to be created, houses had to be built and renovated, and new businesses had to be started up. No comprehensive master plans, visioning exercises, or group wish lists would lead to anything. Real people from the Mon Valley had to do something concrete, lead something, and make something happen. If the local people took the lead, I felt that others from corporations and the government would have to help them by becoming willing and enthusiastic partners. Lastly, people from the small Mon Valley towns had to learn to work together. Everyone was in the same boat. Past competitiveness between towns had to stop. The townspeople needed to think regionally and develop regionally while maintaining their small-town identities.

My first step was to listen to community members throughout the Mon Valley. By listening carefully, I would determine what interests the community members held in common (perhaps to create jobs). I would test their commitment to work on a project rather than just demanding that someone else do it. Residents would then agree on a specific strategy (for instance, buying and renovating a building on Main Street and 8th Avenue) and reach out for partners from beyond the Mon Valley (investors, businesses, etc.). There you have it—a strategy. I presented my ideas to Pease and Bergholz. They liked what they heard. I thought I had the support that I needed. Then, they told me that to proceed, I would need the support of the entire corporate board. To gain their support, it would be my responsibility to make a presentation. I would be given 10 minutes.

I knew I needed to package my ideas for an audience that might as well have been aliens from another planet. They knew absolutely nothing about me and I knew very little about them. Before I got my 10-minute window, I wanted to tag along with my bosses to learn the art of effective communication in the corporate world. Frequently, meetings between staff and a CEO were held over meals at the city's most prestigious downtown private eating establishment, the Duquesne Club. This place was the kind of operation that I had seen once or twice in movies. I was to walk the 6 blocks over to "The club" with Bob Pease. He walked so fast with enormous strides and perfect posture. I almost had to run to keep up with him. I felt like the smaller of the two dogs in a cartoon begging the big dog to let me tag along. When we got to the club, I saw giant pillars, the doorman, the red carpet, and I fell flat on my face. That's right. I tripped on the plush carpet. The doorman dusted off my Kaufman suit and kept calling me "sir." Pease didn't notice that I fell; he was already through the brass doors. I had never seen so many chandeliers in my life. The table and servers were waiting; everything seemed to be waiting for us. We were to meet with one guy. We were 2 minutes early. He was exactly on time. I shook his hand. My luncheon companions started talking about golf—doglegs, sand traps, 3 irons, and tee shots. I bowl. Then they shifted to higher education, "Has Jonathan chosen?" One son is leaning toward Brown; his dad was pushing for Yale. Hey, I thought, want to talk about Buffalo State? Then it was on to wives. Charity balls apparently take up a lot of time. I started to sweat. My boss was supposed to be hitting this guy up for money and we were three fourths of the way through lunch and the question of money was nowhere near the table.

Relationships are crucial when you are trying to get something accomplished.

The server went through the desserts. I'm a pie man myself and luckily they had pie. My confidence rose because I could make a selection I could relate to. That is until Bob Pease inquired, "How's the cranshaw?" He turned to the other guy who said forcefully, "What a splendid idea. Let's all have cranshaw." I had no idea what it was. This was terrifying to me because it meant there was a distinct possibility that I wouldn't know how to eat it. I had visions of flames, cream, and special spoons. Five minutes later I saw three slices of melon arrive, bearing a striking resemblance to what I've always called cantaloupe. I felt like I still had a few things to learn. Lunch was over, hands were shaken, and we were walking over the speed limit back to the office. Not once had money come up in the conversation. I guessed that even someone with as much expertise as Pease in this case just couldn't come up with an opening to discuss money. I asked him what went wrong. Pease looked at me like you would look at someone who couldn't open a childproof aspirin bottle. "What are you talking about? We got the money." He explained that he would be sending a letter asking for it officially, sliding it in with a rehash of the luncheon topics. He said simply, "We already had the relationship." It was a lesson I needed to remember. I especially needed to remember it during my 10 minutes of fame.

The day of the presentation, I got to the Duquesne Club 20 minutes early. The same doorman was on duty, and this time I didn't trip. The only person in the special private meeting room of the special private club was David Roderick, CEO of U.S. Steel. He was staring at the agenda. He had circled the discussion item number three, the Mon Valley Proposal—M. Eichler. He never looked up at me. The others filed in. We ate quickly. (Macaroons—no cranshaw.) It was my turn. Everything had a soft haze around it, like before the medication kicks in prior to oral surgery. The chairperson was friendly to me and introduced me in an upbeat, eager manner. I hit on all cylinders. I spoke crisply and confidently. The chair said, "Thank you very much. Any questions?" Only one meaty hand rose. The heads all turned. It was Roderick. He was red. The gist of his reaction was that he felt the Conference had no obligation to provide any help whatsoever. There would never be a future for this region, and that was that in the eyes of Roderick. I knew he was about to conclude. He was driving the last nail into the region's coffin and my body was down there, too. The boys were picking up their shovels. The chair glanced back at me as if to say, "Good luck kid, I wish you could climb out of the coffin, but I don't see how." I remember seeing Pease at the earlier fund-raising meeting. These men did not have a relationship with me. They had a relationship with Roderick. If I disagreed with him, I was dead. If I remained silent, I was dead. I looked him directly in the eye and pretended as best I could that we were lifelong pals. I acted as though I had the relationship. I pointed my finger at him and with every ounce of confidence I could convey, I said enthusiastically, "You are absolutely right, Mr. Roderick, and it is for all those reasons that you so eloquently mentioned that we have to begin this program immediately!" Well, what I said made no sense whatsoever. It just had to look as if there was no conflict or difference of opinion between the two of us. Lots of these corporate leaders actually wanted to help. They just would not risk ruining a business relationship. The chairman emphatically intoned "Fine, all those in favor?" Bang! Approved! I had my program mandate. There was reason to celebrate. Cranshaw for everyone!

When in doubt, agree!

Issue analysis requires an ability to focus on something that can hold the interest of a lot of people. Remember not to choose an issue *you* think people should be interested in. Instead, choose something *they* are interested in. Suppose you are working for a social service agency that is located in a building that is hard to reach for most of the population you are trying to serve. If you went to your supervisor with the goal of making the services more accessible, you would need to strategize about the nature of the issue. There is a huge difference between telling your boss the issue is the agency's insensitivity to the clients; rather you should frame the issue as meeting the funder's goal of serving 500 families. In the first case, you have alienated the clients from your supervisor and the funders. In the second case, you have presented a way for them all to see eye to eye. OK, we've reached one of those occasions when a diagram might help a bit (see Figure 3.1).

---

1. Listen to community members (one-on-one)

2. Determine the common interests of community members (hearing similar things over and over)

3. Commitment (people are willing to try to do something about it)

4. Agreement on strategy

5. Reach out for partners (bridge social capital beyond the community)

Figure 3.1   Issues Analysis

Reflection Questions

1. What is the difference between an organizer's one-on-one meeting and a client's meeting with a therapist?

2. Why is it important for a poor or working-class neighborhood to increase its social capital?

3. If you wanted to become a community organizer, how would you explain it to your family?

4. Why was Roberto Clemente inducted into the National Baseball Hall of Fame immediately?

5. Why is it important to measure commitment rather than just analyze the problem?

REFERENCE

Putnam, R. D. (2000). *Bowling alone: The collapse and revival of American community.* New York: Simon & Schuster.

4

PROGRAM DESIGN

In this chapter, you will learn:

◆ How to develop a mandate.

◆ How to reach a shared goal.

◆ How to frame your conversations.

◆ How to put everyone in a proper role.

◆ How to begin implementation of your program.

In many organizing models, you seldom, if ever, have to design and implement a program. Instead, you focus on getting other people to do something the way you want them to do it. You pressure them to do their job better. You steer them in the direction the community wants. You tell them what to do (put in a streetlight, provide better police protection, fix the plumbing in the apartment complex), and if they see the power of the people you have organized, they do it. It involves a very different set of objectives if you are practicing consensus organizing. In consensus organizing, you try to build reciprocal relationships around mutual self-interest. Pressure, by itself, may not get you to where you need to go. The best way to arrange mutual self-interest is by partners doing something together. Consensus organizers need to learn to play complementary roles so that those involved can all achieve results from which all benefit. To get to the end point, consensus organizers have to design and implement an intervention that has the parties work together. This requires knowledge of program design. I know you might think that only an executive director of a nonprofit or the head of a for-profit company does stuff like this, but, no, you and a bunch of regular people can do it. So, let's try to see what goes into a program design.

Program Design—How a program will operate step-by-step

As a consensus organizer, I try to imagine how every person I meet could work together with every other person I have already met. Try to think of everyone as having the potential to come together and form a giant human Legoland with every block snapping into the next block to form some giant structure that is beyond most people's wildest imagination. All most people ever see are the small insignificant pieces. You see, however, how they could all click together. In other words, you have to learn to find everyone you meet interesting and valuable, not so much for what they can do by themselves but rather for the potential of what they could do together. You must try to block out your own feelings toward each individual and instead zero in on the possible constructive connection to another. Suppose you meet a pastor. If you are religious, you may really appreciate a pastor who makes comments such as "If the good Lord sees fit to send me here. . . ." and "The Lord in his wisdom has this in store for me." To you, this might enhance his or her value. If, however, you have negative feelings about organized religion, you might find it too "preachy" and you may feel this detracts from his or her effectiveness. It might sound to you like fingernails on a chalkboard. As the pastor keeps praising, you realize that between the amens that the person is pretty tight with a city councilperson. Then, take the example of a block club captain who bemoans the fact that residents, even though they have tried and tried, couldn't get a call back from the councilperson's office. The residents have a legitimate concern and they are being ignored. If you were able to meet the councilperson, you would ask about the pastor and might be told glowingly, "He is the real voice of the community. I know that when the pastor represents a concern, it is legitimate." At this point, I look at the pastor in a whole new light. I don't notice any shortcomings. Preachy? No, not at all. How could anybody say that pastor is preachy? Why, that pastor is a saint.

Bill Maher, the comedian and political commentator, tells a great story about Don King, the huge, wild-haired, bombastic boxing promoter. Maher talks about how he always looked at King as self-serving, a shameless self-promoter, a guy who never shut up, and an all-around pain in the butt. One day, Maher is on a cross-country flight and who should walk onto the plane but Don King, drawing attention to himself, with loads of bodyguards, "homies," and a whole entourage, carrying on like they are with royalty. Maher scrunches down and mutters to himself about how he has the worst luck in the world. As he sits there grumbling, King stops right in front of him and looks down at him. Then he blurts out, "Bill Maher is on this flight. Folks, right in front of me sits Bill Maher, the funniest, wittiest man alive!" King's not stopping. He is pointing, gesturing, jumping up and down. Bill Maher starts soaking it in and concludes, "You know, I started to really like Don King." The point is that relationships are positive when they are helpful, and any relationship can become positive in a flash. Just ask Bill Maher.

As you start to see how relationships have the potential to develop, you can imagine what it is that the pastor and the block club could do together. The best way to do that is to find out what the pastor is trying to achieve and what barriers are blocking the way. Then, you look for how the block club can help to achieve the desired result. Suppose the pastor is trying to convince a congregation that they should start a day care center. Members of the congregation think they will get stuck with too much work. Now, you have some potential for mutual self-interest. The block club likes the idea of a day care center and can provide volunteers. The pastor can arrange a meeting between the councilperson and the block club members and together they can achieve what they want. This process keeps going until you have many new relationships, forming and deepening. Now, let's try to really break down program design into a series of logical, doable, steps.

DEVELOPING A MANDATE

Developing a Mandate—Everyone pulls together in the same direction toward a shared goal

When everyone in the community pulls in the same direction, you have a mandate. Mandates do not occur spontaneously. You will see loads of things that need to change. You will see an almost unlimited number of needs that should be addressed. You might even be able to see a number of potential interventions that are just lying there in front of you. In consensus organizing, however, you are still nowhere. You are nowhere until you begin to develop the motivation of a variety of people to actually do something about something. You will never be able to achieve success unless people want you to. By "people," I don't mean just one powerful player or one loud or pushy group. I mean that a significant mixture of potential partners want to do something. These potential partners have to have an interest that is genuine. An effort will not be successful if one partner, out of kindness, wants to help another partner. That dynamic does not produce a solid, constant, unwavering mandate. Instead, it produces a temporary, shallow paternalism. You are on your way to a mandate when all partners see real benefit for themselves. Every party has to see the potential to get what they want. Every party has to be up front about their agenda. Every party must be willing to work. Every party must play a role they are comfortable with. When you have all of this in place, you are on your way to a mandate. For instance, there is a huge difference in the two following scenarios. In example one, the powerful head of the local chamber of commerce says, "We at the chamber believe that we have an obligation to help our residents who are poor. That's why we are willing to do what we can to provide some type of support. We are not sure to what extent we can commit, but we want to reassure the impoverished in our community that we are concerned." In example two, members of another chamber of commerce working on a similar project in another neighborhood say, "Our businesses will not succeed if our residents can no longer afford to shop with us or use our services. That's why today we are instructing our executive director to work on this 4 hours a week. We are signing support letters on our letterhead and we are making a $1,000 commitment to match dollar-for-dollar any money other nonprofits raise." See the difference? You will find plenty of examples of number ones. Only the type of action described in example number two, however, will lead to a mandate.

SHARED GOAL

Shared Goal—All parties can get what they want by reaching the same end point

All parties have to be up front and direct about the reasons they want to be involved. They all have to put their cards on the table. The goals can't be cloaked in flowery, do-gooder language. ("I always try to help young people. After all they are the future." Or, "We are all interested in expanding the capacities that are in each and every one of us." Get the idea?) Instead, everyone's agenda must be stated bluntly. I always like to hear statements like "Let me tell you what has to happen" or "Unless we are here to do X, I am not interested in coming back." The magic moment in setting a goal is when all parties get to their own bottom line. Then, you and everyone in the group can compare the bottom lines. If the bottom lines can all be achieved through the same activity, you have the shared goal. Now, everyone can explain the same goal to everyone outside the group. All of the people can pull toward the same end point. They actually have created a genuine, real, tangible, shared goal.

FRAMING

Framing—Repackaging the same goal in slightly different ways to appeal to each person

First, you measure your wall space, then you go to the art supply store . . . no, this is a different kind of framing. If you have developed your shared goal, you now get to really begin the "art" of consensus organizing. I learned I had to remember that each person is unique. I just couldn't go on automatic pilot. Each conversation needed to be unique. I couldn't sound like the main character in the film *Napoleon Dynamite,* who after becoming his pal's campaign manager in his run for class president, says over and over again in a robotic monotone, "Vote for Pedro. Vote for Pedro. Vote for Pedro." Instead, you have to repackage the benefit of voting for Pedro in hundreds of different ways, each crafted to appeal to the self-interest of each person. To person number one you say, "Look, you want to be prom queen, and no one takes you seriously. I know how that must make you feel. That's exactly the way Pedro feels now." To person number two you say, "Hey, I know you don't think much of Pedro. But Keith, the bully who throws you against your locker every day, wants Pedro's opponent to win." To person number three you try, "You are one of the only minority kids in school. If Pedro wins, he will represent everyone fairly and that will open doors for other minority freshmen and sophomores." Stop me or I'll get to person number 621.

You get the idea. You keep reframing Pedro and the election differently. You enlarge the number of people who agree with the shared goal: Vote for Pedro. The difference is you are no longer speaking in a monotone. You are no longer a robot. You have created new relationships and a new spirit by strategically reframing.

PROPER ROLES

Proper Role—Utilizing each person's special skills to maximize the success of the group

---

No matter what kind of community effort you undertake, you will have to harness a good deal of talent to achieve success. As we know, the sports world is full of teams loaded with talent. Some of those teams, despite loads of talent, still lose. On paper, talent looks unbeatable but many times, another team wins. Often the winning team has a kind of chemistry that produces "role players" with each player's talent adding up to success. Not everyone is in the starting lineup. Not everyone can play the same position or enter the same event.

A consensus organizer has to steer everyone into a role. You have to judge the available talent and place it so that each role is complementary. Think of it as assembling a giant interlocking human puzzle. When each piece locks together and is placed in exactly the right spot, a beautiful picture develops. People will almost always assume the role you need them to assume if you tell them one thing over and over: "No one does this as well as you do." Don't you like to hear people tell you, "We can't do it without you"? Of course you do. It's actually even better when the person who says it to you means it! Yes, the consensus organizer always means it. So that's what you do. You show each person the big picture. You show how all the pieces fit together. You show that each person is indispensable and no one, and I mean no one, can carry out a given role as well as he or she can. In addition, you begin to position all parties into spots where they can teach others what they know. Who isn't flattered to be seen as having ability or knowledge so valuable that others would love to learn what they know? This builds the capacity of the group to carry out the project. It gives depth and values experience at the same time. Try to develop the habit of pairing a less-experienced person as an understudy with each talented role player. So the best bring along the rest while they play the roles of both program implementer and teacher. Give the experienced people credit for developing the talent and capacity of others.

IMPLEMENTATION

Implementation—Carry out the activity with cohesion and interdependence

After developing a mandate, setting shared goals, framing, and role selection, you are finally ready to do something. All this strategizing should have you at a spot where you can execute some collective action and make some improvement in a community. This is one of the most satisfying moments for a consensus organizer. You get to watch something happen that never would have happened without you. But that isn't even the most important thing you have done because that satisfaction is shared by the entire group of people you have recruited, motivated, and assembled. That is because, no matter how significant your involvement has been, you cannot succeed without everyone else. That feeling of cohesion and interdependence, when everyone realizes how essential everyone else is, is pretty special. It rarely happens in our society. So often we are divided and so often we are conquered. We are constantly reminded of how uncooperative, competitive, and cutthroat our world has become. Well, when you work with others toward a common goal, there is a feeling of satisfaction that is hard to describe. If you were fortunate to be born into a close, loving family, you might begin to understand. You all felt good about yourselves and one another. When we connect, we can achieve success. Here is a simple way to see program design (see Figure 4.1).

It is the implementation, the doing of something specific, that brings satisfaction. When you can get to this sweet place, you remind all those involved of how far they have come. You remind the people of how significant their work really is. You tell them their project is noteworthy. You tell them it is more than just the renovated apartments, the newly recruited business, or the new playground. You show people that the completed project has resulted in much more than they obviously set out to achieve. Instead, it is about how they have changed how others view their community. It is about how others will now look at them, as individuals and as a group. These suggestions can be effective whether you are a

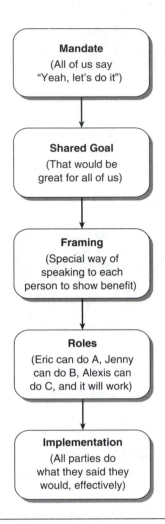

Figure 4.1   Program Design

community organizer or an employee of a social service organization. There are opportunities to use consensus organizing to help clients within every adult services, child services, or family services organization. As a staffer, you can be in excellent position to use these steps to help people. You are perfectly positioned to see the needs and desires of the clients and the needs and desires of the agency. You can be the catalyst in developing the mandate, sharing the goals, framing, assigning roles, and implementing. Remember what's important here is learning the process, not reaching enormous scale. Starting small is not only acceptable, it also is preferred. Get your feet wet. Small will lead to big. So now let's go back to western Pennsylvania.

If there ever was a community that needed a successful program design it was the Mon Valley. Let's go back to 1985 and see how it was done.

THE ODOR CONTROL CAPITAL OF THE WORLD

Well, the hard part was over. Now all that remained was the revitalization of the entire Mon Valley. Inside each of the small towns that dotted both sides of the river were people capable of tearing down the negative stereotypes that Pittsburghers held. The stereotypes centered on an image of the steel-workers as lazy, malingering, slow-thinking people with strong backs and little else. There was even a derogatory slur that people used. They called the steelworkers "mill hunks." This phrase had the same sting as other national slurs for racial groups. We had to showcase people in the Mon Valley who were smart, strategic, forward thinking, and innovative. I knew they were there. I also knew they needed to be organized.

My plan called for hiring organizers to get into these towns to find, develop, and organize these people. Because of the deep divisions in these towns, and the skill and expertise that would be needed, I naturally sought out organizers who had experience. I spoke with experienced organizers and found that it was impossible to match them to the jobs at hand. Organizers with previous experience in labor unions, environmental watch-dog groups, or politics all followed a pattern of thinking that showed they were already justified in their political conclusions and their opinions already set in stone. All of them already knew why problems existed in the Mon Valley and, of course, they already knew the solutions. All of these activists' solutions fit neatly into their ideological bent.

Ideological Bent—People's political beliefs that shape how they think a problem came about and how it should be solved

---

No one was open to developing new relationships in new ways. A prede-termined cause and solution would not tear down the stereotypes or build any new leadership. By default, I realized that I had to move away from orga-nizers with experience. Instead, I had to go after young, smart, trainable people. I decided youth and enthusiasm would be marketed as strengths. I told everyone that's what we had needed all along.

The second big decision regarding organizers was whether they should be outsiders or people who were born and raised in the Mon Valley. Now, what do you think? Before you give a knee-jerk reaction, I ask you to think it through. Sure, it sounds like coming from the same community that you work in would be a huge plus—except for one important thing. Invariably, you and your family would already be entrenched in one of those three ideological camps mentioned earlier: pro-business, pro-labor, or pro-minority rights.

Pro-business—Business people and their organizations are the people with solutions

Pro-labor—Unions and their members are the people with solutions

Pro-minority rights—Minorities and organizations that protect their rights have the solutions

---

Thus, using insiders would put a strain on effectiveness. It would be hard to get such organizers to work with the other camps. Outsiders, on the other hand, would have no camps, no predetermined issues, and no predetermined conclusions. They might know absolutely nothing about the Mon Valley, but I knew they could learn. They would learn by listening, meeting, talking, and respecting people in all of the camps.

The training for the assembled staff of organizers was kept simple. Think of a new coach with a team full of freshmen. The coach designs a few basic plays and practices them over and over. That's what I did. I drew six circles on the blackboard and told the organizers to fill each circle with potential sources of stereotype-busting people. The circles consisted of homeowners, renters, businesspeople, churches, social services, and large institutions (hospitals, community colleges, anything with a large physical presence). The idea was to find a small number of Mon Valley people with the same outlook and bring them together (see Figure 4.2).

All the people selected would bring different perspectives and constituencies, but the organizers would identify their similarities and their potential to work together. The trainees were concerned that because of the residents' differences and divisions, the people, once brought together, would not get along. I told them that the people would get along if their values were similar. Look for the same values within people. Look beyond the obvious differences. It became the bedrock of their work.

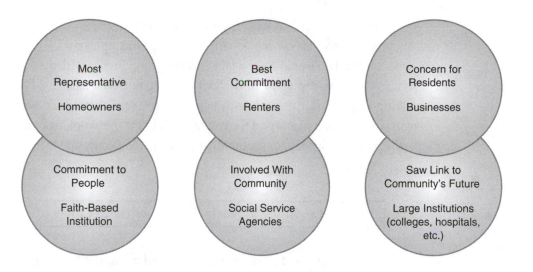

Figure 4.2   Six Circles of Leadership

Find groups and individuals with the same values and link them together.

As the organizers began their painstaking searches, I anticipated that when the volunteers finally got together they would have to do something together. Leadership can only be built through action, not just through planning and reflection. It is the action that bonds people. Look at relationships that last throughout the years. Old friends talk about what they did together—the trips they took, the teams they played on, what happened when they walked, drove, swam, ran, flew together. In the Mon Valley, "doing something" would have to be a visible, tangible project that would have value to the community and be respected by others outside the community. The idea would have to be generated by the volunteers and would be successful mainly through their efforts. The idea would also be supported by the helping roles played by outsiders.

Don't just let people talk. Get them to "do" something.

Remember the real estate project and the key role the broker played? Previously, he was an outsider. To build the confidence and determination of the volunteers, the organizers would need to be coaches, parents, children, cops and bullies, therapists and cheerleaders. One thing they could not provide, however, was technical support—they lacked knowledge about law, property acquisition, job development, and housing.

Such expertise would be crucial when the group finally settled on a project. So it became my job to think about where to find that expertise. I began talking to professionals with such expertise to see if they would want to work with the organizers and the volunteers. I knew this wouldn't be a walk in the park. We develop professional expertise in our society and then we are taught to hoard it.

Find experts willing to teach their expertise to others.

We mystify, deify, and place a high priority and price on dispensing expertise. We do not "spread the wealth." We "hoard it." Many technical experts feel that because they have spent their money obtaining expertise, they are not compelled to give it away for free. I needed to find the small number of experts who were willing and able to transfer their expertise. I needed to find people who wanted to teach others what they knew, and would enjoy the experience of seeing others grow in confidence and leadership ability. If we were unable to acquire this transfer of professional knowledge, how could we tear down the stereotypes? Outsiders needed to respect the people of Mon Valley. The respect had to come because it was merited. The merit would come from effort and gaining expertise. It takes a special individual to willingly transfer expertise. Many lawyers, architects, business developers, and construction companies were willing to help, but their idea of help was very paternalistic. "I feel sorry for what they have gone through...." "I have ideas that will work...." "The residents could review my plans...."—these are all examples of what wouldn't create the change we were after. I had to keep looking and looking. Eventually, I would find someone with technical expertise who would instead say, "It's not that complicated. Here's how it works." Or instead say, "Anybody can learn how to do this."

Jerry Altman had national standing as a lawyer who understood real estate and economic development. He immediately grasped our goals and responded enthusiastically. I would bring Jerry anywhere. One of my fondest memories was Jerry painstakingly working with a volunteer in an auto parts store. Jerry and the auto parts manager would constantly be interrupted by requests regarding fan belts, batteries, and motor oil. You have to admit—that takes a certain kind of attorney. Jerry once instructed a volunteer committee about real-estate finance late at night at a recreation center. There were eight overweight grandmothers robotically and rhythmically dancing to M. C. Hammer's song, "Too Legit to Quit." Eventually, Jerry and a handful of Pittsburgh professionals teamed up with the community organizers. The technical experts could teach and train while the organizers could motivate and mobilize. We called the entire conglomeration the Mon Valley Development Team.

Now, all we had to do was get into the towns and do our work. The Mon Valley town closest to Pittsburgh was Homestead, Pennsylvania. You may have heard of it. It was the site of the famous Homestead steel strike, when management brought Pinkerton security guards down the Mon River to break up picketing workers. People in Homestead still talked quite a bit about it even though it had happened more than 100 years earlier. When you entered Homestead from Pittsburgh, there was a sign on the bridge that read, "Welcome to Homestead, the odor control capital of the world." Now that was a marketing firm's nightmare if I ever saw one. Even more ironic, the hulking Homestead Steel Works was completely closed. Only security guards remained, but the sign still stood. I kept thinking all we had to do was tear down the stereotypes. The Mon Valley Development Team said that it was ready.

WHAT ABOUT LARRY?

Homestead, Pennsylvania had a population of only 5,000 in 1985. When the mill had been at full throttle, it operated 24 hours a day. The total number of workers employed within a 24-hour period was more than the population of the town. Local residents would tell you that the Homestead steel mill was a major factor in beating the Nazis. It produced much of the steel that made our armed forces superior. It produced the steel that helped build the Golden Gate Bridge. As mentioned earlier, when Soviet Premier Nikita Khrushchev was planning his historic visit to the United States at the height of the Cold War, he told the U.S. government that he wanted to see two things, Disneyland and the Homestead steel works. Imagine that. Now here it was, empty and rusting. Imagine the corporate owner puzzled as to why people didn't just move.

Our Homestead organizer showed up, trained and ready to fill in the six circles. She got off to a good start. People liked her. She was developing a pattern of similar interests—except from one key spot—the business community. She started out searching any and all of the business organizations. She found the address of the chamber of commerce. She went up a dirty staircase to a locked second-floor door. After knocking and knocking, the door finally cracked open and a person's voice sounded bothered. Not a good sign. She went up and down 8th Avenue and no business owners seemed to have the time or interest to participate in a revitalization effort. They did, however, frequently recite what I came to call the "Eight Deep" speech. They told us that when the steel mill was open, there were so many people out on the sidewalk that they were eight deep. They had no time to talk about a strategy for the future of their town, but they had time to give the "Eight Deep" speech. Offhand, at the end of her many futile contacts, the organizer said many people asked, "What about Larry?" They were referring to a hardware store proprietor from down the street, Larry Levine, whom she hadn't yet met. The business owners thought he was the kind of guy who might be interested in working with us. They definitely seemed to respect him. I told the organizer that she needed to check with contacts in the other circles to see if they also knew and respected Levine. I asked her to dangle his name when she talked to people who were not the business owners. It turned out that public housing tenants, school activists, and housewives all knew or had heard about him. Almost everyone reacted positively when his named was mentioned. He had connections to the minority community and was a member of the local NAACP chapter. Everyone respected him. Trust of him was evident among representatives from all of the six circles. He joined the volunteer effort.

The first project the volunteers proposed, with assistance from the Mon Valley Development Team, was the renovation of a commercial property. Homestead, Pennsylvania, of all places, was to become the new home of the Pittsburgh High Technology Council, a trade association for high-tech companies. The council was willing to sign a long-term lease for an abandoned property that the local volunteers were willing to purchase and rehabilitate. The banks, however, were dragging their feet about making the loan. Larry saw momentum slipping away. I was working feverishly to get the Allegheny Conference to help influence a bank to make the loan. I could not reassure Larry that we would be successful in changing the bankers' minds. Larry had a conversation with me that he said was to remain private. He did not want what he was about to tell me to be shared with anyone. He said that he would be willing to advance his own money to purchase the building on one condition—I could not tell anyone where the money had come from. When the bank eventually made the loan, he would then expect to be paid back, with no interest. Now that was a stereotype buster. The bank eventually came through and the corporate community helped recruit additional tenants. Trust, real hard-earned trust, was beginning to be built. Fourteen separate towns up and down the river formed new community organizations. Real projects were proposed and successfully carried out.

We then decided to push the envelope. In a region noted for a lack of cooperation and deep divisions, we brought all the "Larrys" together from all the towns. Because of their similar values, work ethics, and, most important, their individual organizational successes, we felt we had sowed the seeds for cooperation. It was crucial to bring people together only after they had acquired a sense of success. Bringing people together who have experienced only failure can easily lead to bigger failures. Bringing people together who have had success can lead to greater success. This new group strategized and agreed to form a coalition; they called themselves the Mon Valley Initiative (MVI). Government, foundations, and corporations supported the MVI. Relationships deepened. Slowly, the Mon Valley began to change. New investments occurred, and people decided to stay. The towns still existed long after David Roderick's pronouncement that people should just leave. Fifteen years later, I typed MVI into my computer search engine. The board and staff of the MVI had changed almost completely over the years, but their accomplishments continued. I also decided to click on the list of contributors and immediately went to the letter L. There was Larry Levine, still supporting, and still helping, his community.

So remember, a consensus organizer always needs to get people together and get them together for a specific purpose. It takes three steps:

Step 1. Organize like-minded individuals into a group.

Step 2. Do something tangible and specific.

Step 3. Find expertise and transfer that expertise to the group.

Reflection Questions

1. Why be forced to implement? Isn't it better to just pressure others to do the work?

2. Should everyone pick out the role they want to play on a project? Why or why not?

3. When people benefit from a project, should they withdraw their participation because of conflicts of interest?

4. What do you and Bill Maher have in common?

5. What role does a consensus organizer play in project design?

5

CULTURAL COMPETENCY IN CONSENSUS ORGANIZING

In this chapter, you will learn:

◆ The importance of your own history.

◆ How to use differences to gain perspective.

◆ How to bring people together using both their differences and their similarities.

In consensus organizing, you work with a large number of very different people. You have the opportunity to see how differences in race, age, gender, ethnicity, and sexual orientation cut across consciousness. Sometimes these differences can divide us like thin paper shredded on a windy day. We live in very different worlds and very divided times. Some people prey on any difference they can find to put wedges between us, making our separateness feel natural, inevitable, and even sometimes desirable. Many times after the 9/11 attacks on the World Trade Center and the Pentagon, conservatives portrayed liberals as "pro-terrorist." Liberals were portrayed as so soft that they opposed efforts to protect the United States from attack. Being kept apart is neither natural nor inevitable. It is unnatural. As humans, deep inside, we yearn to come together. This desire is what consensus organizers uncover. We try to make it blossom and grow. We have many forces to battle. Just remember that the desire to come together is strong. Those forces attempting to pull us apart do so against our deeply held preferences as social animals. We want to be part of a group and the more people who join us the stronger we become. That is our natural goal.

Let's take a look at politics. Does a politician have a vested interest in all of us coming together to do something collectively? Absolutely not. The politician wants 50.1 percent of us to come together to vote for the politician. Politicians will do whatever effectively leads to their coalition of 50.1 percent. Guess what that means? It means they try to divide us. Through division, they attempt to reach their goal.

Sometimes politicians use division to achieve their goals.

Let's say I decide to run for political office ("I like Eich"). I suddenly look at the world in a way that needs to see the value in making me U.S. Congressman Eichler. If I consider taking a stance in support of legislation that allows prayer in public schools, I know that civil libertarians won't like me, many non-Christians won't like me, and atheists won't like me. If, however, 50.1 percent now *do* like me, I don't care about any divisions I have deepened. With polling techniques and focus groups now so advanced and accurate, I can find that 50.1 percent very quickly. It doesn't even matter what I think about the issue, I just want to reach that magic 50.1 percent of the vote.

Take the law profession. When was the last time you saw a trial lawyer say, "Judge, both sides are saying some things that are similar and I think the truth is that they are both partly correct." I think you are probably more likely to hear, "My client is the reincarnation of Mother Teresa. Your client is the second coming of Attila the Hun." In other words, lawyers take adversarial relationships and exacerbate divisions that already exist. They are paid well for their efforts. No wonder that law students practice creating "us" and "them" situations. They learn to see differences and not similarities.

How about our educational system? Do we have equal schools and equally successful students and equally compensated teachers and administrators? Do we even try to reach the goal of equal education? We might have the rhetoric, but we don't commit the resources. Instead of seeing all young people, all parents, all teachers as having the same goals, we divide into separate camps. We dwell on our differences. We try to place blame. Although I teach college students, you can bet my "colleagues" at Yale and Princeton perceive very little in common with me. Because I teach students from mostly modest backgrounds at a public university, I am not even expected to have the same credentials and abilities as my Ivy League pals. Instead, we all focus on our differences; how our situations are so far apart.

Our society divides us and does so quite comfortably. Sometimes these divisions appear while attempting to help others. Sound contradictory? Not really. Let's analyze the structure of cultural competency. It's good that we are sensitive to differences in each of us that have been shaped by our experiences, right? It's also good that we understand how our ethnicity, race, and sexual orientation shape us, right? Of course. We need to understand our own history and roots so we can have a higher awareness of how our attitudes toward one another have been shaped. We must become very self-aware so we can analyze how racism, sexism, and ethnocentrism can creep into our attitudes toward others. Could it be, though, that the more sensitive and aware we are of our differences, the less likely we are to see our equally evident similarities? Consensus organizers have to do two analyses. We have to work just as hard as all caring people to become culturally aware and sensitive to the differences that exist and, at the same time, we have to look hard for similarities that will lead to new partnerships, mutual self-interest, and social change.

A consensus organizer must be culturally aware and sensitive to differences while also looking hard for similarities.

For the next few minutes, pretend you are a kid again. Think of it in terms of two steps. Take out all your building blocks from your toy chest. Look at each different block. They have different sizes and colors. Picture yourself spreading all the blocks out on the floor. Put each block in your hand. See and feel the differences from block to block. That's the first step you do when you try to relate to people. You need to know and understand differences. As a kid, you wanted to have a lot of blocks because each had value because they were different. If they all were exactly the same, it would have limited what you could build. What you could build would have been dull, boring, and repetitive. Consensus organizers then take a crucial second step. We take those different blocks and use the differences to build something more interesting, stronger, and more long lasting. We take the second step of using the differences to create something that benefits us all (see Figure 5.1). Similarities and differences are of equal importance.

Step 1: Learn about your own history.

Step 2: Learn to use differences to work together, while deepening similarities.

Figure 5.1   Cultural Competency in Consensus Organizing

Let's talk about both of these steps so you can see the process clearly. In the first step, you learn about your own history—a vital process before you can lay claim to be able to do anything else. Often, people skip this beginning point. Why do you suppose many skip it? I think people like to see themselves as typical, normal, and middle-of-the-road. They define the middle and they choose the road. They then compare everyone else to themselves. If they are similar to you, they are normal. The less similar to you they are, the more abnormal they seem. Let me give you a real example. I was raised as a Catholic and attended Catholic school. In grade school, we learned that when we entered the church for any reason (for mass, for private prayer, to find the janitor, or to use the bathroom), we were to be absolutely quiet. If we had some life or death reason to talk, it had better be in the lowest possible whisper. I remember thinking that if an elderly neighbor had a heart attack in church, he or she would have to die quietly. Our teachers drilled into our pea brains that church was a very holy place and that silence was a sign of respect and reverence. Well, after having this repeated over and over, even I eventually "got with the program." When, as an adult, I go into church, I keep my trap shut. Many years after Catholic school, I fell in love with a terrific Jewish woman and I had the common sense and good fortune to marry. She is religious, so out of respect for her, I attended synagogue services. Prior to meeting her, I had never entered a temple. So there I was, entering for the first time, sweating, nervous, yarmulke on my head, feeling as though I had the letters C-a-t-h-o-l-i-c stenciled on my sweater. As we walked down the center aisle, the first thing that hit me was the noise. People were talking. Actually it was a little more like shouting. They blurted out deeply religious stuff like, "Did you get a deal on that hotel in Florida?" and "Oy, that deli's pastrami was so lean!" I was shocked. Didn't these people know that there was a religious service about to start? Didn't they feel they were in the house of the Lord? What was wrong with them? Of course it was a very short step for me to feel that they were disrespectful. I remember that this bothered me a lot. It bothered me enough that I didn't want to share with my wife how I felt. I didn't think she would agree with me. Well, luckily I kept analyzing my feelings. I didn't want to be "politically correct" and act like it didn't bother me. I slowly remembered my own upbringing. Was it always wrong to talk inside any house of worship? More interesting, was it always respectful to be quiet? What about how my uncle always fell asleep when the priests talked? He was pretty quiet. The next time I returned to the temple, I met many people whom I classified as deeply religious even though they yakked and yakked before the service. Many of these people led devout, exemplary lives. I finally began to understand. I wanted to find people who respected their religion (good) but I had been using the wrong measurement (bad). I first had to understand my own culture before I could have insight into another.

Once we begin to understand our own history, we should begin to relate to everyone else we meet with respect, warmth, concern, empathy, genuine interest, and curiosity. We do not initially need knowledge. That would come later.

Once we understand our own history, we should begin to relate to others with respect, warmth, concern, empathy, curiosity, and interest.

People will be most suspicious of you when you are a stranger. Their guard will be up. As you show your true self in a nondefensive, comfortable manner and you show real interest in the person you are talking to, you start to feel the progress. You are increasing the chances for a real discussion to take place. You do not have to feel pressure to do everything correctly. Rather, the challenge is to have a genuine interest and make a genuine effort to understand.

Have you ever traveled overseas and attempted to speak a language other than your own? Almost always your effort will be appreciated rather than your competency. You are appreciated because you are trying to do something they can already do. In gaining cultural competency, you are appreciated because you are showing value in others. We show genuine interest in learning and understanding our true selves. We then begin to understand others. Through exposure and opportunity, we gradually gain insight. Try to be comfortable with the knowledge that there is much to learn. Never, ever, fake understanding. It's almost always detectable and very unfair to others. Remember, people like to enlighten or teach others about themselves. The interest just has to be genuine. Cultural competence should not be measured by correct answers on a scantron sheet (that is, those answer sheets used for standardized tests like the SAT and GRE). It should be an interesting challenge we face throughout our entire lives.

For consensus organizers, the second step in this two-step process is crucial. As we gradually learn how and why people are different, we begin the second step. We now show that despite these differences, in fact *because* of these differences, we are going to work together successfully. Many times advocates of cultural competency stop at the point of gaining understanding. Wouldn't it be much better to use our differences to achieve collective benefit? That's our goal (see Figure 5.1).

Consensus organizers create a series of relationships that lead to intervention and program design. Our role is to show that our differences help us achieve results. If all the participants were similar, we would lose the different perspectives, skills, outlooks, and styles necessary to create change. Your effort would be one-dimensional. It would probably fail. By blending differences, you have more talent, more thinking, and more creativity.

By using our differences, we gain additional perspectives, skills, outlooks, and styles necessary to create change.

Consensus organizers create opportunities for double benefits. First, people benefit from their differences by understanding them, appreciating them, and putting them to good use. Second, as we gain insight into differences we find strange similarities we never saw before. Let's go back to the synagogue. I learned I appreciated the concept of devotion. I learned that I respected devout people. I learned that silence is one form of devotion. I learned, however, that it is not the only measurement. With this new realization, that there is a broader measurement, I saw there were more devout people around than I previously had thought. That news made me happier. I used to have one measurement—silence in a house of worship. See how I was limiting myself? In the temple, people conversed loudly on secular topics. But I now saw that they showed devotion in the way they led their lives. The differences lead to the similarities. This is a very profound thought. We live in a society that refuses to do the "two step." We take one step, or none at all. We do not usually make much progress in gaining cultural competency. We almost always do not take the "two steps."

Think of it. Maybe you have labeled people as enemies for all the wrong reasons. In my case, Jewish people yelling in the temple made me uncomfortable. It made me feel that I was surrounded by disrespectful people. It made me want to leave and be surrounded by people "like me." I wanted the comfort of familiarity. To achieve true cultural competency we have to expand our experiences with others. We have to look in strange places, under rocks, and behind closed doors. We have to search out differences. These differences are what the consensus organizers use to make blends. Most important, we see that these differences, once they are understood, are the glue that will hold us all together.

Sometimes, after analyzing differences between oneself and others, we see the differences as insurmountable and use them as a rationale for inaction. We say, "Now that I see how different the resident, or client is from me, how can I even begin to understand them?" When we do this, the awareness of differences can set us back rather than take us forward. Our sensitivity can lead us to conclude that we can't help. Talk about ironic!

It is crucial that we understand cultural differences. As we begin to understand, it puts us in the position to be able to take action more effectively. All organizers know that to be successful, we must bring different people with different skills and perspectives together. As our understanding of differences increases, so does our obligation to take action to help improve the lives of others.

All organizers know that to be successful, we must bring different people with different skills and perspectives together.

Never use increased understanding, awareness, and sensitivity as an excuse for inaction. Rather, try to think of these realizations as an opportunity you have created for yourself and others. Remember, people are more successful when moving toward something than they are when moving away from something. Consensus organizers operating from a "strengths" perspective put divergent people together around a specific issue. We create change by using each person's gifts and talents in helpful ways.

So as forces in our society divide us, they zero in on our misunderstandings and our lack of familiarity with one another. They look for anything that aggravates us and tell us our aggravation is justified. We all suffer together as a result. The rich are all lazy. The poor are all lazy. The blacks are all lazy. The whites are all lazy. The immigrants are all lazy. It never ends. Consensus organizers try to go in the opposite direction. We create real opportunities for disparate people to come together through mutual self-interest and benefit from relationships with one another. As parties work together toward a common goal, they progress toward cultural competency. This is done through achieving mutual goals, not by attending seminars, memorizing steps, or simulated exercises. People begin to see that through differences can come strength. Differences are embraced and celebrated. Most significant, people learn that beyond these real differences, lie many, many more similarities than we ever felt were possible.

Imagine that you have brought together 20 diverse volunteers who all would like to start a day care center in their neighborhood. In this group, you have a person who tends to go on and on when making a point, another who is abrupt and likes to get to the bottom line quickly, and another who is always passionate and emotional. The participants also have different ages, ethnicities, and sexual orientations. To get the day care center off the ground, you also have to build positive relationships with bureaucrats, philanthropists, and parents needing day care. One volunteer may match up better in one situation, and another volunteer better in another situation. As a result, each volunteer sees that differences help achieve success toward a mutual goal. As the volunteers see that they benefit from their differences, they begin to see their similarities as well. They see that their similarities outnumber their real differences. The day care center opens and is a huge success.

OK, on paper this all sounds sensible. But what does this really look like out in our big, messy world? Well, partner, saddle up your pony. We are going deep into the heart of a big state, y'all. Let's head south to Houston, Texas.

THAT'S A TEXAS GRAPEFRUIT

I felt good about the work the development team had done in the Mon Valley in Pennsylvania. The technical assistance providers actually taught all of the volunteers the skills that they had built. I saw their confidence increase as they learned the basics of real estate and business development. The community organizers were effective even though they did not have previous experience. Their enthusiasm, effort, and genuineness had carried the day. As the volunteers stepped forward and took responsibility, as the external resources, such as foundations, corporations, and government, played key partnership roles, I wondered whether these patterns could be duplicated in other parts of the country.

The Local Initiatives Support Corporation (LISC), a well respected financial and technical assistance national intermediary, was one of the external resources that had helped develop the Mon Valley. By the mid-1980s, they had expanded their national program and were involved in more than 20 cities. In most instances, they raised money from local banks and large employers and then matched it with money they received from national sources, such as the Ford and Rockefeller foundations. They then established a local program that provided loans, grants, and technical advice to neighborhood development corporations.

I was interested in trying out the model in another location, away from the industrial areas of Buffalo and Pittsburgh. I flew to New York City and met with LISC officials. They explained that they had a handful of cities where demand for their services had not been as great as expected. This presented a serious problem for them because the local funders were expecting to see new businesses, houses, and apartments in areas of their cities where the need was evident. If there were no organized neighbors wanting to become developers, they were in trouble. Perhaps a new grassroots effort to create demand for their services was needed. I claimed that I had some experience in doing that. I left the Allegheny conference on good terms. I saw Dave Bergholz one last time in his office. He was warm, funny, and supportive. LISC gave me a one-way plane ticket to Houston, Texas.

Have you ever been to Houston? It's a pretty big city. Everything is pretty big. A glass of iced tea holds a quart. The city limits claim more square miles than entire New England states. Houston has an annual rodeo that lasts almost two weeks. The first night I arrived, I stayed at a bed and breakfast in the city. In the morning, the hostess served me a grapefruit and I said, "Ma'am, that's a very good breakfast and this grapefruit is huge." She broke out in a broad smile, brimming with pride, and said, "Son, that's a Texas grapefruit!" That same day it rained a bit. The weather service routinely announced that the total 24-hour rainfall amount was 10.79 inches. Everybody went about his or her business as if it was just a steady drizzle. My first week there, I purchased a small electronic pocket address book and calendar. I put it in my suit coat pocket and walked outside. It stopped working. I took it back to the electronic store and spoke with the manager. He looked at me like I was an idiot and scolded me, saying "You took this outside, where it wasn't air-conditioned, didn't you?" I sheepishly admitted the crime. He screamed, "You can't do that, son. It melted!" Did I mention Houston gets a tad hot and humid? I had to get used to it. I began to be able to tell the difference between a 96-degree day and a 98-degree day. The oil executives liked to tell stories about how in the 1940s their companies used to offer "combat pay," extra money to employees willing to move their families to one of two cities, Calcutta, India, or Houston, Texas.

LISC's local corporate partner in Houston was a loose equivalent to the Allegheny Conference. It had a board composed of the leadership of all the major Houston companies. I felt at home speaking to them. They looked at the poor and the communities they lived in as places with some hope and potential, but most past and current programs aiming to help were misguided, and a great deal of money was spent with little result. Even though Houston businesses were different from Pittsburgh businesses, it seemed their outlooks were surprisingly similar. I was glad to see my experience with other corporate leaders brought some credibility, even down in Texas. I learned that Houston was not Dallas. I sprinkled my standard introductory speech to them with lines like, "The first day I moved to your fine city, it rained 10.79 inches. I called a friend back home, and he said, 'Mike, you've been living in Texas less than 24 hours and you're already exaggerating'." I love some of Houston's phrases. "That guy thinks you hung the moon" (that's good), "That other guy thinks you are all hat and no cattle" (that's bad).

At the neighborhood level, I could walk miles and miles and only hear Spanish spoken. There was Spanish on the billboards, and Spanish in the shops. I had never experienced that before. The poverty in some of these neighborhoods was devastating. In the old 4th Ward, hundreds of shotgun shacks still stood, occupied with real living families. The houses are referred to as shotgun shacks because you could open the back door and see the front door (no hallways, little privacy, and very small rooms) and fire a shot through the whole house, through one door and then right out the other. I had only seen pictures of scenes like this, and they always seemed to be in rural areas, not in the shadows of downtown skyscrapers. Some social workers estimated the homeless population at 25,000 people. These were the unfortunate souls who were unable to live in a shotgun shack. On one occasion, while waiting for the bus, a pickup truck sped by, and three guys in cowboy hats yelled, "Yee haw!" Houston was not the Mon Valley, but I made it my new home. I got my library card and registered to vote. My precinct had its residents practice democracy on Election Day by voting in a Mexican restaurant. The clerk found my name on the registration list under a jalapeño pepper.

LET'S ROAST THE GOAT

To be effective in Houston, I knew I had to understand the social context and political culture. I read both local newspapers daily. I listened to local radio and watched the local television news. I had to do everything I could to absorb the local scene, understand the people, and relate to their psyches.

> To be successful, I had to understand the social context and the political culture.

Those first few months there, before even attempting to hire organizers, I noticed a number of startling differences in attitude, outlook, and behavior from what I was used to. I had to think through these differences and let them sink in. From this process, I shaped my five commandments of Houston. Commandment one, don't trust the police. Houston was the first place I lived in where the majority of residents feared the police. I'm talking about a majority of the law-abiding citizens. In my neighborhood in Houston, it was not uncommon to see people purposely crossing the street when they saw a police officer. It seemed that "suspects" had to be shot to be restrained more often than in any other metropolitan area. Commandment two, newer is better. In Buffalo and Pittsburgh, older was better. In those cities, it was assumed that old things stood the test of time, whereas new things were untested and not a sure thing. In Houston, it was always the new idea, new product, new car, and new house that got the attention and admiration. Commandment three, divide and conquer. With a multitude of minority groups and ethnicities, whites kept power by aligning themselves in one group, while freezing out others, to create a majority and keep the power. This caused a very high degree of mistrust and division among racial and ethnic groups within the neighborhoods. Commandment four, bigger is better; smaller is worse. With this fascination with size, would it be difficult to convince people that a small housing or economic development project would be beneficial? Commandment five, bravado is a sign of strength. Whenever I heard anyone talking "big," either at the neighborhood or corporate level, about all the wonderful things they were going to do, my white, ethnic, Northeastern, blue-collar roots took over and I thought "This guy's talking out of his ass." I was used to everyone around me drawing the same types of conclusion as I did. In Houston, everyone admires this bravado type of person. He or she is seen as confident, successful, and a visionary. Years later, Enron did not surprise me in the least. There was little if any stigma attached to failure. The key measurement was not failure but your response to it. The idea was to talk even bigger after failure, proving your tenacity and spunk. Bankruptcy, foreclosure, and loss were admired if they were followed with resiliency.

Constant attempts to understand and adjust to these commandments kept me on edge. The key was not to get people to see these issues as I did, nor was the key to get them to think differently. Rather, the key was to adopt an organizing method to match their attitudes. I knew that adjustments had to be made, but it was not easy or natural. I had to find the organizers by starting to build a local network of contacts. I found three that I thought had potential. One contact was found through her activity as a mother and volunteer in the public school system. Another contact was found through working on a community beautification project. The last contact was found as an active student at the University of Houston school of social work. I thought his talent had the potential to match the Mon Valley staff. The professional technical assistance providers were, however, much harder to assemble. I was very put off by the big talk, fast results personalities. Finally, we assembled the team. The organizers were trained to analyze the Houston low-income communities and select the six that had the greatest chance for success. The volunteers began to be recruited; they had pride in their communities and they were willing to work hard and learn. The corporate leaders were willing to support their efforts. One group in a predominately Latino neighborhood developed a pragmatic housing development plan. Members of the group obtained site control and proceeded to work strategically. They succeeded, and the construction began. The buyers were selected and finally the whole process was completed.

It was time for a celebration. The families and the entire neighborhood had a reason to have a party. We assembled the families in front of their new homes. Local politicians were present as well as the media. At the beginning of the event, there was nothing but pride and smiles. As the congratulatory speeches, laced with self-promotion, dragged on from the government, philanthropic, and banking dignitaries, grumbling started to be heard throughout the audience of residents. It began in the back and spread throughout the entire crowd. They shifted on their feet, looked down at the ground, talked out of the sides of their mouths, and mumbled to fellow audience members. I whispered to our organizer, "Find out what's wrong." He came back 2 minutes later with his report. It turned out that people from the neighborhood had set up a barbeque pit behind the new homes and had a goat slow cooking in honor of the occasion. He said he didn't know what to do. Another 30 minutes of speeches were scheduled. I said he needed to get up on the stage, and get the emcee to say in Spanish, "Let's roast the goat." The emcee did as requested. A huge cheer went up, as loud as when a goal was scored by the Mexican national soccer team. The whole crowd ran right past the dignitaries and straight toward the goat.

Always try to remember that in every place you work, with every group of coworkers, clients, and volunteers, there will be differences and similarities. You must realize that there is a good deal of skill and experience that goes into sorting out these differences and similarities. You have to become good at identifying both. Identifying differences will make your job interesting. You will see how people's culture shapes their thoughts and behavior. The differences you find will be like individual pearls, each beautiful and valuable, but not quite the same. The similarities you find will be the string that holds those slightly different pearls together. So there you have it. Start stringing!

Reflection Questions

1. Many believe that cultural competency is just an academic term. What does it mean to you?

2. Sometimes people divide us up on purpose. Have you ever seen this done? Explain.

3. What was the original meaning of "Don't mess with Texas"?

4. What is more important—understanding oneself or understanding others?

5. Do you ever think there will be a time when we don't need to think about cultural competency?

6

CONSENSUS ORGANIZING STRATEGIES AND TACTICS

In this chapter, you will learn:

◆ Ordinary people can create change.

◆ Steps to implement strategy.

◆ Measuring potential self-interest of multiple partners.

◆ How to pursue opportunities and judge their chances for success.

B y now you might be saying, "Great, I just bring people together, and no matter how different they are they will work side by side, achieve spectacular results, and everyone will live happily ever after." Well, of course there is a little more to it than that. It requires someone with strategic ability to make it happen and guess who that is? You! You are going to learn how to do everything we have talked about: If you don't have much confidence, let me remind you of one of my favorite *Seinfeld* episodes.

In this one, Kramer tells Elaine a story of how he decided to take a pair of pants back to the store because they didn't fit properly. So he wears them back to the store! On the subway platform, he gets tired of waiting so he goes down into the tunnel and starts walking. He walks into this pile of mud, gets his pants filthy, and turns around and comes home. Elaine gets exasperated and says, "What would you have done if you got to the store? What would you have worn home?" Kramer looks at Elaine like she is from a distant planet and exclaims, "Elaine, weren't you listening? I never got there." That is an absence of strategy.

Key Concepts for Becoming a Consensus Organizer:

Ordinary people can effect change.

Powerful people want to help.

For us to get started, I have to make sure that you possess the one thing you can't learn. That one thing is—you have to really believe in the idea of regular people having capacity and you have to believe that powerful people might want to help. If you don't believe in these things, you will have doubt and that doubt will prevent you from having intent. So how can you test yourself? Easily. Many people feel that working-class and poor people have very little ability or capacity to do more. Some say if they were more "on the ball," they wouldn't be where they are. Instead, they would be more successful. A consensus organizer looks at the same working-class and poor people and sees untapped potential, underdeveloped talents, and lots of exciting possibilities. No book will change your mind about how you think about this. So, I want you to look into your heart and find your compassion, hope, and optimism. I believe it is inside most of us.

There are many people in our society who are completely disconnected from contact with poor and working-class people. Some wealthy and middle-class professionals form opinions only through third parties such as the media. A consensus organizer sees a possibility to create real interactions connecting kindred spirits leading to unusual partnerships. Most of us are capable of seeing these possibilities if we think about how little real interaction there is between the wealthy and the poor. People don't base their negative stereotypes on actual experience. This means there is reason for hope.

Just take a look at how you have lived your life so far. Take a hard look at the values you treasure. Find out if there is a connection between consensus organizing and your beliefs. No one can connect your feelings intellectually or academically. You have to see whether you can embrace and accept the potential to link these kindred spirits. If it is something you believe in, you then have the basic ingredient necessary for a great recipe: You have intent.

OK, assuming you haven't shut the book and moved on to reruns of *Leave It To Beaver* ("Ward, have you seen the boys?"), you are ready to learn the art of developing consensus organizing strategies and tactics. To get you more comfortable, think about it in a series of steps. The following steps will help you get started:

1. Block out your preferences. It really doesn't help if you have a predetermined, detailed idea of what to do. If you really have already developed your own great idea, go bury it outside in your yard next to your dog's bone. Even without realizing it, we start to sell others on what we think. That can be the kiss of death. The more sure you are about what to do, the less sure you are that others have any insight or perspective worth considering. If others come with ideas that are similar to yours, you get to go back in the yard and dig up that idea next to the bone. Otherwise, keep it 6 feet under.

2. Don't focus on the causes. Sometimes people will be willing to come together and get involved to try to change something. Don't assume that this willingness means they agree on the cause of the problem. Every person might have a different "take" on what the causes are. A consensus organizer seeks agreement on a proposed solution and does not attempt to reach agreement on causes.

A consensus organizer seeks agreement on a solution to a problem and does not attempt to reach agreement on the cause.

You will be dealing with people who are working together for the first time because they see everyone else as helping reach a solution. If you go back and peel the onion to look for the cause, you risk the possibility of becoming hopelessly divided. For example, suppose there is a desire to develop recreational opportunities for kids. If you look into why kids have time on their hands that they are spending unproductively, you might have someone say that it is because they don't belong to a Christian church. Another might say the parents are too lenient. Another might say the mothers should be at home and not at work. Another says the minimum wage should be raised. If you can keep the focus on helping the young people, the possibility to create a cooperative working group grows. If you focus on the cause, we will lose the chance for a solution. People will splinter into camps over the cause and be unable to cooperate in formulating a solution. Why? Mainly because they will not like working with people who are so "wrong" in their analyses.

3. Get specific. Nothing is ever accomplished with only general agreement. There must also be agreement and follow-through on specific tasks. These tasks include many things that may not be exciting or flashy. Many necessary steps on the path to success are mundane, repetitive, and even boring. That is why you must make each individual see that each specific task is essential to the eventual goal. Strategy is never general.

Strategy is never general. You must get specific about tasks.

You would never say something vague like, "Will you go over there and talk to him?" Instead you would say, "Are you willing to go over there and talk to him so he unlocks the door for us to meet?" The value of strategy is that it requires everyone to break down the goal into a series of practical steps that people commit to do. They are then held accountable to complete the tasks successfully.

4. Progress through honesty. Consensus organizers do not manipulate people into doing things they don't want to do. Instead, we create opportunities for them to achieve their goals. These opportunities must be presented very directly. I like to put it this way: Consensus organizers do not talk out of both sides of their mouth. Even though we talk to a large variety of people, we have to say the same things. If we suspect that someone wants us to say something other than the truth, we still must tell the truth. If we are asked for an opinion, we must give our honest opinion. I learned a long time ago that people deep, deep down want the truth. They may react negatively at first but, as the truth settles in, they learn to respect it. The people in the room will change. Our strategy of honesty remains the same. For instance, suppose we wanted to open a charter school. We felt our existing public school was too large and impersonal. This means we would have to feel comfortable with what we believe. We would share our honest opinion with others. The only thing that changes is the emphasis. If we talk to a teacher at the existing school we might say, "There is only so much you can do when classes are this large." To a janitor we might say "I don't know how you could possibly keep all these rooms clean." And to a student we might say, "Would you appreciate more individual help in your math class so you could better understand the lesson?" Each person hears a message that a charter school matches their self-interest. We never stray from our belief in the charter school. We would never meet somebody who prefers the old school and then say, "So do we." That would be talking out of both sides of our mouth.

5. *Explore options.* All of us sometimes think there is only one way to do something. We then think that this only way is, of course, the best way. Of course it's the best—because we can't even think of one other alternative. Well, other people interested in the same issue might be able to think of many other options. We now have multiple choices. Now, as a group, we can assess each one and together choose what we think would be most effective. The agreed-upon choice may not have been our own. In my experience, the earlier people hear options, the more open-minded they are. When options are presented later, people stay glued to their original idea. You, as a consensus organizer, need to get the ideas on the table and discuss all of the ideas early. This helps keep the participants creative, open-minded, and better able to appreciate the value of others.

As a consensus organizer, you need to get all the ideas on the table and discuss all of the ideas early.

---

6. *Get commitment.* A strategy is chosen consciously and decisively. It is not decided as a "general direction." People work harder toward a goal when it is specific. This way, they know success when they achieve it. We all work harder when we commit to something. Resist the temptation to keep things general in a desire to preserve unity. We have all been in meetings in which nothing has been decided or accomplished. Some leaders are happy if it appeared that everyone got along and there was no disagreement. They declare these meetings "successful." Well, do not be tempted to go down that path. Real strategy requires real discussions, emotions, trade-offs, reconsideration, reflection, and, eventually, a commitment.

7. *Take the piano off your back.* You do not have to develop the strategy that is selected. As a consensus organizer, your job is to set the wheels in motion and begin discussions that are focused and purposeful. Tapping into the capacities of the entire group develops the strategy. Remember, it is never *your* strategy; it is *their* strategy. If the group has an honest, straightforward, detailed discussion and reaches a strategic conclusion, you have been successful. You, of course, always have the option to make your own

points, and put your own cards on the table, but you do not have veto power over the others. Do not look at this as marginalizing your influence. Instead, look at it as taking the piano off your back. It is not only up to you anymore. If you look at yourself as a creative person, think of the group as your creation. You do not have to create the strategy; you have to create the process that involves everyone. Then your creation, the people in the group, will demonstrate their own creativity.

You do not have to create the strategy; you create the process that involves everyone.

---

8. *EZ credit.* Repeat after me 1,000 times, "We couldn't have done it without you." These must become your words to live by. Think of credit as a big bag of 50-percent-off discount coupons. You have a giant bag to distribute. Don't people follow through better with some type of incentive? You must understand incentive. You know that many more people will walk into a store and buy something with that discount coupon. Well, more people will continue to enthusiastically volunteer if you pass out credit. You can pass it out in three ways:

   a. Privately—People appreciate personal contact when they are told their participation and ideas were crucial and indispensable.
   b. Publicly—People want to hear you say to everyone else how important you feel they are. Every person likes to hear you shout it from a rooftop. (He must have meant it. He told everybody.)
   c. As a part of the whole—Show individuals that their efforts led to another person's effort, which led to another and another. Link up all the credit, so everyone sees that the sum of the parts makes up the whole.

These steps do not mention many other concepts that Alinsky and other conflict organizers believe in. We didn't mention ridicule, embarrassment, or vindictiveness. You attract more flies with . . . or is it you can't lead the cow out of . . . I don't know, I get those sayings mixed up. I do know that people respond very well to a positive spirit. You have the ability to attract partners with a powerful magnet: that you need and appreciate them. Never build strategies around enemies, hatred, or a desire for revenge. Instead, build around the human desire to be important, to contribute, and to be appreciated.

If a group has an honest, straightforward, detailed
discussion and reaches a strategic conclusion,
there is more chance for success.

Saul Alinsky and his organizing principles are still very much alive today. They continue to dominate the organizing profession, and are considered virtually above criticism. Dedicated people throughout the country use his ideas and methods to bring about change, to help the poor and working poor. As they do their work, they are motivated by a strong driving belief that those in power must be held accountable. This accountability, they believe, will only be evident through the mobilization of large numbers of people putting pressure on selected targets. To carry out this approach, a series of tactics and strategies are chosen, heightening the pressure on the target. The target is believed to grudgingly gain respect for the people involved in these efforts and true partnerships can eventually result.

One of the standard tactics is to hold a large rally or meeting and attempt to pack the room with as many people as possible. If one of the targets shows up in response to an invitation, he or she is subject to a series of pre-pared questions that usually must be answered by only yes or no responses. The questions are simplified to test the target's willingness to support the crowd's demands. For instance, if affordable housing happens to be the issue, the target is asked pointedly, number one, "Do you recognize afford-able housing as a priority for our city?" If the target attempts to answer the question in-depth, the response is cut short by the crowd chanting, "Yes or no? Yes or no?" The second question might be, "Do you support an immedi-ate five percent charge to be paid by all developers throughout the city that will be set aside for affordable housing?" If the target wants to say some-thing about his or her actual opinion and the differences between a 2-unit construction project and a 200-unit construction project, he or she is once again cut off by the crowd as it chants, "Yes or no?" Well, you get the idea. There is no expectation of real dialogue. If one of the invited targets (bankers, city officials, developers) does not show up for the meeting, an empty chair is invariably placed upon the stage with the AWOL's name attached to it. Out of this approach, it is believed that community improve-ment is built, power is developed, and eventually power is redistributed.

If, for some reason, this conflict organizing approach falls short, watch where the organizers focus the shortcoming or blame. It is attributed to the low number of people that bothered to show up. It is automatically believed, usually with little actual analysis, that the size of the crowd was lacking and thus the results fell short. Who is to say that this was the key variable? It is almost never a consideration that the premise may have been flawed in the first place. Maybe, occasionally, this approach is not the optimum approach. There is no rigor applied to this model. It is assumed that with a large number of protesters, the approach will always be effective.

Consensus organizers, on the other hand, do not want to back a potential supporter up against a wall, and we certainly do not want an empty chair to prove a point. This different vision requires different organizers and very different neighborhood participants. We need organizers who can look at an issue and see different perspectives that surround it. They have to put themselves into other people's skins. There is no correct perspective or incorrect perspective. Instead, we develop a preferred perspective. We learn to take real pieces from each perspective and we weave each into one intricate, supportive perspective. It should have enough elements of everyone's thinking so that it can become preferred. It is the goal of the consensus organizer to see how skills can be used to find and develop a series of potential solutions with the same preferred perspective.

Consensus organizers take real pieces from each perspective and weave them into one supportive perspective.

The internal organizing (inside a neighborhood) is done by searching for a small number of strategic participants representing different constituencies with the potential to develop the same perspective. This is accomplished by searching for people with similar values gained through seemingly different experiences. Wow, that was a mouthful! To break it down, look at a neighborhood having six different circles of constituencies: (1) homeowners, (2) renters, (3) businesses, (4) faith-based institutions, (5) service organizations, and (6) large institutions. As a consensus organizer, your job is to seek out real participants to fill each circle. In most cases, one person who is a homeowner, another who is a social service director from the YMCA, and yet another who is a small business owner of a flower shop will have many differences. But as you listen to the three of them, you find that they all think kids growing up in their neighborhood get labeled negatively and unfairly. All the kids are seen as gangbangers just by virtue of the fact that they happen to live there. They all have come to the same conclusion independently. All three feel that it is very unfair to the vast majority of neighborhood kids who happen to be good kids. This is a shared feeling. It is an outlook they all have prior to talking to us. They value the decent kids in the community. This is the beginning of a consensus organizing strategy. As you build relationships, you continue to look for the same continuity and block out all the disparities. Your actual project or group activity involves organizing people with common values and a preferred perspective. You could talk to many people who only point out the severity of the gang problem, some of whom place blame on one particular racial or ethnic group. You keep searching beyond these perspectives for your preferred view. In this case, you look for recognition and support for youth who have been negatively mislabeled. So, as you see, this is the mind-set consensus organizers must have. The people are already out there. We see no need to convert, convince, force, or embarrass people to become involved. We weave a perspective that taps their self-interest and their values.

The reason for the mix of the six circles is to bring together a working group that represents different constituencies. No one is more effective in speaking to a homeowner than a homeowner. This holds true for each circle. A businessperson can make a similar point, but initially there will still be a distance that must be bridged between a business owner and a homeowner. Another reason for mixing the circles is that different skills will be brought into the effort. Some from a large neighboring institution (e.g., community college, hospital, large factory) can bring management skills and contacts outside the neighborhood while the renter can make everyone more grounded in reality because they may feel the effects of the issue being addressed much more directly. The renter or homeowner may even be the parent of the good kid who is being negatively stereotyped. The third reason for requiring a mix is this seemingly disparate group will be impressive to the outside world. They will bring the perspectives of the entire community, not just social service agencies for instance. A narrow constituency will run the risk of appearing self-serving to a potential external supporter or funder. A wider constituency will run less of a risk.

For many neighborhoods, a cohesive group of 20 people, with a sprinkling from each circle, can be surprisingly effective. As members of the group learn to respect and trust one other, and reinforced by their mutual preferred perspective, you can begin to scope out the other half of the required recipe—those with resources and influence from outside the neighborhood. You, as the consensus organizer, must be clear about your role. You have to fill the empty chairs with people who want to sit in them.

So, we have come full circle back to the belief that regular people can achieve results and some powerful people might want to help. This belief is the basis for all consensus organizing strategy. When you play the role just described, you will feel quite different. If you work for a nonprofit agency as a program director, you might dream up and design programs. You might not be interested in what you designed. You may not even be proud of it. If you were a development director for a nonprofit, you would try to raise money. You might be successful. You might be praised by the agency. If you were an outreach worker for a nonprofit, you might recruit parents and residents. You might convince people to attend a meeting. But if you are a consensus organizer, you do something different. You show people their true worth. You help people to value and respect one other. You show people that they are interconnected and indispensable to one other. You have them achieve specific results together. This is the true essence of the consensus organizing. You see others in a well-deserved, positive light. Think of how few people can say that. You won't become an effective strategist overnight. It takes practice. Always start small. Maybe there is an issue at your school or workplace that has not been addressed. Maybe you play the role of an organizer right under your own nose. It doesn't have to be a concern that affects thousands. It might just be something that concerns a dozen people.

To improve my strategic ability, I decided to go back to school. Let's say that you all join me back at the University of Pittsburgh's Graduate School of Social Work. Let's take advantage of the excellent faculty. If we successfully complete our degree, we will be rewarded with free plane tickets. I hope you got your passport ready as I told you to. We are then going over to Ireland— not the peaceful, lush green of County Cork but instead the gritty, industrial town you've heard about in the news. We are going to Belfast in Northern Ireland. Oh yeah, it's before the peace accord. So get some sleep on the plane because you need to be alert when we land. Never mind why, just be alert.

Looks Like We Have Three Choices

About 12 years after undergraduate school, I decided it was best that I continue my formal education. I enrolled in the master's of social work program in community organization at the University of Pittsburgh. The main reason for my decision was that it gave me a chance to learn from one of the most talented and inspiring persons I have ever had the good fortune to meet: Mo Coleman. Mo, in other previous lives, had directed a major corporate organization, taught in prison, worked in a settlement house, and advised the automobile mogul, Henry Ford. I found him to be a very interesting guy and here he was, holed up in this very tiny academic program in the city in which I lived. I could take lots of courses from him and get a chance to talk and learn from him. One of the many things that fascinated me about Mo was that he was almost universally liked and respected. Most important, even as a classic "New Deal" liberal, his political opponents respected him and enjoyed being around him. He had built up tremendous power. Hundreds of people came to him seeking his insight and advice. He was a guy that people sought out on a regular basis. On a typical day, he would be in a dozen different situations with every individual or group edging over to him, listening to his conclusions, invariably agreeing, and feeling a part of his conclusion. He built consensus in seemingly effortless, mutually beneficial ways. Underneath all this affability was an extremely purposeful strategist. He used tricks; I think he sometimes used tricks he himself didn't realize. He would bumble along, stuttering, repeating things with a puzzled look. He always appeared to be behind the people in the room, struggling to keep pace when he was mentally miles ahead. He was like a pitcher with two quick strikes on a batter, more than happy to let the next pitch be caught in deep center field for the out.

There were many tricks I learned from Mo. I tried to absorb all of them, but I will always have a favorite. The all-time best one had Mo spending hours with a disjointed, unfocused, argumentative group. He listened and listened then finally spoke. Then he listened and listened some more. Then he sputtered with what invariably looked like absolute spontaneity, "It looks like we have three choices." In all the years I watched and learned, Mo never felt there were four choices, two choices, or one choice. There were always three. I would watch the faces of the rest of the people in the room and you could almost feel the collective relaxation. It was as if they had all the power (Mo didn't appear to decide), they had options (they weren't being forced into a corner), and they had comfortable limits (thank God there weren't hundreds of choices. I wouldn't know where to begin, but I could pick one out of three). Then he pulled out a magician's sword to carve the lady. He made the first choice so radical that everyone in the audience would find it too extreme. For instance, he would say, "Each of you could go out and buy 100 copies of this book." He would then have a third choice, equally radical but in the opposite direction: "You could never buy this book. No one would ever be exposed to anything about this exciting technique called consensus organizing." Then, in between these two extreme choices that had no constituency, he would sandwich in a second choice that sounded moderate, practical, appropriate, and logical.

He would then describe the second choice: "You could each go out and buy just one copy of this book, read it for yourself, and then each decide what you think." Of course, the entire group agreed on the second option, and I would be very happy because I still sell quite a number of books. I'm telling you, I saw him do this hundreds of times. He had enormous power through this skill he had perfected. He always made option number two the approach that would help the most considering the reality of the hand that had been dealt. People always left the room happy, committed, and determined to carry out their decision. There is a special power that is voluntarily transferred to people like Mo who are likeable, seemingly evenhanded, and hardworking. You will notice that their power grows. They create a sense of stability. On the other hand, overzealous advocates have a violent ebb and flow to their power. They gain it through struggle. They usually have it in spurts and then frequently lose it. To them, power is like a spiked fever to a flu-stricken patient. The Mo Colemans gain it steadily and continuously. It is rarely taken away from them.

Consensus organizing requires an understanding that power can grow. I never saw Mo take power from someone or reduce the power of another, yet his own power grew and grew. In the national civic engagement field, the late John Gardner, the founder of Common Cause (the nation's largest citizen lobbying group) and an adviser to presidents of both political parties, was such a person. I had the pleasure of meeting him and explaining consensus organizing. Like Mo, he was a phenomenal listener. He drew quick, accurate conclusions from his listening ability. He told me that people would almost always favor moderate approaches. He said the most lasting improvement efforts were led by people who understood how to package real change and social progress into moderate approaches. People who worried about credit and recognition would stall the very same cause. Mo Coleman grabbed situations and provided the moderate definition. It just happened to always be the second of three choices. Years after realizing how this worked, I was asked to bring together a group of activists from throughout the state of Connecticut. I was under contract to a state government agency. We had a series of meetings in Hartford. There was a lot of tension and distrust in the room at the meetings. Participants had very strong views on how the state should help low-income communities. Let's just say I really had to earn my money. Finally, at one of the meetings, I framed the debate and shouted, "Hey, I think we have three choices." I made choice number one and three some of the worst ideas that had been proposed during the day. Choice number one was the government's muddiest thinking and choice number three was the activist's equivalent. The second choice never looked so good. I had a modest goal—to get out of the meeting alive. It worked.

On my way out the door, shaking hands and thanking God, one of the quietest participants pulled me over and whispered, "Tell Mo Coleman I said hello." It turned out Mo had worked in Hartford a decade earlier. She knew Mo had moved to Pittsburgh; she also knew that I had lived in Pittsburgh. She connected the dots. She wasn't mad. She was smiling. If you want to consider playing such a role, we can now venture outside the neighborhood. Let's go to the external part of consensus organizing.

Their Eyes Are Closer Together

Back in the illusionary pre-9/11 days of safety in America, I would read about the violence in Northern Ireland and shake my head in disbelief. How could these people hate one another so much when they were of the same race? In the United States we understand racial violence and ethnic violence, but come on, the situation in Northern Ireland should be correctable. Well, in life, watch out. Whenever you look at a problem from afar, you run the risk of having someone call your bluff.

In the early 1990s, the secretary of state for Northern Ireland was a man named Sir Patrick Mayhew. His wife was Lady Jean Mayhew. Lady Jean made a visit to the United States and saw various community development strategies. Her hope was to get some ideas and bring them back to Belfast. One of the ideas that attracted her interest was consensus organizing. I had no idea who she was, but I was invited to meet with her and some activists she was working with in both the Catholic and Protestant communities. Sure, where would we meet—Pittsburgh? Houston? No, her office politely suggested Belfast. Great! That should be relaxing, maybe taking a few extra days and turning it into a vacation. One hotel option was to stay in the place that had been the most bombed in the Western world! I checked around as much as I could about this Lady Jean and found out she was greatly admired for her courage and genuine compassion by people on both sides of the conflict. As the spouse of the highest-ranking British official in Northern Ireland, you would think she would have hightailed it to London and waited for her husband to return, but there she was, in the middle of the fray, at great personal and political risk. I accepted the invitation.

Well, coming from a working-class background, the only foreign experience I had was when my brother and I would sneak across the border into Canada (about 3 miles from my house), and bring back illegal firecrackers for the Fourth of July. Maybe the experience with loud noises would help.

I flew to London and then to Belfast. It was a mite tense. There were machine guns at the airport, on the highway, everywhere. I was driven to my first speaking engagement to explain consensus organizing to an audience of about a hundred. As I looked out into the sea of pasty white faces, it hit me. I couldn't tell who was in the audience I was about to address. Were they all Protestant? All Catholic? Mixed? Well, I tried an opener that was designed to break the tension. I said, "Good morning and greetings from the United States. Let me tell you a little about myself. My father was Protestant, my mother was Catholic, and my wife is Jewish, so I'm the perfect person to speak with you today." There was an ever so slight pause, followed by hearty laughter. The speech seemed to go over well. As I shook hands with the attendees afterward, I asked my driver, "Say, was this a mixed crowd?" He nodded affirmatively. I then asked a second question, jokingly, "Man, how can you tell who is who?" He said, not jokingly, "Oh, you can always tell the Catholics—their eyes are closer together." Oh boy, this is going to be a piece of cake I thought as I tried to find some sunglasses.

Lady Jean Mayhew was to meet me the following morning. Someone would pick me up at the hotel lobby at 8:00 a.m. to deliver me to her. Sure enough, a guy oozing with Irish charm came up, asked if I was Michael, and out I went to get into his car. Well, there was no car. There was British military all around me and they had me crawl into a tank! It turned out, we were going to make a few stops in the working-class Protestant neighborhood on Shankill Road. As the gun turret swiveled, we reached our destination. Lady Jean was deeply respected by the activists in the Protestant community. I was impressed with their dedication, their intelligence, and their commitment. It seemed that when the economy went south, they lost their industrial jobs. The Catholics, they felt, got all the help from the government whereas they got none. Sound familiar? There were plenty of impressive community improvement efforts and I felt that many of the people I met were only an opportunity away from dramatic progress. Then, it was time to go over to the Catholic side of west Belfast, the Falls Road. Only one problem—the military vehicle stopped. I was asked to get out. I was required to walk the rest of the way. It was too dangerous for the tank! The soldiers turned around and left. So I started walking, wishing I still had those rosary beads from the Holy Name of Jesus School. On this side, I met people with the same level of dedication and commitment. They, of course, had the predictable and understandable distrust for the police and government leaders. They did, however, have the same deep respect for Lady Mayhew.

After my stops, I was finally able to meet Lady Mayhew. She was very, very impressive—honest, fair, evenhanded, and genuine, and we had a great discussion. She saw that women might hold the key to peace because they had been shut out of formal involvement and they understood the commonality of the problems and the need to come together. As I talked about the situation, I realized what a great task it would be; but I got more and more excited about what possibilities might exist. I could start to see those Legoland blocks. I could start to see roles. I could imagine these people hungry for peace, strategizing together.

There was only one problem—the official role of the British government. In consensus organizing, the government needed to be a partner. There was so much distrust, the situation cried out for inclusiveness. After looking into both Catholic and Protestant neighborhoods on both sides of the so-called peace line, I saw a need to open up opportunities for low-income and working-class members of both religions. I needed to check to see whether the government could be a potential partner. Lady Jean Mayhew invited me back.

On my next trip, I was interviewed live on the BBC. I tried to make my point as tactfully and nonjudgmentally as possible. The interviewer was dripping with venom over my premise that the poor and working-class people needed to lead the effort. I wanted to test the idea that members of the government could open their eyes to seeing a new role for the residents, similar to what evolved in the Mon Valley. The BBC interviewer said sarcastically, "What do you mean when you say that everyone must be involved?" The guy had hate in his eyes. I replied, "I mean everyone. It's a common English word. I'm surprised you've never heard it before!" Funny, but that was the end of the interview and the beginning of believing that the elements for consensus organizing to succeed were not in place. I felt there was still a pattern of reluctance within the British government to allow full and equal participation from the entire community. You can't start a process that creates change by leaving out people who need to create it.

I never accept an assignment if I don't believe I have a good chance to find self-interest. I don't have to feel the assignment will be simple and easy; I don't even have to see how I am going to get there. I just have to believe that self-interest is there.

A consensus organizer must be able to find self-interest.

Consensus organizing requires that both organizing processes (within the community and within the power structure) be done concurrently. If you go into a neighborhood and spend all your time there until a formal organization is eventually formed, you will almost always have a group that will then feel the need to advocate to the outside world. The bonding of group members will almost be too effective. They will look at their own group as "us" and everybody else as "them." In Northern Ireland, the British government's reluctance to trust and involve elements within the Catholic community helped create the "us" and "them" dynamic. Have you ever had advocates approach you? Think of some of the religious zealots, fringe political party members, and social change organizations. When they come at you, their sole purpose (or soul purpose?) is to get you to support their previously developed agenda. Your only value to them is if you do what it is they want you to do. If you don't, you are not only of no value; you become a big part of the problem and a potential future enemy. This is an out of balance, unequal relationship. Even some so-called supporters may be disingenuous and trying to avoid confrontation. Ironic, isn't it? Those trying to combat powerlessness want you to become powerless.

Conversely, if you first organize those outside the community with immense power and influence, you will unknowingly create paternalism. A program will be developed in isolation, designed to help "them," the people who live in the neighborhood. Well-meaning experts hire other experts who know exactly what people want and need. When they are greeted with skepticism and distrust from the neighborhood, they are surprised, confused, and hurt. They cannot understand the response they have elicited. The British government was consistently shocked when portions of the Catholic community refused to trust or be open to participate in neighborhood improvement programs that the government had designed.

To be successful, it takes a dual organizing process done simultaneously. You become a sort of shuttle diplomat, feeding information to others, pointing out opportunities, and building optimism. To see to it that everyone honestly defines and articulates their actual self-interest, you will have to start to define how everyone will benefit and how their power will increase. So there you have it. You can see the mind-set and the method that is required. You have to see the weeks and months ahead as partly sunny days. You become the new weather forecaster. To do this, you can be anyone. You can be a resident, pastor, social service worker, businessperson, teacher, government worker, retired grandparent, but you cannot be pessimistic. You cannot be naïve; you become a realistic optimist.

I went back to the United States and realized that consensus organizing could not be effective in Northern Ireland until the British government became more open to real participation and power sharing among both the residents of the poor Protestant and Catholic neighborhoods. The timing was just not right. They hadn't gotten where they needed to be for the consensus organizing method to be effective.

Over the years, the British government gradually began to understand the need to engage in a dual organizing process. All political elements within both Protestant and Catholic communities were treated equally and seriously. The Northern Ireland Peace Accord of 1998 and continued progress are direct results of a deeper understanding of mutual self-interest.

George John Mitchell, the former U.S. Senator, in his book *Making Peace* (1999), wrote,

> The entire society learned that violence won't solve their problems it will only make them worse. They learned that knowledge of their history is a good thing but being chained to their past is not. Finally, they came to believe, with cool reason, that peace and political stability will enable them to enjoy unprecedented growth and prosperity. (p. 186)

In consensus organizing, you have to look at every opportunity as a *potential* opportunity. Knowing when to continue or quit is an acquired skill. In Northern Ireland, there was some wonderful potential at the community level in both Catholic and Protestant neighborhoods. The residents had the same desire and self-interest to reach out to the British government. At the same time, however, the external partners did not feel as though it was in their self-interest to involve parts of the Catholic community in revitalization and power sharing. That resulted in a "missing piece." Continuing in that scenario would have led to advocacy and not to consensus organizing. Luckily, mutual self-interest later developed because everyone finally came to similar conclusions and got tired of the status quo.

Reflection Questions

1. If we believe nonprofessionals can do the work of professionals, aren't we setting them up for failure?
2. Did Saul Alinsky really have protesters go into all the bathroom cubicles at Chicago's O'Hare airport and refuse to leave?
3. Should strategy be static or evolve over time?
4. What is wrong with the organizer deciding on the most effective strategy?
5. Can you be manipulative and honest at the same time?

REFERENCE

Mitchell, G. J. (1999). *Making peace.* New York: Random House.

7

DEVELOPING EXTERNAL RELATIONSHIPS

In this chapter, you will learn:

◆ Lasting relationships are built on continued mutual benefit.

◆ Definitions of value and worth.

◆ The importance of reciprocity.

◆ To treat powerful people as equals.

I n the next four chapters, you will start to learn how to use consensus organizing techniques to increase your effectiveness in helping others. As always, take your time, read, and reflect. Some of the points may seem a little obvious; but try to think them through and apply them to some of your real circumstances. I know you can do it. Don't restrict yourself to the way you have always thought. Don't keep yourself boxed in. Let's get started.

Partly Sunny

Some activists think that the world ends when they leave the community of supporters. They tend to see everyone from the outside world as non-supporters, or worse, as enemies. They feel that the outside world consists entirely of people and organizations that are the root cause of the issue they are addressing. Consensus organizers look at those very same people and organizations as the potential sources of solutions. We see the opportunity to go beyond our obvious borders as the chance to build new relationships that are needed to reach our goals. We look forward to the exploration of the world that lies beyond our neighborhoods and communities. Many activists are trained to look for those people who are causing a problem and then typify them as negative, uncaring, self-serving, and evil. Of course, there can be truth to this analysis. As consensus organizers, we do not dispute this; however, we go beyond this somewhat limited analysis to take a different look at these people. Do they have the power to help? Oftentimes, they do. If they have that power, we see them as potential allies. Some people may think this is the most naïve thing they have ever heard. Consider this. Is it any more crazy than the assumption that these people are automatically our enemies until the end of time?

Sometimes things are seen negatively because of how they have been framed over the years. Take, for instance, our daily weather forecast. Think of all the meteorologists who predict that Tuesday will be "partly cloudy." One of these forecasters coined that phrase a long time ago and it has been used ever since. We, the people wanting to know what the weather will be like on Tuesday, are used to hearing the prediction "partly cloudy." We are conditioned to see this day as partly negative (or to those of us living in Southern California, completely negative). That's how we interpret the phrase. We see it as better than rain, but nowhere near as good as a sunny day. Isn't it true that the meteorologist years ago had a second choice? Couldn't he or she have analyzed the same isobars and high pressure troughs and called the day "partly sunny?" If we all heard that forecast, wouldn't we be anticipating that same Tuesday as a wonderful day full of great possibilities? Would more people picnic, walk, bike, swim, and jog? Yes, they would. People would approach the very same day with more optimism.

Consensus organizers believe that there are external resources that can be blended into the goals of people from low-income neighborhoods.

Consensus organizers believe there are external resources that can be blended into the goals of people from low-income neighborhoods.

BUILDING LASTING EXTERNAL RELATIONSHIPS

There are lawyers, accountants, builders, doctors, engineers, and countless others with skills that are desperately needed. There are nonprofits and for-profits that have power and expertise. Why should we automatically assume that they don't care, or worse, only want to hurt us? Approach the outside world with an open mind. See the possibilities of opening doors and not finding them all locked. Think of Tuesday as "partly sunny."

So, if there are all of these potential supporters out there and we start to believe that they might want to help us, where do we start? Well, we have to start with a premise. The premise is that help will not come from strangers. Instead, help will come from people we know. This means we need to get to know lots of people. Once they know us, they might help us.

In all my work, I am almost always surprised by how isolated we are. In many cities, our citizens have never traveled to neighborhoods that are 2 minutes from their home. In some cases, people never go downtown. In others, people avoid crossing major highways to see what's on the other side. This isolation leaves us deprived. We are deprived of new contacts, deepening ties, and increased networks. We keep to ourselves. Consensus organizers realize that this lack of contact makes people wary of strangers. It leads to a "siege mentality" in which "we" are "right" and "they" are "wrong." We can't be dependent on the kindness of strangers. Because people we know will help us, we have to know more people. We have to count on friends.

Think for a minute about how we make friends in our personal lives. Have you ever met people who only want to talk about themselves and their own problems, needs, and desires? Amazing! So have I. All the time they talk about "I did this. . . . I want this. . . . I feel. . . ." and seldom is it about you. Despite the fact that there are lots and lots of people in the world who do this, most of the time we do not choose them as friends. Instead, we look for a sense of balance in a potential friend. We are more than willing to help out, listen, empathize, but we want some reciprocity—we want others to help us, listen to us, and empathize with us, as well. You have to think of building external relationships in exactly the same way. You build through reciprocity—helping one another.

We build external relationships through
reciprocity—helping one another.

Rich and powerful people and organizations still need help. Low-income and working-class people need help as well. Would rich people automatically want to help us just because we need help? Of course not. Do you want to help people who are overly needy and want to be your friend or do you instead say something like, "I stopped returning her calls. She always wanted me to do exactly what she wanted when she wanted it. I never could do enough for her. She was just too needy." We do not form friendships when we are required to give 100 percent and get nothing in return. In fact, we protect ourselves by refusing to make or keep friends who put us into this situation. Just keep this in mind as you reach out to new people and organizations. No one "owes" you their time and help, no matter how rich and powerful they may be. They must see benefit to themselves to want to make your acquaintance. Do not try to build a relationship around the community's needs. If you do, you will look around and say, "Hey, where did all my friends go?" Instead, build friendships around reciprocity.

To build a reciprocal relationship, you must first be willing to do it. It is not about tricking someone or manipulating someone. Could you interact with someone rich and powerful, someone who has not been concerned about your issue, someone who might have contributed to the problem and actually want to still help them? I constantly hear people respond, "Well, I couldn't build a relationship with anyone like that. They owe us. They need to make up for everything they have done to hurt us. In fact, I don't think they could ever do enough to make up for it." If you feel that way, you will never be able to build reciprocal relationships. You have to want to do it.

Lasting relationships are not built on guilt, sympathy, or public relations. They are built on mutual benefit.

Lasting relationships are built on mutual benefit.

VALUE AND WORTH

Again, go back to your own personal friendships. Most of the time, our deepest, long-lasting relationships are with people we have helped and who have helped us in return. We talk about these friends by saying things like, "I can count on him" or "They are always there" or "She really understood just what I needed." We feel two things from friends like this and these two things must become the basis for all your external relationships—a sense of *value* and a sense of *worth*. These twin concepts are the foundation of how you create new relationships with people outside your community. Let's take a detailed look at both concepts.

Value—We have to provide real value to someone to be appreciated. Value can be evidenced in a variety of ways. We could be valuable by investing time. We could be valuable because of our particular skill or expertise. We might be valuable because of our reliability. Our value to another can evolve over a period of time. The relationship can deepen as the person receives continued, expanded benefit. People may value us for many different reasons, allowing us to continue to expand our base of relationships.

Worth—As we prove our value to others, we begin to be appreciated. Worth is the reciprocal feeling that comes from being valued. As you are appreciated more, your sense of real worth deepens. This makes you want to be valued even more. Think of your deepest friendships—your favorite aunt, your best teacher? Don't you feel a deeper sense of commitment to "not let them down"? This deep feeling was developed over a period of time in which value and worth were expanded.

This is the same dynamic that must be created when you attempt to develop external relationships. As the external person or organization sees value in you, you feel a sense of worth.

In developing external relationships, a sense of value must be seen to develop a sense of worth.

If, for instance, you were working with the mayor and the mayor genuinely felt that you were essential to his or her success, you would feel a sense of worth. If the mayor then helped you achieve one of your goals, you would value what the mayor did and the mayor would feel a deeper sense of worth. The reciprocity continues to be woven around you back and forth until all the individual threads of value and worth form a tight-knit relationship.

Notice how different this process is as compared to forcing someone to relate to you or your cause? If a person is forced to deal with you through fear or intimidation, there can be little, if any, chance to create value or worth. Many advocates argue that pressure and mobilization are essential to create change. Pressure and mobilization can bring about change. But does that change lead to lasting improvement? If a bank makes loans because it fears bad publicity, there is little respect, trust, or reciprocity. The loan may be approved, but has a relationship deepened? In this scenario, to create additional change you have to create an atmosphere of fear and intimidation all over again. If, instead, the bank saw real benefit to itself in making the loan, the relationship would have a chance to develop through mutual benefit, leading to value and worth. You could increase the chance for additional benefit to the community.

It may seem logical to try this with people who are similar to you. You could picture this happening between people or groups that are somewhat equal in power and size. But what if the relationship involves someone much more powerful than you are? Now, that you may find to be more challenging. You might feel that you would be crushed and taken for a naïve, weak, unequal partner. When we deal with a more powerful entity, some of us become reticent and deferential. We think the external person or organization knows more, has more resources, and can't even begin to picture us as equal. Others go to the opposite extreme. We feel the external people or organizations know nothing about the community, are unethical, and treat people as insignificant. We then rationalize pushing them around and making demands. Both reactions are unproductive. Both eliminate the opportunity to create value and worth. In the first case, when we are intimidated, we allow the powerful to treat us paternalistically. It's as if we feel we have unlimited needs and little ability whereas they have all the resources and answers. Almost nothing makes me sadder than watching the rich and powerful treat the poor and working class paternalistically. You can see it especially in immigrant communities, where people with a lack of fluency in English are treated like children (come over here now and have some of the food we brought). In the opposite case, we see the rich and powerful as adversaries and we treat them as enemies. (Will you agree to our demands? Yes or no?) The elites need to be beaten and forced to do what they don't want to do.

Social workers and people in other helping professions are often seen as dedicated people working long and hard to help the disenfranchised and those suffering from poverty and injustice. When society gives you credit, it is credit for your effort. It is not credit for results. Sometimes this recognition for effort does not do you or your client much good. It can leave you locked in a small room together and prevent you from going out into the community and beyond to build new external relationships. Push yourself beyond the walls of your office and the building housing your agency. Push yourself into making new contacts and establishing new partners. I want to share four "tips" to help you do this (see Figure 7.1).

> **Tip #1:** Show how you can help them.
>
> **Tip #2:** Make them comfortable.
>
> **Tip #3:** Have specific tasks for them to consider.
>
> **Tip #4:** Have fun!

Figure 7.1   Tips for Building External Relationships

Tip number one: More people will be open to you if you show how you could help them. Remember, it is the other person who gets to define what "help" is, not you. So, contact them and show them your potential value. Tip number two: External resources often feel out of their comfort zone in a low-income community. Help them to feel comfortable by inviting them to visit and meet some impressive people (the people you are trying to help) in the targeted community. Tip number three: Be very specific. People get a little overwhelmed when they are asked to do broad, sweeping things like "revitalize the community" or "eliminate joblessness." Make sure you offer them an opportunity to play a role they understand and have the confidence to perform. Tip number four: Have fun. Nothing can be funkier than pulling a real mixture of people together. Our huge gumbo of a society allows us the opportunity to mix and match very different people to achieve a common goal. Think of what a real meeting would look like and how satisfying it could be to have people benefiting from helping one other, no matter how diverse their looks and behavior.

Does this mean it is possible to have positive relationships with everyone? Just as everyone cannot, will not, and should not be a friend, not everyone outside targeted communities will help. Many people will not see value in working with you. When this happens, consensus organizers just move on. We are not zealots looking for conversions. We are looking for natural relationships built on mutual self-interest and deepened through value and worth.

How about trying it? Start by choosing people you do not know but feel would be helpful in accomplishing something important to you. Your first step is to find out what their agenda is and what they want to accomplish. You have to be the helper first. Then you become the "helpee." Step two is to look into ways you could help them achieve their goals. During step three, you actually deliver the help. In step four, you reveal your agenda in detail and present opportunities for them to help you. You then exchange roles. In step five, you now trust each other and work together on new projects that meet the requirements of mutual self-interest. It is a relatively simple process that consensus organizers use repeatedly in many contexts.

JUST SOUP

The first time I got a call from a powerful person from a private foundation, I was working in a basement in Perry Hilltop, a neighborhood on the north side of Pittsburgh, Pennsylvania. I panicked; why did he call me? What did he want? I was worried that I was about to be ripped off because powerful people might try to take advantage of someone like me. What if someone saw me talking to him? He called from a local family foundation, and he wanted to meet me. In my old organizing framework, I thought anything that would come out of this would be bad. What was he trying to do anyway—buy me off? I was to meet him at a restaurant I would ordinarily never eat in. It was much too expensive. Of course it had to have a theme; in this case, ducks. The restaurant had ducks everywhere, creating a sort of tweedy, hunting club atmosphere. I was, of course, early; you never know if the bus is running on schedule. He arrived, of course, right on time. He seemed rich, stiff, and overly polite. He dressed like the kind of guy who would collect wooden ducks. I knew enough to listen intently. I was worried about everything. The menu was large, like the kind in movies in which the actor quizzes the waiter incessantly, "Is the salmon fresh?" As I looked over the entire expanse of choices, I realized I only had enough money for a cup of soup. The amount of money in my pocket wouldn't even cover the cheapest sandwich. The waiter hovered. I ordered the cup of soup. My lunch companion had a large salad, a prime rib sandwich, and a cocktail. I figured I had better sip the soup slowly. I was so green and so out of place that it never occurred to me that he would expect to pick up the tab. I thought I had to pay because he didn't announce that he would pay. It never occurred to him to say he would pay because he figured it was obvious. In the "WASP world," this is just understood. In my world, if someone planned to treat they would bellow it so loudly the dishwasher would hear "It's on me." We would want everyone to know when we were being generous on a particular day. I was learning the confusion that understatement can sometimes cause. He asked about my work. He understood some of what I explained and he seemed sincere. I began to see the distinct possibility that we could benefit each other. I had to learn pacing; I had to learn how to convey knowledge and confidence. This was challenging, but the biggest challenge, by far, was sending a strong message that I needed him. If I couldn't show that I needed him, it just would never work. I could feel the importance of it. All you had to do was look into his eyes. He needed to be necessary to our effort. It was natural to make a resident, an uneducated or poor person, feel indispensable. But I had to push myself to give this man the same feeling. Without careful intervention on my part, he would never have revealed his agenda to me. It was as if he would feel it inappropriate to do so. I had to be careful not to misread this and assume he had no agenda. He had his suit, education, position, and wooden ducks. He still needed something from me and the effort I represented. I had to learn how to get him to gradually reveal his agenda by being indirect and circular. After catching on to this requirement, he became the major funder of a multiyear community improvement effort.

Building relationships with outside resources is a simple task if you are willing to cross the line that makes you treat powerful people as equals. If you make them feel irrelevant, they will find someone else to make them feel relevant.

> Building relationships with outside resources requires you to treat powerful people as equals. Reciprocity is key.

The experience of many of these external people tends to be more in fields like the arts and fund-raising rather than poverty fighting and community development. External people with potential resources will search until they become comfortable. If you make them feel either superior or inferior, they will become uncomfortable and will not be able to articulate why. There are things they can do that you can't and things you can do that they can't. As I talked to my luncheon companion over my cold soup, I found the groove that is needed to build a reciprocal relationship. We found a special way to help one another's self-interest. We talked about how we could help each other. I started to like him a lot.

Years later, as I started to deal with national foundations and government and civil rights organizations, I learned that reciprocity was the key. If I was at a meeting with an external resource and I had nothing to offer him or her, it just would not click. It would be friendly, and might lead to a request to meet again. It might lead to an "expanded conversation." But it would be useless. If there was nothing I could do to help them—even if they couldn't see it—we would not be able to build a true partnership.

So let's do a little traveling and expand on these points. Let's start out in "my kind of town," the windy city of Chicago, Illinois. I want you to meet someone you may have heard on the radio. Later we'll head over to Midway

Airport (never go to O'Hare unless you have to). From there, it's a package vacation to Las Vegas, Nevada. Remember what happens in Vegas stays in Vegas, even if it doesn't happen on the strip or even downtown. Why go to the places everyone else goes? I know, let's go to a strip mall!

THE REST OF THE STORY

Human beings are wired in such a way that we understand if we get something, we need to give something back. It is the glue that holds society together. Marketers definitely understand this. Just check your desk at home for all those free calendars and mailing labels that you received, that you didn't really want, and never asked for. They were sent to you because, whether you realize it or not, you are more likely to give to the causes that send you unwanted crap. When you get something, you are more likely to give something in return even if you don't want it. Imagine how strong this bond is when it's something you actually do want.

I had to make a presentation to a national foundation in Chicago, and the room was filled with board members and staff. The staff wanted a detailed, technical explanation of the work I was proposing. As I tried my best, I noticed I was losing the attention of a tall, distinguished man. He started to drift visibly and obviously had no interest in what I was saying. The attention of the rest of the audience started to drift as well. That one guy, however, looked strangely familiar. It finally hit me. He was board member Paul Harvey, the radio commentator, heard by hundreds of thousands of people every day. He had made a very successful career using his amazingly theatric voice to read dramatic human-interest stories to people like me. I couldn't go the rest of my life unable to hold Paul Harvey's attention. So, I shifted gears. "Ladies and gentleman, your questions could best be answered by a story about a small-town hardware store owner in western Pennsylvania." I told them about Larry Levine. Harvey suddenly fixed on me with rapt attention. The only thing that could have made it better was if I had a voice similar to his. When I finished and thanked the staff and board members for their time, I saw Harvey get out of his chair. He was following me out into the hallway. He towered over me, looking like a giant American eagle. He put his hand on my shoulder, squeezed it hard, and with that deep radio tone and unusual cadence said, with genuine admiration, "Mike, that was a good story." I had created reciprocity with Paul Harvey. I had given him what he wanted. I received a large grant, and that was the rest of the story.

SUPPORT WITHOUT UNDERSTANDING

The most important premise of consensus organizing is that you can successfully appeal to people who have money and power but little or no understanding of what is happening in low-income neighborhoods. If they have little understanding and lack the interest or capability to gain more understanding, you can still get their support by determining their self-interest. A big mistake that advocates and activists make is assuming that there can be no help unless the helpers really understand the problem. Some activists take this so far that they will only accept help if there is an agreement about the cause of the problem. Some of the strongest, deepest commitments to communities can be made by appeals to the self-interest of helpers that have little to do with the actual issues in the community. People with money and resources have needs that go far beyond your problems. The trick is how to understand their goals and frame your ideas to make a successful match. This is a much different tactic than attempting to get someone converted to your cause. This is not about constructing litmus tests to determine worthiness. I always feel that when you have the opportunity to deal with potential external resources, you have to do your homework. You have to figure out what they need and want. Surprisingly, they are trained to act as if they have no self-interest. They are told their job is only to listen to you. Don't let them get away with their own illusions. They *do* have agendas. It is about time they just spit them out.

For instance, funding sources may be very concerned with tangible results. It becomes their mantra. They may phrase it differently, but it's still there. One time they might say, "These neighborhoods look the same even after all this money has been spent." Later, it might be, "People come to us year after year needing more and more help." Then, they might conclude with, "We never see efforts that eventually stand on their own." What are they really saying by making these statements? I think they are saying that they want to see something that works and will continue to work in the future after they no longer fund the effort. The fact that at some point their continued support will not be required may be more important than the help your program provides. You take those funding sources' self-interest and say similar things to them without compromising your goal. You say, "What we want to do is set up something that can continue without you. We have seen our neighborhood held back by our inability to build our capacity to become independent" or "We cannot rely on others. We have to rely upon ourselves," or "We have to prove our desire to continue before we deserve your support." Time and again I have seen activists respond instead,

"There is no problem more important than the problem we are about to address." They follow it with 30 minutes of statistics and personal testimony showing how serious the problem is. Then they conclude by repeating over and over that no one is addressing this particular problem. Remember, no one wants a lecture. I know you don't. Nobody wants to be told how uncaring he or she has previously been. I know you don't. Most important, no one wants to be made to feel guilty. Do you? Trust me, very little real help and respect is developed through the use of guilt. Most lasting support is generated out of self-interest.

Most lasting support is generated out of self-interest.

It Must Be Good Because Everyone Says So

Another truth I see time and time again is that supporters are more inclined to provide support when they see a lot of other supporters. This means you should talk about who is helping you, instead of talking about who isn't. There really is such a thing as a bandwagon. You want others on your wagon, not jumping off of it. Tell potential supporters how much they will miss out on if they are not a part of the crowd. All marketers understand the concept of social validation. Human beings have a greater desire to participate in something when other people are participating in it. Remember the classic example of one person looking up toward the sky? A certain number of people will look up as they pass the first person. As a larger and larger number of people look up, almost everyone passing by looks up. When others do something, we feel we are missing out if we don't. If no one is doing it, we believe it is probably wise that we also refrain. The windmill-chasing advocates blame everyone for a lack of support. Don't make the mistake, however, of telling potential resources that you have no resources. When they hear that, they tend to back off. It is human nature, not the decision of someone who is uncaring. Don't fight it; use it. Please do not interpret this advice as meaning that you falsely butter up potential supporters, telling them whatever they want to hear and trying to ingratiate yourself through lies and exaggerations. All consensus organizing relationships are built on honesty.

All consensus organizing relationships are built on honesty.

SEND IN THE DOGS

One time, Richard Barrera and I were attempting to raise funds in Las Vegas. A colleague of ours set up a meeting with a potential supporter. He gave us the address and told us there was a chance he would be late and, if so, we should begin without him. We got to the address he gave us and thought there was something seriously wrong. We were standing in the middle of a nondescript strip mall. You could guess what the stores were. They were the same stores you see in any strip mall. We got to the specific address and there were curtains across the entire window with absolutely no signage. There was just a small, unmarked door. We looked at each other and were convinced we were lost and must have gotten the address wrong. Our contact told us that this local foundation had the resources to be a major donor (more than $100,000) if we played our cards right. Such a funder couldn't possibly be located behind an unmarked door in a strip mall.

I opened the door; inside was an unattended secretary's desk and two folding chairs. Behind the phantom secretary, there was another door slightly ajar. Then, out of nowhere, we heard this tiny, crackly, old person's voice say, "Back here, boys." Remember, this was Las Vegas. I had this vision that we were about to be rolled and lose our money instead of raising any. Should we go in? We walked in like two patients seeing their new dentist. We didn't want to enter, but, after all, there was a reason we were there. We entered to find a very, very, old pasty-skinned woman staring at us. I couldn't take my eyes off her mouth because her lipstick had been applied at about a 45-degree angle; it covered only the middle of her lips and was smeared above and below her mouth like a red teeter-totter on a playground. She said it was about time we had gotten there and screeched, "What do you want anyways?" It was just the three of us and her tone indicated we'd better cut to the chase. I wondered if she sat there every day like this or only came to this playground on occasion.

I tried to hit all of our key fund-raising points, but she kept interrupting me, contradicting me, and, in general, was about as rude as she could be. I tried to stay the course, but she just wouldn't let me. She asked what cities we were working in and where we had been successful. Social validation was ready to kick in. If I could show her others had supported us, we would increase the chance that she would support us as well. I mentioned New Orleans. She countered, "That hellhole?" She asked me for a detailed program design and, when I gave her a description, she blurted, "Ha ha, you think that will work in Las Vegas?" Richard later said, "I knew we were in trouble because the vein in your neck started to pop out." He said he knew from experience that I was about to blow a gasket. I finally had had it.

I interrupted her. At that point, anyone catering to her and telling her she was right to doubt us would invalidate social validation. It was Vegas. I gambled.

I said firmly, "Look, we are trying to give you an opportunity to help people with a proven approach. Other funders have been very happy with our work. If you keep on interrupting and acting like you know everything, we will leave and withdraw our offer to let you participate. If you are rude one more time, we are out of here and we are never coming back. We do not need your attitude." I remember thinking that I was feeling the same way I do in blackjack when I split twos. It may work perfectly; it may backfire, but all the others at the table will second-guess you. You make the decision; you live with the consequences. She looked at me stunned. I stared back at her with every ounce of determination I could muster. She finally spoke. "How much do you boys need?" I told her. It was considerably more money than our contacts had suggested we request. We needed a total of a little more than $250,000 and told her the entire amount. She said, "Go out and try to raise the rest of it from other places. Work as hard as you can for a month. If you come up short, I'll put up the rest." We had just secured a commitment for more than a quarter of a million dollars. She then got this strange, demented look in her eyes. Out of nowhere, she deepened her voice and screamed, "Send in the dogs." At that moment, I grasped what it was like to be in a David Lynch movie. A door miraculously opened from what I had thought was a closet and two giant Great Danes came racing out toward us at breakneck speed. Admit it; we all think from time to time how we will die—car accident, heart attack, or a nasty fall. Well, at that precise moment for me, it was a dog mauling in a Las Vegas strip mall. The dogs flew straight past me toward Richard, and they started licking him. They licked for what seemed like an eternity. Our donor was obviously pleased, and so were we. I told Richard later, when we couldn't stop laughing, that it came out to about $10,000 a lick. We were successful by believing in what we were doing and pointing out that many others believed in us as well. She decided to climb aboard our wagon. So remember, if you follow this advice, some day a woman wearing crooked lipstick will command a giant dog to come out of the closet and lick you all the way to success.

The easiest job we can create for ourselves is one in which we would spend all day only with people who thought just like us. Wouldn't it be easy to be surrounded by supporters and like-minded individuals and never venture out into the shark-infested waters beyond our little private beach? There are more than sharks in those waters. There may also be a raft and the supplies that save us from slow death. Push yourself off your island out into those waters. It may involve some risk, but it will also make you more engaged, energized, and successful.

Reflection Questions

1. Why do we have to prove our value to other people before they help us?

2. What is wrong, if anything, with asking the rich and powerful for help and having them receive nothing in return?

3. Explain the importance of value and worth in relationship building.

4. What makes your best friend your best friend?

5. Could somebody please tell me why the television show *Friends* was so popular?

6. Which city is windier, Chicago or Buffalo?

8

FORMING PARTNERSHIPS

In this chapter, you will learn:

◆ The consensus organizer's definition of partnership.

◆ Six specific steps for forming partnerships.

◆ The proper roles of partners.

◆ How to "flip" an issue.

Talk about a buzzword! Partnerships. This word is so overused and overworked that it's almost to the point where it has lost all meaning. Want to buy a new car? Form a partnership with Chevy. Want to make more money? Form a partnership with an on-line program to start a business. Fall in love? Move in with your partner. It's almost as if any human interaction you have in your life is now referred to as a partnership. Any word that broadens to that degree can lose most of its meaning. For our purposes, we need to tighten up the definition a little. My guess is it won't include most Chevy dealers.

Consensus organizers must bring together people who are very different from one another to work toward a common goal. Oops, I guess you could call that a definition. We need to think of partnerships as people coming together to achieve mutual benefit.

In consensus organizing, partnerships bring people together to achieve mutual benefit.

HOWDY PARTNER

Beware of broad, squishy definitions that might include things like better communication, sharing of ideas, discussions, and so on. According to consensus organizers, partnerships exist when the partners receive tangible benefits. Anything short of that may still have value, but it is not our definition of partnership. Do partners have to be equal in power, numbers, or stature? No, they don't have to be equal. They all just have to receive benefit. For instance, suppose a block club forms a partnership with the local phone company. The block club may want a new vegetable garden and the phone company may want more customers. You can have a great partnership even though everything about the partners is different.

Finding potential partners should be exciting and fun. Read through these steps and see what you think:

Step 1. The first step is to plot out your agenda. You must be able to put on paper or on the computer screen your goal and the steps needed to get there. Don't even talk to a potential partner until you have done so. Without your agenda written out, it will be impossible to analyze potential partners. You wouldn't even be able to discuss their roles. First, know what you want to do. If it turns out you don't even need a partner, congratulations. Sometimes it is possible to reach a goal by going at it all by yourself. If you can do it by yourself—great. There is no reason to have a partner. Most of the time, however, it is hard to reach your destination alone.

Step 2. List all of the tasks and functions that have to be performed to achieve your goal. Be very complete. Don't leave anything out. For instance, if your goal is to create a summer soccer league for kids, list everything you would need to do to get it off the ground—secure the field, uniforms, equipment, and referees; recruit kids; buy insurance; set up a refreshment stand;

and so on. Some people tend to leave out the task that might divide the partners, for example, how the league president will be selected. Maybe it's the task that two partners feel most qualified to carry out. Maybe it's the task no one wants to do. Don't leave out the crucial, controversial action that must be taken. Don't just say a prayer of hope and close your eyes. Don't avoid anything that must be done to achieve your goal.

Step 3. List everything that you and your existing supporters will achieve if you accomplish the above tasks successfully. Make sure that someone on the team has the ability to perform each function. Do not stretch the truth or overburden your group. Either you have the capacity or you don't.

Step 4. Analyze the gap between what you can do and what you can't do. Maybe you need some additional help to reach your goal. Your existing partners may have the desire but not the capacity to achieve success. Is there any pattern in all the additional things that need to be done to accomplish the goal? How long is the list of remaining tasks?

Step 5. Who has the capacity to fill the gaps that you have found? What is their self-interest, if any, in contributing to the project? It may have been simple to determine who might have the capacity you need, but that person might have no self-interest in becoming involved. Keep looking until you find the individuals or organizations with capacities and interests that are complementary to your goals.

Step 6. Recruit the partners. Make sure the project is of interest to them and butter them up. Tell them you can't do it without them. As always, be very specific. Prove your value to them by showing what your crucial contribution will be. Make sure that reciprocity has been established.

As you go through these steps, try not to limit your conceptions of potential partners. Don't just look at the obvious choices. Be wary of only going to the "usual suspects." They may be tired and already overextended. Limiting your thinking about potential partners might cause you to miss a person or persons who might have been willing to help. Your partner may be someone you could not even imagine working with. Perhaps it is someone you don't even like. The point is to find someone, anyone, to help you complete the particular tasks necessary to achieve success. The more unusual a partnership appears on the surface, the better. Consensus organizers call this the "unusual partner." This is the partner that raises eyebrows, the partner that makes others sit up and take notice. Think about a project like MTV's *Rock the Vote*. In this effort, popular rock and rap musicians tried to inspire young people to get involved in the political process. Their participation was surprising, thereby making it more effective. The surprising nature of the partnership enhances the level of commitment of the participants. It makes the effort special and interesting. When seeking partners, never box yourself into considering only the usual cast of characters. Instead look for the surprise—just like the prize in the Cracker Jack box. You never want people stepping on one another's toes. You need to have each partner in a different lane in the same swimming pool. Never place someone into a role just because you don't want to do it yourself. There is no sense in that. Everyone wants to feel competent. If you place people in roles they are not able to do, they will do a poor job and your effort will fail. You can't plug holes with just anyone. So take great care to make sure that each person has the ability to do his or her specific task. This will lead to a successful group effort. Successful partnerships place people in roles in which they are comfortable and effective.

Successful partnerships place people in roles in which they are comfortable and effective.

Another buzzword is "collaboration." Watch out for this one. Often in the helping professions, funding sources look at all the grants they are making in a low-income community and all the nonprofits they are supporting. Supporters may see what they label "duplication of services" and feel that it is important to send the message that the group they fund needs to collaborate. Supporters may be accurate or inaccurate in their analysis, but either way they have created an atmosphere like parents do when they impose a forced marriage upon their children. It is as if the parent says, "Trust me, it is for your own good and you will learn to love each other as time goes on." It could happen. In most cases, it won't. Beware of this dynamic because it does not create a true partnership. Frequently, nonprofits collaborate only because a supporter demands it. They see no other value in it and come in mumbling and grumbling, expecting the worst and often finding it.

For most collaboration to be successful, the participants need all the motivations discussed so far in this chapter. Only with real self-interest and complementary roles determined can collaborations succeed.

So you may now be asking, "OK, I see the immense responsibility required here, but where is the fun you promised?" The fun is in beginning to see the possibilities of working with people who are enormously different from you. Consensus organizers make a big mistake when we seek partners who are mostly like us. Remember earlier, when we were talking about knowing yourself first and then proceeding to understand others? Well, here's your chance. You want to look for that one similarity that will motivate your potential partner to join in the effort even though it may be one reason and one reason only.

COME ON DOWN, Y'ALL

After I had worked in the Mon Valley in Pennsylvania and moved on to Houston, Texas, I needed to boost the confidence of the Houston participants. I considered using a variety of local people in the role of "confidence builders" until it finally hit me. The volunteers in the Mon Valley had already achieved a great deal of success. Their success was unknown in the rest of the country. Their confidence had grown with the completion of each project. They had continued to reach out and develop more and more partners. What about putting the Mon Valley people into a new role, switching them from "determined to prove themselves" to "experienced and successful"?

I could see that it was in the self-interest (and would boost the egos) of the people of the Mon Valley to play this new role. It would help people in Houston and in the Mon Valley at the same time. Members of the Houston contingent might initially think they had little in common with the small-town, Eastern European, and African American volunteers from the rust belt, but exposing members of the two contingents to one another could change that attitude. They would build relationships with one another. It was very simple but profound. No one had thought either group could be successful! In Houston, many had labeled members of the targeted neighborhood as stupid immigrants from backward, Third World countries, whereas the residents of the Mon Valley had been stereotyped as stupid mill hunks with strong backs and weak minds. There was a potential unbreakable common bond. So, I flew a group from the Mon Valley to deep in the heart of Texas. It was more fun than you could ever imagine.

First of all, one of the most dedicated volunteers in the Mon Valley, Karen Lovich, from the tiny town of Monessen, Pennsylvania, stopped at the airport gift shop immediately after she deplaned. She bought a Texas hat, bumper sticker, scarf, shot glass, book cover, and T-shirt, all of which she proudly displayed throughout her visit. One of the Houston volunteers made tamales. It was a blast. Everyone was put into effective roles and everyone benefited. After the 2-day visit, the Mon Valley group went home. I returned to my apartment, exhausted from the effort, but very satisfied. The Mon

Valley people had distinguished themselves in their roles as teachers and motivators. The confidence level of the Houston people visibly improved. I put on my TV, looking for something challenging like a rerun of *Leave It to Beaver*. ("Why did you do it Beav? I, I, I don't know, Wally.") There, on my screen, on the public access channel, up popped Karen Lovich! She was pounding on a podium, shaking her fist, and telling everybody that they could do it. She was urging people to save their own neighborhoods. She was positive they would succeed. It felt oddly comfortable to be sitting in an apartment more than 1,500 miles away from the Mon Valley and see what a good partnership could do.

Always be clear about what you want and need in a partner. Make sure people understand the role you are asking them to play. Good partnerships are never casual. Instead, they are detailed and structured so that everyone sees how the pieces can fit together and everyone can agree with the fit.

Good partnerships are detailed and structured so people know their roles and how the pieces fit together.

Never bring people together and assume that things will just fall into place. Be up front and specific. You will all benefit as a result. Confusion leads to inertia and inaction. Certainty can lead to positive change.

You want to look for partners who match up at the right place and the right time. Partnerships are based on timing and do not have to become permanent. Think of a partnership as a great match for a particular set of circumstances at a particular point in time rather than something that must last forever. Consensus organizers believe that relationships deepen through mutual benefit, not through obligation or burden.

Relationships deepen through mutual benefit, not through obligation or burden.

Usually when people benefit from their work together, they will appreciate one another's value. This will increase their chances of working together in the future but does not guarantee it. You do not want to put any pressure on forcing the relationship to continue. Relationships will continue successfully if and only if mutual benefit continues.

Think of a partnership as a date or a series of dates in which both parties are happy and satisfied. I guess a partnership could be considered "going steady" for a period of time. It is not an engagement or marriage. If you propose, the other party may not be ready for a commitment. You are not attempting to create a perfect match on exhausting sets of criteria. You are only making a complementary match based on a very specific goal.

This approach will help you become constantly vigilant and aware of unique, surprising partnerships. It will teach you to analyze everyone's perspectives on issues where agreement does not exist. For instance, wouldn't it be interesting if women's rights organizations and right-to-life organizations found something to do together? Of course they can't come together on the issue of abortion, but how about something else, anything else? Having trouble thinking of something? How about campaign finance reform? I think it would also be great for environmental groups to work with chemical companies. *We have to at least start understanding the perspectives of others and realize that despite differences on some issues, there may be fascinating similarities as well.*

If we expect perfect matches leading to perfect partnerships, we will keep reinforcing the divisiveness that permeates our society. We will continue to seek out only those in agreement with us. Remember the trip the people from the Mon Valley took to Texas. There was a bond created that no one ever could have previously imagined.

So, let's take a closer look at all of this and go on a little trip to partnershipville. First, you'll hear a little story about a city that shall remain nameless. The reasons for the secrecy will become evident. Then, it's off to the Big Apple. If you can make it there, you can make it anywhere. So put on your Billy Joel CD and let's take a ride together.

There Is No Film in the Camera

One of the most challenging requirements of the consensus organizing model is the absolute necessity of dealing with people you don't like. You have to deal with many people effectively, including some you do not respect, admire, or care for. Traditional community organizing lets you off the hook on this point. Traditional organizers get to constantly blow off steam by attacking targets composed almost exclusively of people they do not like. On the other hand, consensus organizers have to form partnerships with a variety of people. Our criteria do not afford us the luxury of excluding people we do not like. Simply put, we are stuck dealing with some people we do not enjoy. It is crucial to match the self-interest of others regardless of our personal reactions toward some partners. Other professionals understand this and accept this. Lawyers take on clients, doctors have patients, and business-people have customers they don't like. Traditional organizers, on the other hand, get to remain "holier than thou." They decide who merits help and who deserves hatred.

By now, you know I'm about to suggest how to handle the need to deal with those you don't necessarily like by telling a story; but this one is a little bit tricky. I want to tell you about someone I had to deal with that I really, really, did not like. This is a true story and the person is still on the planet, so I can't be too obvious. I do, however, want to assure you that—despite being careful—the story is factual.

I once worked with someone who had talent, charisma, and charm galore. I recently heard a quote, "There is no smaller package than a man wrapped up in himself." For some reason, this quote seems most appropriate and, from this point on, I will refer to the person as "Small Package." I just did not respect this person. Call it working-class bias, but Small Package, I suspected, did not really care about poor people. I felt that Small Package stumbled into his career by chance. Working with poor people was just a stepping-stone for Small Package's eventual political ambition. Of course, I may have been wrong, but I doubt it. I could never shake my feelings. It even bothered me that other people, who I did respect, liked and admired Small Package. My gut reaction was to spend hours proving that I was right and they were wrong. I fought against it and tried instead to concentrate on the fact that Small Package was actually helping the poor. It was impossible to deny that this person's immense skill was truly benefiting people. So there you have a classic dilemma for a consensus organizer. I believe this is the very issue that holds back all types of activists. The environmental activist refuses to work with a company that has previously polluted. The union official can't respect the company official and vice versa. The homeowner's association can't work with the nonprofit homeless organization. This inability is cloaked with statistics, histories, and past encounters that we use to justify our perceived superiority. Well, put me in the same emotional boat. I want to teach you a trick so we can all paddle together and no one has to drown.

How could I live with myself? Small Package was egotistical, self-promotional, and cocky. All these tendencies were things that I did not want to see in a work partner; but there was no way for me to avoid Small Package. Talk about ubiquitous! Small Package was everywhere there might be potential attention and possible publicity. His advance staff, which handled public relations, had a full-time job promoting, promoting, and promoting. Members of the advance staff came to see me about a pending promotional trip. Their requests were the standard requests. Small Package was traveling to another town and I had to arrange meetings with the mayor, top corporate leaders, nonprofits, and civil rights groups. The press needed to be everywhere Small Package would be. I had to cooperate, but I don't remember anyone saying I couldn't have a little fun. Fun is the key to justifying the tension of dealing with this type of consensus organizing situation.

My fun revolved around my promotional duties. I had to set up the meetings with important people. I had no choice. I had to have the press show up. I had no choice on that either. Then it hit me—Small Package loved to have his picture taken. I figured—how about even more attention? In addition to inviting the press, how about hiring an additional photographer to follow Small Package around the entire trip? Nothing would be more impressive than a camera constantly documenting his every move. Get off the airplane, "click," eat breakfast, "click," turn and wave, "click, click." Well, that would be a definite plus for Small Package but wouldn't it gall me even more? Well yes, but not if I told the photographer to take the film out of the camera. That's right; all day I followed the entourage around saying, "Please turn this way. This will be a great shot," and, "We've got to get this one with you and the governor." Man, that was fun. We were both feeling like pigs in . . . you know, where pigs like to be. We both had grins on for 10 hours. The happier Small Package got, the happier I got. We must have looked like old pals joined at the hip. It was a win-win situation. It was such a shame about the "technical problem" that prevented the film from ever being developed.

Seriously, you will have to figure out your own ways to handle people you don't like. It is not acceptable to avoid or exclude them. That would hurt the very people you are trying to help. Some of you may find this aspect of consensus organizing even more difficult than I do, but I urge you to understand the importance of casting a wide net. The problems in our society are too great to exclude anyone who might help, regardless of our own personal feelings toward them. We have to overcome the arrogance and the rush to judgment that many activists display. We have to drive away a tendency to avoid the "impure." If you can build this discipline, you will get great satisfaction in seeing people helped by those you do not necessarily like or respect. You will feel an even deeper sense of satisfaction and accomplishment. Just remember when it really gets tough, be creative, and have some fun. Oh yeah, just one more thing. How come the publisher of the book didn't put more pictures of me in it? They took a lot of pictures, but for some reason they didn't use any. What's up with that?

Then They Need Us

Williamsburg, a neighborhood in Brooklyn, New York, is one of the most interesting and captivating neighborhoods I have ever worked in. It is also home to some of the most astounding people I have ever met. Right across the East River from Manhattan, the Williamsburg Bridge takes you to the heart of the community. Subways take you across. Many people walk. It is the home of a thriving Jewish community, mostly Hassidic, a thriving Latino community, and a still-strong Italian community. There is a high school right over the bridge aptly called El Puente Academy. The school was proposed and developed by dedicated community members who believed that all students should be involved in their neighborhoods as a vital part of their education.

I had met a talented young organizer, Paula Rojas, who was not originally from Williamsburg but loved the neighborhood the minute she saw it. She was intrigued and interested in learning more about consensus organizing. She had built positive relationships at El Puente. I hired her and placed her in the school. The students took to her and formed a group to decide on what community issue we would address collectively. They named their group "YO!" (Youth Organizers!). Each student expressed anger toward many of the small food store owners who did not live in the neighborhood, had inferior merchandise, charged exorbitant prices, and treated the customers as if they were less than human. As you can imagine, the students wanted to "go after" the store owners. Just like the adults who held the same opinion, they had no real long-term strategy. They saw an injustice and wanted to correct it. They felt their job was to point out the injustice, target the store owners, and put pressure on them to stop. After all, they had watched television their whole lives, viewing numerous protests. Wasn't this their only choice? Paula, as an expert does, took them through options, getting them to gain a deeper understanding of the complexity of the issue. Somewhere in Pittsburgh, Mo Coleman was smiling.

One student offhandedly commented about how different the various street vendors were from the predatory store owners. In front of many of the apartment buildings in Williamsburg, tenants would set up makeshift tables on the sidewalk and sell food, crafts, and clothing. These vendors, the students remarked, treated people with respect and charged fair prices. If someone turned out to be unhappy with a transaction, these sidewalk vendors would do whatever they could to mollify the customer. After all, the students reasoned, the customer knew where the vendor lived. Paula wondered out loud whether there was any help the students could provide the vendors. In consensus organizing, there is a key point in the process in which the issue must be "flipped."

In consensus organizing, there is a key point in which the issue must be "flipped."

The organizer takes the interests of the residents, in this case the students, and flips it into a stereotype-busting, creative direction. Paula took their animosity and flipped it into a creative, positive direction.

From that spark, the high school students of YO! took action. They realized that they had to get to know the vendors. They had to establish trust. They introduced the vendors to one another, proving that the vendors could support one another rather than compete. The students urged the vendors to work together and organize. The vendors formed a coalition. The students, mainly bilingual and bicultural, moved with precision and expert strategy. They seemed almost natural consensus organizers. They built up the vendors' confidence. It was evident to the students that the vendors needed technical help in planning inventory, pooling resources, and joint marketing. They understood the consensus organizing dual functions of linking external resources to an internally organized group. Paula taught them how to find all the various organizations that claimed they could provide help. She prepared the students to analyze and judge which of these groups might be the best to help the vendors.

My role was to fly into New York City and review the students' strategy. I was cautiously optimistic but worried that we might be expecting too much from young kids. As I walked toward the school, my mind raced. Paula felt these teenagers were taking to the model better than most adults. She thought our expectations must remain high. She said that they could get out of their insulated world and be able to make external matches. After all, this step had proven to be an Achilles' heel to many others. Could they do it?

The students were bouncing off the walls waiting for me. They had chosen their potential partner, the extension service at Cornell University. A staff member would come to make a presentation to the vendors. I asked them, "Why Cornell?" One kid shook his head and seemed disgusted. He gave me the same look he had probably given his teachers. "Mike, you just don't get it, do you?" He continued emphatically, "We didn't choose it because it was Cornell, we chose it because of who Cornell agreed to send." Now, I was getting excited. It appeared that they not only understood how to do this, they understood the nuances as well. They told me the person's name. It sounded French. I pointed out that there were no French vendors. Another kid said, disgusted with my naïveté, "Man, you really do not get it! The lady they are sending is Haitian and she came to the United States as an immigrant." Now my internal grin stretched over the entire borough of Brooklyn. I played devil's advocate one final time. I pointed out that she wouldn't be able to speak Spanish. A third YO! screamed, "Don't you see, that means she needs us." We had a room full of 16-year-old kids that understood consensus organizing to the core. They grasped the cornerstone concept of mutual self-interest. Paula had done a superb job, believing in them and shaping their thoughts. But it was the students' natural ability to grasp what others struggled with that caused me intrigue. They had clarity and strategic ability.

After the meeting, everyone worked very hard. They were determined to be of value to their neighborhood and to the vendors. The wonderful details of their work could be a book in itself. To summarize, the vendors did hit it off with the staff member from Cornell. They were such a good match that they created a peer lending effort and had joint sales displaying their goods collectively in a city park. The vendors' profits increased.

During the effort, a particularly devastating hurricane ravaged Central and South America, affecting many of the vendors' native countries. They decided to send a contribution to help the victims. They also sent a letter to the White House, explaining that they were able to do this because of the organizing help of high school students from El Puente Academy. Someone from the office of the vice president of the United States got a copy of the letter. He showed it to Vice President Al Gore. Shortly thereafter, a large motorcade traveled through Williamsburg. It stopped at El Puente Academy. A picture hangs at the school (this time there was film inside the camera) that shows the YO! student organizers, with pride on their faces, standing with a man who was a heartbeat away from being president.

I was so intrigued by all of this that I suggested to Paula that we fly a couple of the students to our next board meeting, which was to be held in Atlanta. She called and said that the students had a proposal for me. I wasn't positive, but I could have sworn that she giggled. On my next trip to New York City, I took the subway over to hear their idea. They designated a spokesperson. She said, "Mike, you could send two of us by airplane to meet with your board in Atlanta, or you could send all of us by train and save $30. So which option do you prefer?" Now, they were out-consensus organizing me. It was getting spooky.

Paula and all of the YO! staff took the train. They didn't get a lot of sleep. Then again, other than Paula, they didn't need any. One kid said, "Man, Atlanta has a lot of trees." Their presentation to the consensus organizing institute was fascinating and surprising. One of our board members with a long corporate and business background, after listening intently, asked a student, "It sounds like your life changed for the better once you started thinking like a consensus organizer. Am I right?" The young boy, named Raphael, stuck his hands onto both sides of his head and replied laughing, "Are you kidding? It's a curse! I can't turn it off. I used to get home from school and my mother would start yelling at me. I would get miserable, try to block her out, and blame her for all my problems. Now I find myself thinking, 'What can I do to prevent this? What does she need? How can I get what I want by giving her something she wants?' Then, the next morning I would go to school. There is a kid I used to beat up, but I don't do that anymore. I figured out how we can help each other. It never stops." The board looked like an audience watching an excellent magician. Their faces said it all. They couldn't believe what they just had seen and heard. It was right then and there that I promised myself that someday, somehow, I would get an opportunity to work with young people again. They had no political correctness or ideological barriers; they were natural consensus organizers.

HUCKING A *CHAINIK*

In the same Williamsburg neighborhood, a collaboration of nonprofit organizations was attempting to match unemployed residents with local jobs. I was asked by a foundation in New York City to convene the groups, and help train them in consensus organizing techniques. I thought this was a very good opportunity. I always liked working in New York. I found people there to be very demanding yet very fair. They were open to new ideas they thought had some chance of working. It is not a parochial place. You hear less "That's the way we are going to do it because that's the way we have always done it." Also, one of the organizations was a coalition of Hassidic organizations. I had no experience at all working with Orthodox Jews. I thought it would be a challenge.

Rabbi David Neiderman led the United Jewish Organizations (UJO). I had heard a lot about him. At the first collaborative meeting, he wasn't hard to spot. He had an unbelievably tangled beard, cold black eyes, pale white skin, a too-small black felt hat (kind of like a 1970s African American baseball player with a cap), and a black coat that hung on him like moss on a tree on a humid day. The coat looked like it weighed more than he did, and he weighed a lot. The rest of the group looked like a New York City street corner—a little bit of everything.

There was quite a bit of chatter and milling around before the start of the meeting and I remember thinking, so far this is like any other group I've worked with. The people seemed like they were beginning to get along. Maybe this would be easy. I nonchalantly asked everyone to be seated. As they began to pick seats, my eyes drifted to the rabbi. He wasn't sitting. To his right was a woman, who I would later learn was fairly adamant about issues concerning women's rights. The last empty chair was next to her. Well, as I would learn later, the rabbi, according to his religious beliefs, was not allowed to sit next to a woman. It is fair to say that this particular woman had a hard time relating to this particular religious belief. The conversation between the two of them was approaching a spot at which it could take an unpleasant turn. Here I was, the master of the technique of consensus organizing and I couldn't get two of the collaborative members to even sit down next to each other. You could say I had a bit of work ahead of me. I had to do something fast. It was at this precise moment that I thought about my wife. I thought about her in this instance, not so much to draw on our deep love but more to draw on her deep knowledge of Yiddish. See, this Catholic boy was fortunate enough to have a Jewish wife. Now, her family is not Hassidic; they came from a more liberal wing of the religion, but they do know Yiddish. On many Fridays I had gone to Shabbat at Aunt Betty's, where I was referred to, very good naturedly, as "The Pope." They flung around Yiddish at such a machine-gun pace that all the way home I would ask my wife, "What did Uncle Ernie mean when he said it's a 'big schmeggi'?" As the rabbi stood defiantly over the empty chair, I blurted "All right all right, quit hucking a *chainik*. You can have my seat." There was about a 5-second silence, like when a group pays tribute to someone who has just died. Then this big, loud, belly laugh came out of the rabbi. It was infectious. Everyone at the table started laughing, including the women's rights activist. What I had told him in Yiddish was to stop "banging a kettle." God bless the saving power of Yiddish.

I got to know the rabbi and I learned to admire him greatly. He is a genuine leader. Years before, he had joined a coalition with Latinos and prevented a garbage-burning incinerator (a serious pollution hazard) from being situated in the neighborhood. He had to cross a line and reach out to the entire community. He had walked out of the Hassidic segregated section of

Williamsburg, and went straight to the Latino part, breaking the long tradition and teachings of his faith, stating, "We all breathe the same air." A reporter wrote that when Rabbi Neiderman did this, it was the local equivalent to President Nixon visiting China for the first time. He fascinated me, and consensus organizing fascinated him. He had come from a background and culture in which the ideas of consensus organizing were not practiced or even considered. Yet, here he was, using consensus organizing techniques and finding that they worked.

I was often proud of his friendship but never more so than when the employment collaborative had to hire an organizer to work for all the participating organizations. It was a common belief that this hiring process would actually destroy the coalition. No one felt that a woman would be given a fair chance to compete. The women believed the rabbi would veto any attempt to put a woman in the role. The Latino members wanted a Spanish speaker. Some insisted that the organizer be a longtime Williamsburg resident. The more I grappled with this, the more I understood the skeptics' points of view. The hiring of this one organizer had the potential to dissolve the entire collaborative. How could there ever be an agreement? My job was to make recommendations on how to construct an interview committee. I thought that the best place to start was to clear the air and state the obvious. There was the potential for deep disagreement. Could we at least start out by writing down all the qualities we were looking for in a candidate?

We agreed to leave out issues that were divisive. I then tried to get a member of each group to talk about the pressures they were under from their own organizations. This technique provided the chance to depersonalize differences and personalize similarities. We gradually, painstakingly, got everything out on the table. The groups agreed to interview a number of potential candidates. Most were bilingual. There was one extremely qualified candidate who, in most settings, would easily have made the cut. But we had an unusual partner that made this selection seemingly impossible. She had great experience for someone so young. She lived in the neighborhood and was fluent in Spanish. Her resume was dotted with liberal causes. This would usually be a positive factor, but, again, not necessarily in this case.

I decided to ask each person in the room if this woman could be included as one of the people to be interviewed. I thought it was best to save the rabbi for last. Then, at the very last second, it hit me. I needed to get his reaction about this before presenting it to any of the other participants. I didn't want to increase the chances that the rabbi would feel threatened or become defensive. He did suggest her as one of the final candidates to be interviewed. She was called and told she would be brought in and given a chance. The following week she would face the rabbi.

The male candidates did well in their interviews. When it was finally the young woman's turn, she was very poised, confident, thoughtful, and motivated. She spoke quietly. The interviewers leaned forward to hear her answers. I thought she was handling everything perfectly. But did it really make a difference? Hadn't the rabbi agreed to interview her as a token gesture to his collaborative partners? It would be hard to conclude she wasn't the best candidate, but again, it was doubtful whether that mattered at all.

I knew it was coming. It was just a matter of where and when. Initially, the rabbi showed no signs of discomfort. He asked appropriate questions without dominating the process. Then, he finally got the chance to ask his real question. When he asked it, he was direct and pointed. "How can I recommend you, when you are a woman who knows nothing about and has no appreciation of our community?" I prayed she would not overreact. If she became even the least bit accusatory she would never get the job. In her calmest, firmest voice, looking directly at the man with the felt hat, 2-ton overcoat, and tropical rain forest beard, she said, "Rabbi, how will I ever learn to help you or your community if I don't start now? I need your help to be effective. Together, you and I can help get jobs for your people and people throughout the entire neighborhood. I know I can become effective with your help. You have to decide whether you want to provide the help." Now that was a consensus organizer's answer. She placed no blame; there was no unfairness or political incorrectness. She made a genuine appeal to reciprocity. If you do something, I'll do something. It was brilliant. The committee was enthusiastic and unanimous. They offered the job to Paula Rojas. That's right; she was the same person that would later organize the kids at El Puente Academy. She deserved the opportunity.

As a consensus organizer, the word *partnership* should mean a lot to you. It shouldn't be a word that just sounds good. It should be something that you use all your abilities to achieve. You want to be able to bring people together to reach mutual benefit. You should strive to put people into roles in which they are both comfortable and effective. You hope to see people stay together in partnerships through continued mutual benefit. So start to see the possibilities. There are thousands of opportunities to form partnerships. Just open your eyes and begin.

Reflection Questions

1. Can partnerships be created through funding opportunities? Why or why not?

2. Why did the people from the Mon Valley want to go to Houston?

3. Why can't partnerships be permanent?

4. Who were better partners—Bonnie and Clyde, Ben and Jerry, or Siegfried and Roy?

5. Why did Raphael from El Puente Academy refer to consensus organizing as a "curse"?

9

BUILDING PERSONAL RELATIONSHIPS

In this chapter, you will learn:

◆ Class is an important factor in the way we view others.

◆ We need to work with people who are different from us.

◆ Focusing on skills, abilities, and connections.

◆ Easy steps to building new relationships.

To be a successful consensus organizer you have to meet, listen to, and get to know a lot of people. Some of them you will not like. Some of them you can take or leave. Some you will enjoy. Some you might find interesting, maybe even fascinating. All have the potential to be beneficial to your efforts. The people who you will like the most and find the most interesting will probably follow a pattern. The pattern will be simple. They will tend to be the people who remind you most of yourself. This may sound funny to you, but I think the more you reflect on it, the more you will see what I mean. All of us like people who see things the way we do. We like people who enjoy the same movies, vote for the same politicians, and follow the same trends. The challenge lies in building personal relationships with others who for whatever reasons see the same sets of circumstances and yet draw completely different conclusions. We see these people in a more negative light. We cloak our displeasure by labeling them as "difficult," "self-serving," "cocky," "not a team player," or even a "bad influence." They may be none of these things and instead may turn out to be key people in helping to achieve success.

Class Dismissed

It is often the individuals with differing opinions who are key to achieving success.

The real analysis needs to focus on why we think negatively about people who draw different conclusions than we do. We need to do this analysis because we usually can't get a lot done with only those who are mirrors of ourselves. There just may not be enough of those similar to us to do all the work that is required to create change. We will need to develop many more new and varied relationships to be successful. Let's start by looking at whether there is a pattern among those we agree with. I think that the closer a person's experience is to our own, the more we tend to see things similarly. The further apart our backgrounds, the more dissimilar our experiences and the less chance there is for us to be simpatico. What are the variables that tend to make our experiences more similar? Age is a big one. Ever talk to someone who lived through the Vietnam War and you didn't? Ever have the subject of health come up with someone who is 50 years older than you are? Race and ethnicity are obvious factors. Studies have been done on reactions to police that vary immensely depending on race and ethnicity. Gender and sexual orientation many times can bring us closer together. We understand male bonding, girls' night out, gay vacation spots, and so on. Another factor bonds us together (and of course keeps us apart), however, and that is the dreaded "c" word, rarely uttered in America. I am referring to class. We live in a society that refuses to admit the importance of class distinctions. Class discussions (not class*room* discussions) make many of us surprisingly uncomfortable. It's like some dark family secret that we don't share with others. We know it's there. We feel its effects every day. We just don't want to talk about it. In Alfred Lubrano's (2004) excellent book, *Limbo: Blue Collar Roots, White Collar Dreams,* he talks about those of us born into working-class families who become professionals through education and hard work. He says that many are caught in limbo, looked at by the upper-middle class and rich as not quite equal, while at the same time seen as abandoning our roots by our own families and neighbors. I believe that reaching across class lines may be even more difficult than crossing racial, ethnic, age, and sexual orientation divides (see Figure 9.1).

- Age
- Life Experience
- Race
- Ethnicity
- Gender
- Sexual Orientation
- Class

Figure 9.1   Variables That Influence Attitude

Class behaviors and expectations are taught to us. The teaching has placed all of us into an ever-deepening river with swift currents and sharp rocks. Many of us see this river and find it too difficult to cross. We stay with "our own" on the safe shore. I will argue that often when we say, "There's something about him I just don't like" and we can't be specific, the reason behind our discomfort often lies in class differences. Let's start with some very tiny examples. One time, I was eating at a nice restaurant with my wife. My parents and friends from the old neighborhood would have referred to this restaurant as a "fancy" restaurant. This would not be complimentary. It meant that they would be uncomfortable, the portions would be small, and it would look nice but taste bad. The hostess and waiter would be "stuck up" and "snooty." It would not be nearly as good as the fish fry we could have gotten by walking down to the local tavern. At a fraction of the price, we would have gotten three times as much food with cold beer and "nice" people all around. My in-laws would have enjoyed the restaurant my wife and I were in and found it attractive, with imaginative recipes, nice presentation, and impeccable service. Most of my wife's friends would have agreed. Most of my friends from the old neighborhood would not. So, anyway, there we were, ordering our food and enjoying the ambiance. The food looked delicious and as I started to dig in, a piece of meat flew off my plate and landed on the floor about 10 inches from my foot. My first impulse, after my embarrassment, was to bend over and immediately pick it up. After all, I was the moron who dropped it. My wife looked alarmed, not because I had dropped the food (it turns out that rich people do it all the time), but rather because I was starting to bend over to pick it up! It was as if her mind was trying to beam into my brain, "Don't do that. That's why they have restaurant employees." It was a classic case of seeing the same situation completely differently. She felt we were paying good money for service and I felt I was paying good money so I shouldn't mess up. I identified with the poor sap that had to work harder picking up after me. She identified with the paying customer. In all seriousness, it was killing me to leave that piece of meat on the floor. Imagine multiplying that situation times a hundred. Do you see how easy it would be for both of us to say, "There's something about him or her that I just don't like?" It all comes from our class. I feel like the busboy yet I have become a customer who can afford to eat in the "fancy" restaurant.

One more restaurant story: When I eat alone at a restaurant, I will sit wherever the host or hostess seats me. Without even thinking, I must feel that it is their job to choose the table and my job to sit there. When I eat with an upper-middle-class or wealthy person, he or she will choose a table and the host follows. Now I am not saying I am polite and they are impolite. In fact, I do tend to sit a disproportionately large number of times next to the swinging doors to the kitchen or the large garbage dumpster. One time I asked a waitress friend of mine and she said, "Oh, rich people never sit where we suggest. I think they want to show us who is boss." Of course, this friend's upbringing was working class.

One time my wife went with me to a wedding on my side of the family. My wife loved the bride's dress and complimented her on it. She was curious to know where she had shopped for it, where she had found it, who had gone with her to pick it out, and so on. Well, the dress was handmade as was the case with many other brides in my family. They didn't have the money for something "store bought" because they thought they would be ripped off by the store owner who would think they were rich. Lubrano (2004) tells scores of stories to show how pervasive class differences are and how hard of a time we have reconciling these differences.

You might notice differences in people when they eat dinner or, as we called it, "supper." I like to eat earlier than my middle-class friends. It comes from years of watching my dad come home, "washing up," and then immediately eating. Why? Because after a hard day of physical labor, he was very hungry and very tired. Notice also when people make a selection or purchase. An upper-middle-class or wealthy person expects lots of choices and options. A working-class person tends to feel uncomfortable with, say, 25 pairs of shoes scattered on the shoe store floor.

In addition to all these differences, we have some classical behavioral tendencies as well. I am used to people yelling. My middle-class friends are used to discussing. I like to kid around and tease. Others like to show their sensitivity. I think all these seemingly minor things are important because when you are around people who are different from you, you might be uncomfortable and not like them. If you don't like them, you may never develop a personal relationship with them. Then you have lost all their potential help and assistance.

CLASS IN THE COMMUNITY

Let me show you how these class differences can play out in a community. In San Diego, two professional planners from upper-middle-class families worked for a nonprofit that operated a multipurpose community center in a low-income neighborhood.

> Class plays a key role in how people react
> to one another.

To analyze how effective their programs were, the professionals designed a questionnaire to be distributed to community residents. They compiled a series of questions to test out how well they were doing and to see what changes the residents would recommend. The questionnaire was appropriately bilingual. When the surveys were returned, the planners invited the community to hear about the compiled results and have the opportunity to provide further input into the programming of the agency. So far, so good. The planners were well prepared. When they had all their equipment set up and were ready to begin, they politely but firmly asked the audience to delay any questions or comments until after their professionally prepared PowerPoint presentation was completed. They were genuinely interested in feedback, but they wanted it in an orderly, appropriate manner. During the PowerPoint presentation, some of the residents left. When the planners' presentation concluded, the remaining residents stared down at the floor and remained silent.

What had happened? The planners had insulted the poor and working-class audience and didn't even know it. When this example is talked about in a college class, I can recognize the students from the middle-class and wealthy families right away. They are just as dumbfounded about the audience's reaction as the planners had been. Students from poor and working-class families, however, would shoot up their hands. They would say that the planners might just have well have said, "Shut up and listen to us. We are superior to you." Amazing. Even though this was not the planners' intent, it still had the unintended result. In this case, the racial and ethnic background of the planners was irrelevant. It was a class issue.

So, if you are starting to see the significance of this, good. Awareness, however, is not the same as coming up with a solution. Try this. Take a look at your own class background and begin to look at three people you have had to deal with that "bug" you (see Figure 9.2). Take a really close look. What is it about them? Then take a look at their class background. How similar or dissimilar is their background from yours? If they are from a different class, try to imagine being them. How would you behave differently if you had their job? What sensitivities and insights would you have that they do not? Does this pattern apply to all three of the people who bug you? Do you see behaviors you would want to change in each of the others?

As consensus organizers, we must work effectively with people who are very different from ourselves. Remember the phrase, "There is not enough of yourself to spread around"? As we see the necessity to reach out to those different from us in class, ethnicity, race, gender, and sexual orientation, we may have to deal with people who look at the world differently. We have to deal with people we don't completely like or understand. We have to get to the point where we may still be bothered, but maybe just not as much. Every time you figure out why someone's behavior bothers you, you will be able to handle it a little better. You start to move past your differences and value the working relationship because it can help lead to success. You will also be gaining insight into yourself and others, and a better understanding of why you are who you are. You can measure progress by how much you can move beyond superficial stereotypes.

I was once working with two volunteers in Palm Beach County, Florida. One was a WASPy, "blue-blood" banker born into money. He had a certain air about him that said sailing, polo, and charity balls. He had perfect posture and diction. The other volunteer was working class. He also had an air about him, but that air was sweaty, profanity-filled, and loud. The point is—these guys were different. They had gotten to know each other by working as volunteers over an 18-month period. One day, out of nowhere, the banker's bank

Name	Similar Class? Yes/No
People you admire	
1.	
2.	
3.	
People who bug you	
1.	
2.	
3.	

Figure 9.2   Class Background

announced that it was downsizing. He was being laid off. It was officially referred to as "corporate restructuring." At our meeting, during a break, the banker told the other guy what had happened. As it turned out, the still-employed, working-class guy was a member of a competing bank's community reinvestment committee. He offered to put in a good word for his laid-off associate. The banker was deeply grateful and was rehired to do banking as a specialist, lending in low-income communities! It ended up being a much more fulfilling job for him. The two of them continued to help each other for years to come. This could only have happened because, despite their differences, they had both been asked to volunteer on the same project. No one changed through force. The poor are not "pure" and the rich "impure." We all need one another, precisely because we are different.

> Consensus organizers need other people because they are all different.

This gives you a lot to think about. Never close yourself off to anybody because everybody has the potential to help you. You have to look at every opportunity to meet new people as a crucial opportunity to gain more help. If you have met people whose age, class, ethnicity, and so on are different from yours, then so much the better. As a consensus organizer, you do not have the luxury of surrounding yourself with people who are most like you. You have to get to know as many people as possible. You have to value everyone.

What if you have the misfortune of having to build a close relationship with someone you can't stomach (and you will)? Do not focus on your dislike. Certainly do not try to totally eliminate your dislike for the individual. Instead, focus on the person's skills, abilities, connections, and so on.

Relationship-Building Skills:

1. Value everyone.

2. Do not focus on dislike.

3. Focus on skill, ability, and connections.

The person who has relationship-building skills has the potential to help others. Keep focusing on the specific factors in the person that can lead to helping someone else. If you really care about your client or the neighborhood residents, you will find that the appropriate focus should help you stay consistent and willing to work with a person you really don't like or admire. Keep seeing clearly that there is help down the road. It should help you swallow the medicine and achieve the cure.

Think of people as a set of precious coins. Some coins are from foreign countries. Some are hard to exchange. Some have undetermined value. Does that mean you should throw away all of them except the ones with George Washington's head? Think of how foolish you would feel when someone told you the true value of all those coins you threw in the garbage.

Try to look at every stranger as having some future potential value. Don't try to turn everyone into your friend. Don't become a person without preferences, superficially claiming, "I like everyone." Just remember, you do have to push yourself past just those you are comfortable with being around. The more relationships you have, the more you can mix and match. This will increase your opportunities to help others. So what if it means you will have to tolerate a few differences? It will make your life a lot more fulfilling and a lot more interesting.

So you are ready to build new relationships. Maybe you are shy. Maybe you aren't sure what to do first. Let's break it down into some easy-to-follow steps.

1. Listen a lot more than you talk. Most people like to talk about themselves. You want to get to know them. Sounds like a match made in heaven. Just ask leading questions and they are off to the races. Some of my favorite leading questions are, "Why did you take this job? What gives you the most satisfaction? Why is this important?" See, it's pretty easy.

2. Repeat the things you understand. All people you encounter wonder whether you can understand them as they talk. If you don't get what they are trying to tell you, they really are wasting their breath. For instance, if they had said for the last 5 minutes that they think more people have to become involved, you could say, "Oh then you are saying we need to do things like call everyone on the block?" Keep building the relationship by proving to the person that you have been listening. Saying, "I see," or "Mmm, please continue," does not prove you were listening. Anyone can make those comments and never pay attention. The person talking needs proof that you are listening.

3. Say you agree when you agree. Say it's interesting when you don't. Watch out for the public relations nightmarish, "That's just what I think too," when you are really thinking, "Yeah! What a jerk." Never build a relationship on false flattery or false statements. If you disagree, keep people talking by saying that you are interested. This allows you to gain further insight into why they believe what they believe.

4. Mix and match. After gaining understanding of what makes people tick, match them up with someone who they do not know who thinks similarly. This builds your power because you brought them together. If both people benefit from your matchmaking, you will find both wanting to help you. You have just doubled your supporter network with a single match.

5. Come back. Never meet someone, see some potential value, and then fail to follow up. New contacts always wonder whether they will ever see you or hear from you again. People want to know whether they are important. If they can help, they are important, so you need to call, e-mail, or see them again.

So, to make this a little more real, let's go visit two people. One you probably have never heard of. The other one you have probably seen on TV. This time we'll be going to Las Vegas, Nevada. This time you will be playing blackjack. I know you are saying, "I don't gamble. All I do is put a couple of quarters in a slot machine and that's it for me. Then I'm off to the buffet line and a Cirque du Soleil show." Well, cut it out. You're not at your kitchen table. You're in Vegas! Take out some cash and remember, always, always split the aces.

YOU COULD DO THAT

When you get into the habit of thinking like a consensus organizer, you notice some differences in the abilities of individuals. There are considerable differences in each person's ability to be creative and strategic. You can find someone who works hard, believes strongly in something, and is a pleasure to know. That does not mean they are creative or strategic. Some people just think creatively and some just don't. For you to be effective, some of the people you work with must be creative. You cannot be the sole source of innovation.

There is a very funny and ironic scene in the great film *Wag the Dog*. Dustin Hoffman, playing a Hollywood producer, has been asked by the president of the United States to stage a fake war to increase the administration's popularity. In one scene, Hoffman looks down at the array of people he has assembled to fake the war. He has brought together music composers, film editors, writers, and commercial jingle creators to "produce" a fake war. He looks down at the assemblage and beaming with pride states, "I just love it when I bring creative people together." Well, you are the movie producer. You will, it is hoped, bring people together for a slightly higher purpose. The point is you are not assembling a group of your followers. You are putting together a group that follows a vision they create. You only construct the purpose for which they are assembled.

I have observed that people love to be a part of a creative process. This is especially powerful for those experiencing it for the first time. In our society, we are very used to being led. Pastors, marketers, bureaucrats, elected officials, corporate executives, advertisers, and administrators all lead us. And let's face it, many are not that creative. When someone comes along and tells a group that you really need them to think, strategize, and lead, and you mean it, they can't believe their good fortune. They are ecstatic—they respond, they participate, and they think.

When people are asked to think, strategize, and lead, they respond, participate, and think.

When I was working in Florida, a leader of a corporate group was made aware that the county government was preparing to tear apart a historically African American neighborhood. There were plans being developed for a multilane highway. We had a consensus organizer in the neighborhood who was building trust among the residents. The organizer could have easily stirred up the resentment and alienation the community felt, and then directed that toward the devious county government. Instead, the organizer presented the information about the unhappiness in the neighborhood to the corporate leader. At no time did he suggest what the corporate leader should do. If we expected him to do something or said that it was his responsibility to do something, I believe he would have made our attitude the issue and ended up doing nothing. He would have argued that our expectations were unrealistic and unfair. Instead, we said that we didn't understand what the county was doing or why. This made him more than just important; it gave him the opportunity to be strategic. He called his friend at an engineering firm. The company president sat on his corporate board. Together, they helped the residents make a remarkably effective presentation to the county commissioners. A pro-community newspaper editorial miraculously appeared in the local newspaper. The highway plans were scrapped and in their place new water and sewer lines were put into the neighborhood. Don't you agree with Dustin Hoffman?

Well, that's the fun part, but what about all the other people who might want to help with certain issues but come up three bricks shy of a load as strategists? Remember, not everyone can do this. My friend, Rob Fossi, and I worked together in New Orleans, Louisiana. Rob was the program officer for the Local Initiatives Support Corporation and was responsible for putting together the financing and technical assistance for housing developments proposed by local community groups. Rob is effective and very talented at doing 95 percent of what his job requires. When people around him don't step up to the plate and do their fair share, however, he has a tendency to become what some people refer to as "a bull in a china shop." He lets his strong desire for justice and fairness charge forward, leaving more than a plate or two of broken china in his wake. The thing that makes this complicated is you would probably almost always believe that Rob has a valid point. You would, like me, admire his determination. The fact is, however, you would be watching a train wreck.

I learned a technique that was transparent but still effective. Instead of screaming at him "Are you out of your mind?" or "Why don't you just put a gun to your head?" (OK, so I tried both, but telling him to stop made him more determined to prove he was right), I tried to do something more creative. So one time I tried, "You *could* do that." I then told him that there were other alternatives, maybe 50 or so, he could also try. I felt all 50 were to some degree better than his first choice, but I always let him pick. I never attempted to tell him or force him into doing something. It began to work. In one case, he chose suggestion number 45 (10 percent better), then, eventually, suggestion number 10 (80 percent better). After he saw the pattern, we would both laugh at each other. It got to the point where he would reveal his indignation over a very valid concern, string out a series of expletives, and propose something that would set his cause back 20 years or so. He would then look at me—stop, laugh, and say, "I *could* do that, but maybe instead I shouldn't."

The point is we all can work with a variety of people who have concern, compassion, and a willingness to act. We have a much smaller number of people we encounter out there who are effective strategists. Your job is to melt the butter in the frying pan. The other ingredients will follow. The recipe will come together. You are not the entire meal. Just put the butter in the frying pan, sprinkle in the ingredients, and mix thoroughly. Treasure those people who are truly creative and strategic. Put them into your recipe. At the same time, remember that one key ingredient does not make an excellent dinner. It is always the combination. Nurture, develop, and work with all those who have big hearts, are genuine, have real caring, and want to help those in need. For all the nonstrategists out there, steer them, by telling them that they *could* do that.

How to Play Blackjack With James Carville

Consensus organizers have to build positive relationships with an unbelievable variety of people.

Consensus organizers have to build positive relationships with an unbelievable variety of people.

You have to notice people and have genuine curiosity. Then you must ingratiate yourself to the poorest, richest, the most obscure, and the most famous. For some of us, we can do this with the poorest and most obscure, yet fail miserably with the rich and famous. Some have trouble with the poor and obscure and are only interested in knowing and relating to the rich and famous. I believe difficulties occur when our behavior is inconsistent. As humans, we crave and seek out consistency. When we are inconsistent, we are off of our game. We get uncomfortable and we lose our effectiveness. I think we even disappoint ourselves when we behave inconsistently. Try to understand this desire we have for consistency. No matter whom you deal with, try to be consistent. I strive to say the same things on the same topics to completely different people. You have to discipline yourself to do it. If you are not careful, you lapse into "selling" things to people or telling them what you think they want to hear.

Consistency must become one of your skills. It is a building block to determining mutual self-interest. When I tell the same thing to two seemingly disparate people, I watch to see if their reactions differ. If they differ, I don't make the match. If they have the same gleam in their eye, the same fire in their gut, the same determination etched in their face, I have a chance to develop potential partners. If I had behaved inconsistently, telling them two different things to try to ingratiate myself with them, I would have no idea where to go next. All I have created is two opposite reasons for the connection. Remember, the point isn't that they both bond with me; the point is that they bond with each other. After they see value in each other, they will be indebted to me.

I can best illustrate this by talking about the political strategist James Carville. He's the bald guy from Louisiana that kept saving President Bill Clinton. Let's just say that I have always been a big fan. I was forever in his camp, when, at the height of Clinton's shenanigans, Carville faced the national press. Someone in the back shouted, "What kind of advice can you give the president when the vast majority of Americans no longer trust a word he says?" Carville scratched his naked head, squinted, grimaced, shuffled his feet, and drawled, "Trust? Now trust is a very funny thing. Americans have lost a lot of trust in many things. For instance, they lost a lot of trust in you guys [the media]. Take the FBI. When I was a little boy, my brother and I used to run around the woods with imaginary guns and badges and pretended we were FBI agents. Shoot, we didn't know J. Edgar Hoover was running around his office in a skirt!" The entire press corps was in stitches. They were a long way from where they started. He sailed them down his own river. I was amazed at this guy's strategic talent.

Well, a few months after Clinton left the throne (I noticed Al Gore didn't hire Carville), my wife and I took a short vacation to Las Vegas. It was the last day of our trip, and we were heading home on a 1:00 p.m. flight. Now when I go to Las Vegas to gamble I set a limit on how much I'm prepared to lose. That morning, I was prepared to lose $100. Once I lost the $100, I was done. On your last day of vacation in Las Vegas, you never really think you can win, do you? Well, with that mind-set, I descended the elevator in Caesar's Palace with plans to meet my wife back in the room at noon. My plan was to play 25-cent video poker. To stretch out the 100 bucks, I decided to read the paper and have coffee first. On the front page, I learned the Democratic National Committee (DNC) was in town for a meeting. I chuckled to myself about Clinton in Las Vegas. It seemed like he would be in his element there. As I headed over to the machines, I heard a distinctive high-pitched voice. I heard that choppy Louisiana cadence. I saw the black T-shirt and bald head. It was James Carville. He was walking with a short guy I didn't recognize. They were walking briskly, straight toward the blackjack tables. What do I say? "Hey, aren't you James Carville?" No, whatever you do, don't say that. My legs were leaden. I finally got to the tables, walking like Sean Penn. I thought the anonymous slot gamblers were muttering, "dead man walking." Carville and his companion had already sat down at a $25 blackjack table. All the other seats were open. I sat down at the opposite end of the table from Carville, with the short guy between us. James was playing his hand with only one red $5 chip. I tried to gather my wits. The minimum at the table was supposed to be $25. I moved my $100 bill toward the dealer. Should I ask for $5 chips like Carville had? I knew about the $25 minimum and I debated whether to point to Carville and tell the dealer, "Oh yeah, how come I have to play for $25 and he gets to play for $5?" Probably not a wise idea if I wanted to build a relationship and stay at the table. I took four $25 chips. I could not draw any attention to myself. If I did that I knew they would leave.

Now, for those of you who have never sat at a $25 blackjack table in Las Vegas, let me tell you that I could easily lose four hands in about 40 seconds and there wouldn't be much in this book about playing blackjack with James Carville. James was in the seat that got the first card. It turned out that the guy I didn't know was a "whale," a big-time gambler. He was betting two hands at a time at $200 per hand. For the uninitiated, that means he is worthy of attention, by not only the dealer, but by the cocktail waitress, the "pit boss" (manager), security, and everyone else, too. On the first hand, James wins 5 bucks, the "whale" wins $400, and I lose $25. The cocktail waitress comes over; James orders a Virgin Mary. He looks right at me and says, "Eva have a Virgin Mary heah? They good!" I'm now in. I am one of the guys. If only I can stay at the table. The "whale" increases his bet to $500 a hand. Carville gets cocky; he bets two $5 chips. He loses. He looks at me with mock disgust, "Oooeee, whenever I make a big bet my luck goes south." We are all laughing. The "whale" wins $1,000, and I win $25.

In what can only be considered a miracle, my four chips last an entire hour. They have now roped off the entire table, not allowing anyone else to sit down beside the three of us. A crowd has now gathered because James has been noticed. I get a kick out of the fact that people are trying to figure out who I am. I start conjuring up colorful nicknames for myself. Carville is down 15 bucks and his friend is up $60,000. I look at my watch. I'm supposed to be back at the room, meeting my wife, and heading for the airport. The "whale's" cell phone rings. Now you are not supposed to answer cell phones at the blackjack tables in Las Vegas. In this case, the pit boss nods his permission. They do not want the "whale" to leave with $60,000 of their money. The whale puts his hand over the mouthpiece and says, "James, they want us over at a meeting for the presidential library." So I now figure this guy must be a big contributor to the Democratic Party. James looks at me, he then turns to the "whale" and says, "Library? That's too boring, man. The three of us is gonna stay out and have some more fun!" The three of us? Man, we are one for all and all for one. It does not get any better than this. I look at my watch, and I realize I'm supposed to be in a cab, with my wife, halfway to the airport. I muster up all the responsibility in my married body, and push six chips toward the dealer to cash out. I then feel a firm hand squeeze mine. It's the "whale." "Hey, buddy, you brought us good luck. You can't leave us now." Carville gave me a look he must have given Clinton a thousand times. The look said, "Son, don't mess up now." I sat back down. The two of them applaud. The "whale" goes up $75,000. Carville declares, "Yeah, you right. After we finish, let's all have lunch at da Palm!" The Palm restaurant, just the three of us, just like old times.

I apologized, but I really had to go. So I never got to the Palm, the DNC, or to smoking cigars with Bill Clinton. But I absolutely know that I could have. You could have, too, by being yourself. Treat everyone the same, special but not too special.

Lessons on blending in:

Treat everyone the same—special, but not too special.

The janitor, the actor, the corporate leader, the store clerk, the public housing tenant, and the presidential adviser (James Carville) all have to be motivated and brought together by you. You can do it. Maybe like me you can win 75 bucks in the process.

Be yourself —always. Be genuine—always. Do not try to guess, "What do they want to hear?" Instead, imagine, "I am really interested in meeting this person." You cannot be phony and succeed as a consensus organizer. You are not in public relations, sales, or motivational speaking. As a result, you try your best not to be a different person to different people. Most lasting relationships are built on honesty and trust. So just keep it simple: Be honest, truthful, and yourself.

Reflection Questions

1. To build a relationship, is it necessary to impress the other person with your credentials and knowledge about a subject? Why or why not?

2. Have you ever noticed differences between two people caused by class?

3. Should you ever, under any circumstances, utter the phrase "I think of myself as a people person"?

4. When you meet someone new, should you listen more or talk more?

5. Describe your own class background. Were your parents and grandparents from the same class?

6. As a consensus organizer, how would you approach people differently from the way you have approached them in the past?

7. Which song more closely resembles relationship building in consensus organizing? "Love the One You're With" by Stephen Stills, "Glory Days" by Bruce Springsteen, or Mariah Carey's "I'll Be There?"

REFERENCE

Lubrano, A. (2004). *Limbo: Blue collar roots, white collar dreams.* Hoboken, NJ: Wiley.

10

BUILDING INSTITUTIONAL RELATIONSHIPS

In this chapter, you will learn:

◆ How to deal with bureaucracies.

◆ How to work effectively with for-profit and nonprofit organizations.

◆ How to build relationships with private philanthropies.

W e've talked a lot about how to get to know an individual, find out his or her self-interest, and then match it to others. Many times, out in the community, we are faced with a more complicated task. We will have to attempt to build a relationship with an entire organization. That organization might be a school, a whole department within city government, a for-profit business like a bank, or a nonprofit like a civil rights organization. We might desire a positive relationship with a particular organization because of its power, prestige, skills, money, or expertise. It may not be enough to have the support of Juanita who works for the Urban League. We may need the support of the Urban League.

Consensus organizing involves building relationships with entire organizations.

For many of you, the idea of even contacting some of these organizations may seem daunting. That's OK. In some ways, this may be preferable to others who say they are comfortable in approaching them. Those comfortable people may need to unlearn a few things to become more effective. Most initial contact with organizations leads nowhere. It is often hit or miss. It may start out with some potential significance but will lead nowhere. A consensus organizer wants a relationship with an organization that becomes institutional—as permanent as possible, yet evolving, and meaningful to everyone. In this chapter, we will divide up organizations into different types. These categorizations might help you get your arms around this function and allow you to begin to see yourself in this role.

Inside each community, there are numerous individuals who have tremendous assets and abilities. These assets and abilities need to be mapped out and linked to others with complementary skills, wants, and needs. A teenager needs to be linked to an elder who needs his lawn mowed. A single mother needs to be linked to a woman who loves children and has the time to baby-sit. John McNight and Jody Kretzmann made a career out of pointing out the need to see strengths and assets in low-income communities rather than just problems and pathologies. In *Building Communities From the Inside Out* (Kretzmann & McNight, 1993), they very convincingly show how the elderly, youth, artists, the handicapped, and others are poised and ready to be linked to neighborhood improvement efforts. Even in communities with lots of social capital (networks of relationships of trust), however, there still need to be ties to more clout, power, money, and expertise and that means finding some "external partners." These external partners oftentimes are organizations as opposed to individuals. They may have buildings, offices, and staff removed from the community. The process of finding these external resources is essential because there just may not be enough clout and power within a low-income or working-class community. There are limits to what can be achieved through self-help. The consensus organizer wants to go beyond self-help and build new relationships with entire organizations that lie outside community boundaries. To do this, you have to think of yourself as an explorer. What is out there in the vast ocean? What adventure awaits you? Where is Russell Crowe in his role in the film *Master and Commander: The Far Side of the World* when you really need him?

Outside the community, there are many resources within many organizations. Some are found within various levels of government and others are found in organizations that are not governmental. Think of it like this:

Governmental

- Federal (Departments of Housing and Urban Development, Education, etc.)
- State (Departments of Community Affairs, Children, and Family Services, etc.)
- County (Departments of Environmental Health, Health and Human Services, etc.)
- City (Departments of Parks and Recreation, Police, Fire, etc.)

Nongovernmental

- For-profit businesses (corporate foundations)
- Large nonprofits (YMCA, Salvation Army, Catholic Charities)
- Private philanthropies (family or community foundations)

Consensus organizers need to understand how all these potential resources function. We need to get into their "heads" and understand what they value and what they are trying to accomplish. We want to understand organizations in the same way we try to understand individuals. There are many similarities between building institutional relationships and building personal relationships.

> There are many similarities between building institutional relationships and building personal relationships.

There are, however, also some important distinctions in building relationships with entire organizations. Let's get started.

INSTITUTIONAL TYPES

Government

Many people in today's society hate "government." Ever since Vietnam and Watergate, what used to be called public service has been replaced by the negative term "government." Let's go back to the early 1960s for some perspective. That was the era when it was considered a high calling to seek a career in public service. There were programs like VISTA and the Peace Corps and countless other opportunities. Many people chose the public sector for their careers because of high ideals and deep social consciousness—not to seek maximum salaries and benefits. In the course of a single generation, we have seen the concept of noble public service replaced by a negative image. Many now see the public sector as filled with lazy bureaucrats, doing nothing all day except getting in our way, pushing tons of paper, and sucking up our paychecks through unfairly high taxes. What a swift change. It would take a whole book to catalog the reasons for this 180-degree turnaround in perception. I think that being lied to during the Vietnam War and being lied to during the Watergate scandal built a foundation of disrespect for the entire public sector. To many people, it seems that we have not had any kind of admirable leadership to successfully alter such attitudes ever since. We still have thousands of public sector employees and programs. Does that mean the entire profession attracts only liars, cheats, and malingerers? Of course not.

One current negative stereotype often has us imagining some fat, lazy, career employee pining away for an enormous pension (at our expense) and coming up with insane rules and procedures designed to prevent us from receiving real help. I'd like to take a little deeper look into bureaucracy and where and why it all began. Did you ever wonder why there is so much paperwork and so many rules and regulations at every level of government? Egos run amok? People with nothing better to do? Actually, the imposition of rules and procedures originally emerged as a reform effort. In the 19th century, the United States government was extremely corrupt. Big cities, especially, had political bosses and political machines that did everything under the table. To try to clean this up, the Progressive movement was formed, and it pushed for merit hiring and competitive, open bidding for contracts so that people had an equal shot. It was considered protective of fairness to have more paperwork and structure. It was considered to be worth it because anything was considered better than corruption, bribes, and kickbacks. We stand in lines in government offices so that no one gets to cut in front of us (Schorr, 1997). This is a very important observation. It is for the purpose of equal treatment and the elimination of favoritism that we live with bureaucracy. This means that consensus organizers see most government procedures as well-intentioned and most government employees as trying to treat all citizens fairly.

So what mistake do many activists and advocates make when they have to interact with government? They demand special treatment! Do you see how this backfires? They consider their cause so important, their need so pressing that they will not stand in line, fill out forms, or abide by rules. What do bureaucrats do in response? They become more bureaucratic. If this weren't so important, it would be pretty funny. It's kind of like a cartoon. The advocate is in the role of Wile E. Coyote and the bureaucrat is in the role of the roadrunner. No matter what strategy the coyote uses to catch the roadrunner, he never succeeds.

So how do you work within government or with government as a consensus organizer? You go to that same bureaucrat and discern a way to mesh his or her self-interest with your self-interest.

To work through government bureaucracy, you must mesh the organization's self-interest with your self-interest.

You say "Could you please explain the rules so I can follow them correctly" (or some variation of the same theme)? This makes the person and the institution feel respected. It makes their goal of fair and equal treatment legitimate. You then really listen and begin to understand what drives the bureaucracy. It even starts to make a little sense. If you interact with government in this way, word travels through other government offices that you were "a pleasure to work with," a "good partner," a member of a "reasonable group." As the word spreads, subsequent governmental meetings become more relaxed and collegial because when people feel respected they will respect you in return.

There are often strong ties among government staff, similar to the ties within police and fire departments. They feel the need to stick together. They will share positive and negative information with co-workers to help one another deal with a public that just doesn't understand all they go through. Your goal is to have positive information circulated about you.

Try to imagine yourself as a government official and how you would feel when people felt they were above the law and told you your rules were stupid. Would you reward them for their pushiness and arrogance or instead would you work with others who were cooperative and respectful? As you begin to establish this type of relationship, you begin to institutionalize it. Each time you work with the same public sector department or program, you deepen your understanding of each other's agendas. You understand each other's barriers and impediments and you work together to overcome obstacles. You are on the same page.

For-Profit Businesses

Some of you have a pro-business attitude and others have an antibusiness attitude. You see it everyday. Some people love the idea of contracting out government services to for-profit businesses (garbage collection, bus service, etc.) because of their belief that the private sector always does a better job, cheaper and faster. When Enron officials were caught in illegal activities, pro-business enthusiasts said things about not letting just a few rotten apples spoil the whole barrel. To the contrary, others worry that the bottom-line profit motive of businesses will always tend to take advantage of the consumer, particularly the poor consumer. Whichever side of the aisle you stand on this, you have to include business organizations as another source of potential partners. For instance, consider that much of the affordable housing developed over the last 20 years would never have happened without private sector involvement.

So what do businesses and corporations want and why would they ever want to develop a relationship with someone like you? Businesses need profit and profit is generated through product and image. You have the potential to help with both. Last time I checked, working-class and poor people still had some money. Just like everyone else, they tend to spend it. They need a bank, a gas station, a supermarket, a drugstore, a barbershop, and even a shoe store. Working-class and poor people can also partner with businesses by helping them convey an image of fairness, concern, charity, and opportunity. So, simply put, businesses might need a relationship with you. They might not know how to create it, but they may be highly receptive to an overture from you. It just has to be the right overture. Remember how government entities needed you to play fair within their systems? Businesses want you to agree that their self-interest is justifiable and they don't "owe" you anything. Nothing ticks off business organizations more than being blamed and hearing that they "owe" someone. You've heard this attitude expressed before. "You make so much profit, you owe us and should support our soccer team." "You have this big warehouse in our neighborhood, so you owe it to us to start a tutoring program." I propose instead that you think in terms of how businesses benefit by being part of your community. Maybe you could suggest that you are glad they are part of your community. For you who are antibusiness, this will be a stretch. Just like it was a stretch earlier for those of you who had distaste for bureaucrats. I've seen a lot of institutional partnerships forged by people who had trouble taking the first step but reluctantly took it anyway. There are loads of potential business connections out there. Most nonprofits speak a language foreign to businesses. Nonprofits use words like "problem," "crisis," "catastrophic," "process," and "widespread" instead of "opportunity," "tangible," "niche," and "measurable." Business organizations respond to concepts they understand in which they can use their strengths to make a difference.

Large Nonprofits

Many large nonprofits such as social service organizations, civil rights organizations, and environmental organizations may have a self-interest that matches your own. This does not mean that they will be searching for you or begging you to join them anytime soon. If you are the "little guy," you will have to be the one initiating the contact. So why would some multimillion-dollar outfit let you get your foot in the door? That's up to you to find out. As nonprofit organizations grow and mature, they may drift away from their mission. They may forget their roots in the community and they may need to reconnect. They may need new blood. They may need fresh ideas. You should begin relationships with large nonprofits in exactly the same way you would with businesses. You have to accept the fact that something must be in it for them. It makes no sense to talk to them about their obligations to the community.

It makes no difference which person you initially contact within a large organization. Start by asking everyone you know if they know someone who works or volunteers at the nonprofit. You can start at the top with the executive director or chairperson. You can also start closer to the bottom with an outreach worker or paraprofessional. Just start somewhere. If you are talking about helping them, they will be receptive. Find out their interests or concerns by reading their newsletter, annual report, and website. Look for a match between their interests and yours and you should be on your way.

Private Philanthropies

Everybody would like to have more money. Some people work for institutions that are set up to give it away. You can be there to help them. When certain wealthy people die, retire, or start to slow down, they sometimes take part of their money and they set up a foundation to make charitable contributions. They do this for two main reasons—tax benefits and good feelings. They may also have a deeply held concern for certain issues or causes and they want to help make progress toward a specific goal. Many of these wealthy people set up a vehicle to distribute grants in the form of a family foundation.

If you have an agenda that matches their agenda, you may be able to begin a new, naturally satisfying relationship. For instance, if you have developed an innovative way to address the health care issues affecting individuals with AIDS and that is the issue of primary interest to a particular family foundation, you can begin a relationship by talking about what you both know and care about. Remember to try to learn from members of a foundation as well as teach them. You should both be gaining skills and expertise. It is crucial to see the difference between this suggestion and what many others will try to do—chase money. When organizers decide to simply chase money, they will see a family foundation, find out its interests, and claim to be interested when they are not. They are just doing it to try to get funding. This is not honest or genuine and will never lead to an institutional relationship. When members of an institution feel there is a genuine connection between their goals and yours and they see you have the skills and abilities to accomplish something, they will begin to treat you with respect.

When members of an institution feel there is a genuine connection between their goals and yours and see that you have the skills and abilities to accomplish something, they will learn to treat you with respect.

This respect has the potential to become mutual. Mutual respect can lead to the beginning of a deep, real, positive institutional relationship.

Community Foundations

These organizations are a different kettle of fish. Community foundations usually set up shop in a city or county by offering to take anyone's money (even yours) and find opportunities for you to give it away by matching your particular interest to a nonprofit that can help you carry out your plan and reach your goals. Let's say you are interested in supporting efforts that provide pregnancy prevention education for young women. These foundations would take your donation and present it to a group they feel is addressing the issue effectively in a particular neighborhood in your city or county. The community foundation positions itself in the middle, building new relationships. You might say that a staffer working for a community foundation is playing the role of a consensus organizer.

You can strategize on how best to begin a relationship with community foundations by looking at their website, newsletter, and annual report. Remember, for them to grow and become more successful, they need to know you and others like you. They need you as much as you need them.

COMMONALITIES

So what do all these organizations have in common? Aren't business organizations pretty different from government ones? Isn't a corporation different from a family creating a charity? In many ways, they are not different at all. They all have an agenda that you might be able to help carry out. Consensus organizing differs from advocacy because you are not trying to convince them to be interested in something they are not. Instead, you are just trying to find someone whose interest is similar to yours. The more people you know, the more organizations you know, the closer you are to being able to develop, over time, institutional relationships. Institutional relationships begin when organizations see value in knowing you over the long term. They begin to trust you. They begin to want to know what you are doing. They begin to look forward to hearing from you. They even begin to introduce you to others who may help you as well.

To get to the point of building institutional relationships, you must realize that the people representing these organizations are not different from you. They have some of the same insecurities, quirks, odd habits, and crazy behaviors as anyone else. They do not know everything. They are not smarter. They make mistakes. They are not "out of your league." You have to begin somewhere and you absolutely have the ability to hit it off with some of them.

So let's finally get down to a town you've been waiting to get to ever since this trip started. Let's go to the "city that care forgot." Let's go all the way down the Mississippi to the Crescent City; the home of Dr. John, the Neville Brothers, Fats Domino, Harry Connick, Jr., and Harry Connick, Sr. Let's stop off and get some red beans and rice and a cup of gumbo, maybe some beignet (don't get the powdered sugar on your dark pants). Yeah, you right, let's get to New Orleans, Louisiana, and show you how quirky things can really be.

Did Anyone Get the Baby?

With the support of a large national foundation, I was able to locate in one of three cities in which I would be working for the next 3 years. One choice was New Orleans. You don't even need to know the other two. I just felt I would love New Orleans. I had a great time when I visited there, but come on—this was an opportunity to live there. New Orleans is a city in which you step back in time and you do so with great purpose. I found an apartment on Camp Street near Napoleon Avenue. This meant I could walk to an oyster house, where the family that ran it lived upstairs, a snoball stand (not a Buffalo snowball, but a thick sticky flavored ball of ice that gives terrific relief on a humid day), Tipitinas, a music hall with terrific music each night and a Cajun dance on every Sunday at 5:00 p.m., and the historic St. Charles streetcar that dropped me off right in front of my office.

My apartment was in what was called a "shotgun double" with my landlord and his family right next door. A couple of days after moving in, I came home to find my landlord and some neighbors visiting on the front porch. I said hello and chatted with everyone for 15 minutes. I then excused myself and went in to make dinner. The next night, my landlord was waiting for me. He was exasperated. "How could you leave the porch so soon?" he moaned. "You were so rude." That was something no one in Boston ever accused me of! I would sometimes stop at a neighborhood bar in New Orleans with a neon sign outside lit up spelling "Laundromat." It had one washer and one dryer behind the men's room. It advertised that it was open 24 hours a day, 7 days a week, 364 days a year. Now that gives you pretty much unlimited access to beer but, of course, I had to ask what was the one day all year that the "Laundromat" was closed? I figured maybe Christmas or perhaps the owner's birthday. The bartender told me with a straight face, "We close every December 31st." I was dumbfounded. I said, "But that's New Year's Eve." He replied, "It might be New Year's Eve to you, but to us, it's amateur night." Yes, that was a small example of local color.

When I went to my first New Orleans City Council meeting, I noticed an upright piano facing the public seating. At the start of the meeting, a smartly dressed man came out from behind a door and seated himself at the piano.

I asked the guy sitting next to me, "What's the special occasion?" He didn't understand my question. Apparently, the piano player appeared at every meeting. The first order of official business for the New Orleans City Council that day was a special recognition for a New Orleanian who was retiring from the U.S. Navy after an especially exemplary career. The pianist played "Anchors Away." Now that is not something you would see in Columbus, Ohio.

But not even that prepared me for my first meeting with a group of corporate bankers. I had scheduled a meeting to explain a program idea to provide affordable housing for the working class to high-ranking executives of five New Orleans' banks. The meeting, scheduled for 10:00 a.m., was to be held at the largest of the five banks. I arrived at 9:50. I told the receptionist my name and who I was to meet. She asked me to take a seat. I remained in that seat at 10:00 a.m., 10:05 a.m., 10:10 a.m., and 10:20 a.m. I carefully inched up to the receptionist's desk. Maybe she forgot about me. Maybe all five bankers were waiting for me at a different bank. She replied, "No, baby. You are in the right place. The meeting wasn't scheduled until 10:00 a.m. They'll be around sometime soon." At 10:25, the rest of the attendees ambled in. I figured, now we will finally get down to business. Instead, the host banker buzzes his secretary and tells her to "please bring it in." What could "it" possibly be? Big charts showing mortgage lending trends? No, it appeared to be a big cake. That's right, it was a giant sheet cake and six cups of New Orleans coffee laced with chicory. Everyone got a piece of cake and ate it. The pace was leisurely. No business was discussed. Then, out of nowhere, the host inquired, "Did anyone get the baby?" Well, now I am up a creek without a paddle. The baby? It's 11:00 a.m. We haven't even mentioned affordable housing and now someone was supposed to pick up an infant? All the bankers shook their heads "no." Concern is expressed. I'm thinking someone forgot to bring along a kid. I remember the feeling I had. When you have no idea what is going on and everyone else does you just have to let yourself become the swimmer who goes into a back float. If you just relax and do nothing it might become pleasurable.

The host, after a thorough polling, decided that no one had gotten the baby. They all chuckled and the host cut everyone a second giant piece of cake. I know if you are a reader from Louisiana, you've figured this out paragraphs ago, but for the rest of you, here's the deal. At 11:15 a.m., 75 minutes after the meeting should have started, banker number three proudly announced to a round of hearty applause, including me, "I got the baby." He then spit something out into his napkin. The bankers applauded like the home team had just come from behind in the bottom of the ninth inning. It turned out that every year during carnival season, prior to Lent, custom required the purchase of King Cakes (specially decorated sheet cakes). They were then devoured at meetings and get-togethers all over the city. If you had the good fortune to have the only piece that contained a small plastic baby, you had to bring in the cake the following day. In this case, with this cake, it took a while to find the baby. Not one person had a problem with the time it took. Everyone was in agreement and everyone was on the same page.

This little episode should show you that you needed, in this situation, to tolerate the lateness and enjoy the tradition. You can be late and eat a lot of cake just as well as any New Orleans' banker. To build an institutional relationship you have to relate to the institution.

To build an institutional relationship, you have to relate to the institution.

In this case, it meant waiting until someone got the baby. Sure, your institution may not be quite as interesting, but all institutions have their own ways of doing things that you must adjust to, accept, and fit into. Just try to figure them out. See what they want. See what they need. See if what they need matches your agenda. Proceed with enthusiasm, lots of napkins, and watch that cholesterol.

DAMN LEO!

When people from New Orleans are in complete agreement with something you say, they shout out their feelings by saying, "Yeah, you right!" It gets to be a habit and you like to hear it because it means that you are getting closer to the other person—that person is feeling a tighter bond with you. When people from New Orleans know you have just moved there, they are very curious to see if you like it. If you do, you are accepted as if you are a native. No questions come about your lineage, your pedigree, or your granddaddy. You like it here? I love it. Yeah, you right!

As my love affair with the town bloomed, I did the things a tourist does first. For instance, I went to the zoo. It is a very nice zoo with special emphasis on Louisiana animals and habitat. You don't see a swamp in every zoo but there was one there. In a somewhat bizarre move, members of the zoo's board of directors decided it would be a real feather in their cap if they got a little more exotic. They thought it would be spectacular to bring in an animal all the way from Australia. They believed this could be their crowning glory and put them on the map as members of the zoo-elite. They proposed the purchase of a koala bear. When this brainstorm was formally proposed, it became a topic of hot debate throughout most of the media and among most of my neighbors. It turns out that koala bears are a tad expensive. Let's just say that you could do a lot of other significant things with the money that it takes to gain ownership of one small marsupial.

Kids throughout New Orleans thought it would be cool to get a koala. A lot of adults agreed. But who would pay for it? The zoo targeted all the major charitable organizations and then created a bandwagon effect, putting pressure on everyone to come up with their fair share of the koala commitment. Sure enough, the money was raised and zoo staff ventured to the land down under and returned with Leo. That's right, Leo the koala. The tiny, adorable, cuddly little guy arrived in the Pelican State with great fanfare. There was almost a frenzy over the fur-ball. Kids did research about him in school. Artists sketched him. Long lines formed well before the gates opened with fans hoping to catch one of the first glimpses. One TV station summed it up as Leomania.

People ran to see Leo on the first day the exhibit opened. They saw the eucalyptus tree. They saw his habitat. They looked and looked but no one could find Leo. He was still in his indoor cubicle. He wouldn't come out the entire day. Zoo management, worried about community outrage, issued a calming press release, revealing that such behavior is typical of koalas when placed in a new environment. They told us Leo was fine. He would be acclimated and happy to greet New Orleans in just a few days. Monday came. Tuesday came. The next Monday came. Each day, all day, Leo did not budge. In fact, he sulked. You got the feeling he had eaten some bad shrimp étouffée. The public was now starting to seriously worry. What if Leo never came out? What if he was homesick and heartbroken? What if he cried himself to sleep at night humming "Waltzing Matilda"? At this point, zoo management was aware that at any moment the crowd might turn on Leo. They might say to themselves, "Hey, is Leo saying he doesn't like New Orleans?"

Separate from this epic drama, I had a meeting with a major corporation in town that I wanted to lend support to an inner-city revitalization plan. I needed to begin laying the groundwork for an institutional relationship and I had the good fortune to be meeting with the organization's chief executive officer. We were halfway through our lunch meeting (oyster po' boy sandwich with turtle soup—delicious), and I thought I was doing fine. We were getting to the point of revealing each other's self-interest, when the TV in the corner cut to the local noon news. Sure enough the camera was at the zoo. It turned out that somebody on the zoo staff suggested that to try to satisfy the public's demand to see the koala, a closed circuit camera could be installed in Leo's hiding place so the crowds could at least see him. Of course, this just made people more upset because "Leocam" just showed him to be miserable and bored. In the middle of my point about how to develop inner-city leaders, the TV report caught my lunch companion's attention. Then it hit me like the proverbial ton of bricks. The company that made the highest contribution to obtain the koala just happened to be represented across from me, elbow deep in a pile of crawfish.

His face, once open with enthusiasm and interest, turned dark and troubled. He got an eerie, distant, hollow look in his eyes, like a person remembering a dark thought from the past that never, ever goes away. He drew in his breath slowly as if anticipating imminent doom. Then he uttered, deep and guttural, slow and measured, "Damn Leo!"

So there you can now see what might happen to you when you enter the world of potential institutional partners. You have to remember that their world does not revolve around your world. They oftentimes will be under other pressures and influences that affect how they relate to you. You have to be keenly aware of your potential partner's particular situation.

As a consensus organizer, you have to be keenly aware of your potential partner's situation.

Potential organizational partners are not dealing with you from inside some kind of isolation chamber.

Eventually, Leo came outside. He climbed his tree. He ate his leaves. The city celebrated. The koala funding sources could finally move on and consider new relationships. I was one of the thousands who made the pilgrimage to see Leo. I thought he was great. I thought the investment was worth it. I was proud of him. In fact, I swear he looked me right in the eye and winked. It was a magic New Orleans moment. Leo and I and fellow New Orleanians: Yeah, you right! It may seem a little daunting for you to see yourself as an organizational partner. If so, just block out the big picture and imagine meetings with one person inside a large organization. That's all you do at first, then it starts to build and build. Just like it says on your shampoo bottle, lather, rinse, repeat. Lather, rinse, repeat. Do not work in isolation.

Find the institution that can help and start your work as though you were opening up that shampoo bottle. You can do it.

There is not a lot you can do all by yourself. You will need some partners along the way. Some of the help you need will be provided by bureaucrats, some of the help from nonprofits, and some of the help from philanthropists. Getting them to see value in you will have them see value in the people you are trying to help. All it takes is some clear thinking and determination to prove that what they want is what you want as well.

Reflection Questions

1. Can a good lobbying effort build an institutional relationship? Why or why not?

2. How can you tell whom to talk with to try to build an institutional relationship?

3. Why is it traditional in New Orleans to eat red beans and rice on Monday?

4. What makes a partner want to remain your partner?

5. Which type of institution would be harder for you to work with—government or business? Why?

REFERENCES

Kretzmann, J., & McNight, J. (1993). *Building communities from the inside out.* Chicago: ACTA Publications.

Schorr, L. B. (1997). *Common purpose.* New York: Random House.

11

DEVELOPING YOUNG ORGANIZERS

In this chapter, you will learn:

◆ How to transfer trust.

◆ Innovation and practicality in program design.

◆ The importance of protective influences.

◆ Incorporating consensus organizing into young lives.

As the consensus organizing model began to take shape and started to attract more national interest, I realized it was necessary to train more consensus organizers. Without more practitioners, the method would gradually fade into the sunset and be slowly forgotten over time. Like most new ideas, it makes sense to test it with young people, so they can take the original idea and hone it, shape it, refine it, and expand it, adding their own insights and applications in an ever-changing world. I felt that consensus organizing would become a more marketable skill over time and that young people could use the skill to help others throughout their lifetimes.

As interest in consensus organizing grew, I began to encounter all kinds of demands on my time. I was even invited back to Belfast, Northern Ireland. Every opportunity seemed too good to let go. I was invited to speak to foundation, social science, and government audiences. Most of these audiences were involved in special events or conferences. Often these gatherings had themes. This role began to suck a lot of time away from doing actual organizing. I started to see how other professionals in the field of community building only gave speeches and never seemed to do anything else. No one seemed to take notice of the time drain. I recognized it was getting out of hand when the discussions at these events got more and more lofty. It was not a good sign to see 3-day conferences structured around themes such as, "Paradigms for Change." I used to wonder what the kids I grew up with would think when they heard the word *paradigm*. They would probably think it was three words and it amounted to 20 cents.

The last straw for me was when I was asked to join an effort led by a coalition of national foundations, entitled, "Reengaging Democracy." I initially agreed to participate on a panel. After agreeing, I got a flyer in the mail from a candidate in a local election. I realized I had committed to attend the conference out of town on the day of my city's primary election. Now, I love local politics, and I did not want to miss the excitement. I called the conference sponsor to apologize and to cancel. Instead, I wanted to meet one of my obligations as a citizen in a democracy. When I begged off, the conference sponsor pleaded, "Can't you get out of it?" The irony was that the conference organizers were more interested in talking about the problem than they were in actually doing something about it. Even worse, my desire to actually do something was getting in the way of their discussion. I was messing up their effort. I started to see that if I did not take care, the real work of consensus organizing would never get done. Instead, it would just become a debating point and a footnote in the history of community organizing.

I felt the model needed to be practiced and taught. I was particularly interested in the second part. The practitioners of other organizing methods teach through their own training centers. Independent of other partners, they train those interested in their particular organizing method. Since consensus organizing looks for partners with mutual self-interest, I wanted to make sure to develop partners who were already obligated to teach. Colleges and universities were potential partners. After all, the place to teach and train should mirror the model itself. I had long talks with members of the board at the national Consensus Organizing Institute. They were supportive of my desire to teach. I got permission from them to contact universities and to come back with a proposal. I saw that we needed to practice and at the same time we needed to teach.

My visits centered primarily on universities with social work schools. There were two reasons for this. One reason was that I had a professional social work degree. The other reason was that a very interesting battle was going on within social work schools. The history of the profession is a proud one. Its roots of commitment to empowerment and policy reform were impressive. Among the issues the profession has concentrated on have been child labor, landlord/tenant rights, and immigrant services. In the past few years, however, the direction of the profession and preparation for entering it had taken a sharp turn. It seemed that therapy, direct practice, and clinical work had almost completely replaced community organizing, community building, and poverty eradication. The shift had begun quietly, but now people were really starting to notice its impact. There were fewer and fewer students trained to enter nonprofits in low-income neighborhoods, and more and more students on their way to becoming licensed private practitioners. More students were hanging out shingles, making themselves available to help people with personal problems if they could pay $75 or more an hour. I wanted to see if there was still a part of the social work profession that wanted to see some new models of community intervention. I wanted to see if someone would look at consensus organizing as one of the ways to return the profession closer to its roots. It seemed feasible that there could be some mutual self-interest identified and developed. I was off on a new adventure, an adventure into academia. My friends told me it was a trip I was totally unprepared for, unsuited for, and, perhaps, pathologically attracted to. Well, if they were correct, at least I would be around plenty of therapists. Let's face it; I was ready to find a new paradigm.

After I visited university upon university, I began to see a pattern. In almost every university, people realized that they needed a stronger connection to their low-income communities. Often, the campuses were located on the edges of these communities. They recognized the need to be a resource to these neighborhoods. They were eloquent regarding their responsibilities, and articulate about the resources they possessed. They even had PowerPoint presentations as proof. They had everything except for one link in the chain. They didn't have a clue about how to build productive relationships.

Most university administrators did inventories of their resources. They e-mailed and surveyed students, faculty, and staff. Although resources were discovered within the universities, I doubted that the administrators could be effectively utilized in the community. Most administrators did not have the patience, skill, or tact needed to deal with community residents. Neighborhoods were looked at as sorts of living laboratories. The people were research fodder. The neighborhood residents frequently looked at the university as an untrustworthy, power-hungry monster. They were only valuable to the university as guinea pigs.

There was also a pattern within the schools of social work. The majority of the faculty had clinical backgrounds and thus worried about students even venturing into low-income neighborhoods ("Go only in the daytime in pairs"). In some cases, students were treated almost like patients, constantly asked how they were doing and how they felt. Clinical skills are certainly crucial for social workers; however, an exclusive focus can lead to limited community practice.

Clinical skills are crucial. An exclusive focus, however, can lead to limited community practice.

There was no openness or understanding among the university people to reconnect to the communities they were trying to serve in new and different ways. So I had to do what we do as consensus organizers—look for the exception to the rule. I looked for a social work school and university that had a different set of circumstances, and key people placed in spots that would find the teaching of consensus organizing helpful in achieving what they wanted to achieve. I did not try to convert or sell anyone. I never feel that people should be talked into doing something that they do not see as being valuable to them.

This process of wading into academia was going to be the ultimate test. I felt I would know the right partner when I found it and this partner would feel the same toward me. The danger in this stage of partner searching is that you may begin rationalizing the value of a potentially interested party. You then lower your expectations and find yourself settling for something less than you originally thought was needed. Don't do this! Keep looking. If you do not meet your standards, consider dropping the idea completely. Come up with a different idea. You cannot succeed in consensus organizing with non-motivated partners.

On a visit to San Diego, California, I visited San Diego State University. I met Dr. Anita Harbert, chair of the School of Social Work. Anita is from a small town in West Virginia. West Virginia is where the coal came from that produced the steel in the Mon Valley. She understood what was accomplished there. She got it. She was very articulate about current issues in the profession. She was interested in consensus organizing and intrigued by the impact it could have on the curriculum. She was interested in an effort that would return the students to the roots of social work. She ran me up the flagpole at a special faculty meeting. The faculty was open and receptive. I also benefited from the Southern California concept of "whatever"—a sort of live-and-let-live attitude, an openness to accept other people and new ideas. I then proceeded to peel the bureaucratic onion until I reached the university president. President Steve Weber has a PhD in philosophy. He likes ideas. I believed he was also genuinely interested and intrigued by consensus organizing. That was my feeling from the first time we met. He was smart and engaging. I liked him very much. San Diego State University, through Weber's leadership, had connected with Robert and Sol Price, local philanthropists, who had a major interest and investment in a low-income, predominantly immigrant community called City Heights.

The neighborhood bordered San Diego State University. The Price's had high expectations. Their money was made through the Price Club store warehouses, and they expected tangible results. Weber was taking millions from Price and needed to produce tangible improvements in the City Heights neighborhood. I had finally found the level of self-interest I needed. Was it time to buy some sunglasses and say "Dude," "Totally awesome," and the dreaded "Whatever?"

I liked the profile of the student body. It had a very large percentage of minorities and lots of first-generation college students. It had a very reasonable tuition rate. If I had grown up in San Diego, I would have told my parents I wanted to go to Stanford. Then they would have said, "Fine, how are you going to pay for it?" And I would have enrolled at San Diego State. I think I would have fit in. You can take the trolley and be in Mexico in half an hour. The school drew students from the Pacific Rim countries. I felt that the school was mirroring what the whole country was going to look like within a generation. It felt like the right place.

A building on campus that houses the social work school was developed as a public works project under the Franklin Delano Roosevelt administration. The unemployed, during the depths of the Depression, were hired to build it. The odds of that connection in Southern California were slim because there were few WPA projects in the area. My father voted for Franklin Roosevelt because of the program that built the building where I would now have my new office. I felt on solid ground on the campus. I was able to negotiate my contract and teach, while creating what would be called the Consensus

Organizing Center at San Diego State. The center would create opportunities for students to practice what they learned in the classroom. It sounded like it would be a challenge and it sounded like it would be fun. I guess you would say I was like, totally looking forward to an awesome experience.

So, there I was in the Pacific Time Zone, staring at the weather page in the newspaper. Monday, High 77 degrees, Low 68 degrees, early morning fog followed by sunshine. Tuesday, High 78 degrees, Low 69 degrees, early morning fog followed by sunshine. Wednesday, High 76 degrees, low 67 degrees, early morning fog followed by sunshine. No wonder my new house cost so much. I sat in my kitchen thinking of all the advice my East Coast friends had given me. "Southern California—Are you out of your mind? People have no roots there. Everyone is so shallow and self-centered. You are going to hate it." Nothing like a little encouragement as you start a new job.

I had done a lot of training before and had been a guest lecturer at universities, but now I was about to be seen as an actual professor. I would be teaching actual courses to a large number of students. How could I get them and keep them interested in organizing? Even more basically, how could I get them to understand the concepts of neighborhood and community? So, with all of this apprehension, where could I find some genuine encouragement? Was there someone who could ground me in the task ahead?

A week before I was to start school as a university professor, my new boss invited some faculty over to welcome me. I felt enthusiastic, excited, and cautious, all at the same time. Would I fit in with the faculty? Would they accept me as a peer? I am not what most people would call an "academic type." I do not always seem to be a serious scholar. I do not have a long list of impressive research projects and published journal articles. I liked the faculty I met. We had more in common than I ever expected. They knew it was my first time teaching at a university and that I would be anxious to see how the students would take to me.

One colleague really made me relax when he said that he had been recently putting a complicated social research problem on the chalkboard. When he turned around, he saw one student enthusiastically waving her hand with a huge light bulb smile on her face. He felt proud that he had gotten through to one of his students. He recognized her, and when he called on her she blurted, "Professor, you got chalk all over your ass." Now that got me ready. That was better preparation than all the faculty orientations and training manuals put together.

I went to work and I loved the students. I learned almost immediately that they had little experience in community involvement. Even the concept of community was new to them. Many who grew up in Southern California were actually raised to avoid involvement with others. Some parents discouraged community activity. It could only bring problems, unwanted obligations, and restricted personal freedoms. I had to start with very basic concepts.

Only the poorest immigrant students picked up on community themes. They remembered their experiences in Mexico, Ethiopia, or Vietnam. The Southern California students had not participated in any type of community organizing or community building. Only those students who had been raised in the poorest neighborhoods had any sense of why you even needed to know about these topics. It was a very challenging task, but not an impossible one. I learned where my starting points needed to be and then I started to click. A small number of students became very interested and wanted to participate beyond the classroom. I needed to create learning opportunities for them in San Diego. I needed to begin to flesh out the Consensus Organizing Center.

In the City Heights neighborhood, Price Charities was making its presence felt. This philanthropy had genuine concern for improving the public schools and was not exactly a shy wallflower in pushing its agenda. The Price's chose to concentrate on a feeder pattern in which all students who attend a particular elementary school collectively moved on to a middle school, followed by a high school. They felt if they improved the education of very young kids and followed them with quality opportunities through high school, they would then see positive results. These three schools had all the typical shortcomings of inner-city schools around the country. The Price's chose San Diego State University (SDSU) as its key partner and was spending $2 million a year through SDSU to improve the City Heights neighborhood.

I now needed to analyze whether community organizing could be useful in helping to achieve the goals of both Price Charities and SDSU. I left my President Roosevelt–built office to check out the high school, ironically named Herbert Hoover High School. My first visit to Hoover High School revealed what I expected. The facility looked like what I had expected, and the students did as well. I met with the principal and talked about his goals and about my experience. I told him that to be a resource for him, the center would need help in connecting to his students. I needed to develop a relationship with someone who already had the students' trust and respect. Then that person would transfer the trust and respect to us. In consensus organizing, you look to use existing positive relationships. You don't want to be "pure" and start from scratch in each situation. Our lives are far too short for that. I asked the principal to introduce me to a teacher. I even described the type of teacher I needed to meet. He followed what I was getting at and made the right match.

YOUR TURN

Now, as a little exercise, you tell me whom I would want to meet. What characteristics would I be looking for? Take into consideration how I would tend to be viewed. The high school teachers would expect me to be some hotshot researcher, seeking a grant, trying to get rich. I would be a leech from the university who wanted them to be a pimp, lining up their best students to be on beck and call to be used for my personal benefit. In a situation like this you do not want to talk to a bureaucratic risk-adverse teacher nor do you want to talk to a "Sounds fantastic, get all the students out of my hair" teacher either.

If you answered instead that you wanted a protective skeptic, you answered correctly. I wanted to meet a teacher who did not automatically trust me but someone who was interested in determining whether I could really help the students. It makes sense that a good, dedicated teacher would be protective of his or her students. I greatly respected Mr. Fehrenbacher. He is the type of public school teacher that we all owe a lot to. He is the type that is unrecognized, undervalued, and doesn't even care that he is. He just teaches, inspires, and motivates. God bless him. When he saw that I cared, too, he transferred the hard-earned trust he had built with his students over to me. He made sure we were not skimming or creaming a handful of top students. He wanted to make sure we at the center believed in what we were doing. I could now put the program together and count on our ability to fill a classroom with students from Hoover that would be motivated to take advantage of an opportunity.

Consensus organizing cannot work if you have the sole responsibility to build trust. You must find people who are already trusted who, in turn, learn to trust you.

In consensus organizing, you must find people who are already trusted, who learn to trust you.

You then have the building blocks for a powerful, permanent, and productive relationship. People do not transfer trust easily. Think of all the people who never open their purse or wallet for others. They are hoarding their money. People protect trust even more diligently. You must cherish the transfer of trust. It's your cup of water in the middle of the desert. Without someone stopping to help you, you will have to walk through the desert alone, dragging yourself to the very distant service station. You may well make it in the oppressive heat but even if you do, you will be in terrible shape by the time you arrive. You need other people to help. You have to be capable of asking for it, and you have to lovingly nurture it if you receive it. So, don't be afraid to stick out your thumb, because the car on the highway may be headed in the same direction as you are.

You are not in a boxing match in which one fighter wins and one loses. You are not an ice skater trying for a higher score than your competitors for your performance. Rather, you are aware of your goals and you are looking into the goals of others. You are aware of the various steps needed for the goals to be accomplished. You are ready to piece everything together (see Figure 11.1).

Stick to something you would like to accomplish. Find others who want the same thing. What would everyone need to do to make it happen (roles and specific tasks)? It gets easier if you practice with something you actually care about. Go ahead and give it a try.

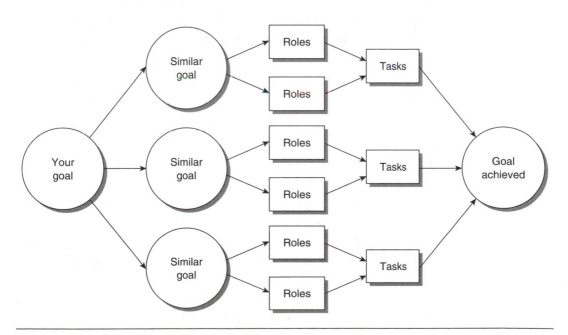

Figure 11.1   Steps Used to Accomplish Goals

So, how about a couple of road trip stories from that part of our country where the sun always shines and the surf is always up? It's the place where half of the classified ads are for cosmetic surgery. It's time for you to go into the actual brains of high school students suffering the effects of endless summer. We are off to the Golden State and America's finest city—San Diego, California.

WE NEED A STRESS CLINIC

Recruiting at Hoover High School was an enlightening experience. Any parent will tell you that connecting with a 16-year-old is quite a challenge. The parents are right. Kids at that age can smell everything coming. They can smell lying, exaggerating, false hope, and ulterior motives. Their sense of smell can rival the feline family. Within the range of a mile, a 16-year-old can smell phonies, liars, and cheats. You must prove yourself first because there is very little benefit of the doubt. Luckily, this should be easy for consensus organizers. We should naturally be thinking of self-interest, and we should be very comfortable with putting our cards face up on the table. We should not be uncomfortable with the truth. So, when members of the Consensus Organizing Center first went to Hoover to recruit, we talked about the potential benefits to the students; but we spent an equal amount of time talking about the benefits to SDSU and the center. I told the students that they were needed because the university had made this big commitment to Price Charities to improve their neighborhood and without their involvement we would fail. This approach is 180 degrees from spouting the general, vague, meaningless platitudes such as "You are the leaders of tomorrow," or "Our future depends on our youth."

So what exactly was our offer? We wanted to teach the Introduction to Social Work class to high school juniors for college and high school credit. We felt that the best way to motivate these kids to want to go to college was to give them the chance to see that they were capable of achieving certain goals. Proving to them that they could pass a real college course, on a real college campus, was the only way. It was a pretty simple program design, right? We had current SDSU social work students interview the high school candidates. We stressed that it would be difficult, and we stressed the commitment it would take. We selected 17 students. They would take the bus to our campus each Tuesday and Thursday at 1:00 p.m. for the entire semester.

All the assignments would match exactly the assignments given to college freshmen and sophomores. Included in the course was a 40-hour community service project. If they passed the class, they would earn three college credits toward their degree. They would become college students at age 16, from the inner city, from a neighborhood where college seemed like an impossible goal. We decided to symbolically entitle the effort the Step Up Program.

On the first day of class, I really did not know what to expect. Waiting with me for the students to arrive were three social work undergraduate majors, who had been trained to help our effort as teaching assistants. They were anxious as well. Would the kids even show up, would the bus be hopelessly late, would they freeze up and realize that it wasn't worth the risk, or would they get lost and just give up? Our classroom clock read 12:59 p.m. We heard noises; they were loud; they were coming down the corridor. The noise we heard was not a disruptive, push-you-into-the-locker type of noise; it was an excited, anticipatory type of noise. As the high school students got to the classroom door, they completely shut up like a second-grade class at a parochial school entering church for Mass. I introduced myself, passed out the syllabus, explained the assignments, and started the class by explaining the history of social work. I talked about settlement houses and the strategies they used to help immigrants. Hands flew up in the air. The students talked about how the social service agencies in San Diego were spread out and the resulting problem of accessibility. They understood the hardships that this created. They talked about professionals not understanding their neighborhood. Not once in the entire 75 minutes, however, did a kid make a comment about feeling like a victim. When an inequity was pointed out, the students were extremely matter-of-fact about it. They discussed proposed solutions quickly and skipped over rhetoric and ideology. I was a happy man.

The students' first lengthy written assignment was due in 6 weeks. Each student was to assume the position of a social worker. Each had to create and design a program intervention in the City Heights neighborhood on an issue of choice. Now this is not an easy assignment even for older college students. They are much more comfortable writing about a program design that someone else has created. They like to repeat and discuss someone else's efforts. We were expecting high school kids from a school in which the vast majority of students never went to college to design and create a program of their own. We were expecting them to succeed. I wanted the bar to be kept high because we had to have them feel that their efforts actually meant something.

The week before the assignment was due, the students were much quieter in class. They knew the pressure was on. All the papers were handed in on time. Almost all the papers were superior to the papers produced by our college students—a few were vastly superior. The biggest differences were in the levels of innovation and in the practicality of the program designs. College students fall into a pattern of writing about programs that disseminate information or expertise from the professional to the client. The professional has "It," and the client needs "It." The Hoover High students instead talked about how the clients were the source of the solution and that partnerships needed to be formed with professionals to achieve real results. They understood roles. They knew the importance of the real political and social circumstances that existed. They understood context. To be able to do such things, you need advanced analytical thinking skills.

One student, Jessica, wrote about her plan to create a stress clinic at the high school. At first glance, the idea seemed a bit mundane. But what she wrote in her paper made me very surprised. She said most of her fellow students had a desperate need for sex education. She said that the school was located in a very conservative city with an extremely conservative school board. Any officially approved sex education program would always be watered down, generalized, be inoffensive and ineffective. She wrote that activists and advocacy groups pushing for sex education would always be ineffective. They would be more interested in the justification of their cause than in getting a curriculum approved.

So, in this context, Jessica proposed a very low-tech intervention in an unused classroom at the high school. Counseling, public health, and social work students from San Diego State would staff the intervention. The effort would be labeled as a stress clinic. Isn't everyone willing to support an effort to reduce stress? She felt that conservatives and liberals would agree. If one of the causes of stress occasionally touched on a sexual issue, well, Jessica said, it would just be naturally addressed.

Imagine reading that from an inner-city 16-year-old from a school that was seen as failing. Do you think we all need a young person like her to work for a school district, local government, or nonprofit? Does she need to see that her skills are valued? If she were the only student in the neighborhood with this kind of ability, it would still be noteworthy. It proved not to be an isolated talent. Again and again, throughout the semester, these kids came down that corridor and continued to advance. Their fieldwork (40 hours of community service) was equally outstanding. I had them analyze the efforts that were beginning to be made to improve their neighborhood elementary school. Kids at this school would eventually become Hoover High School students. Again, they saw through all the rhetoric and very accurately analyzed which improvement efforts were effective and which were not. Our students felt that the school's strategy to involve parents was ineffective. They felt there was too much pressure and guilt put onto parents. (If you care about the education of your children, come to a meeting tomorrow at noon, etc.) Instead, the students suggested inviting the parents to do "fun things." This would make going to school an enjoyable experience that entire families would like to repeat. For instance, for immigrant families, the students suggested holding "ethnic nights," in which parents and students would talk about their native countries, share pictures, play music, eat the foods of native cultures, and reminisce. The idea was to show the parents that the school was celebrating their pasts, not blaming them for them.

I felt that this talent had to be harnessed. These students had to go to college. We could not allow them to end up working in a fast food restaurant, hotel, or tourist attraction their entire lives. As a city, a state, a country, we needed them to do more. It was in our mutual self-interest.

At the end of the semester, all 17 students passed the course; there were even a few A's. This was a monumental achievement for students whose families, high school, and neighborhood had no expectation of them ever attending college and succeeding. These students were expected to end up in dead-end, menial jobs at less than a living wage. Now, they had proven to themselves that they were capable of succeeding in college and were on their way to a professional career. We had a small celebration picnic at a neighborhood park. Some of the students brought their younger brothers and sisters and parents. A new self-fulfilling prophecy was beginning to be created. For the first time, younger kids saw someone just like them changing their lives in a positive way. They could imagine following in the footsteps of their brothers and sisters who destroyed negative inner-city stereotypes and had now begun to create new futures.

When these students reached their senior year of high school, we, at the center, got slapped in the face by certain realities. Despite their successes, they could still fall through the cracks. Some had no money so they felt they couldn't go to college. They had heard that financial aid was available, but they assumed it was not available for them. Others, despite their success in the program and their communities, still lacked confidence. Our college students worked with them and kept encouraging them, refusing to let them slip away. By May of their senior year, all 17 were accepted into college. This achievement flew in the face of the rest of their graduating class in which 75 percent of the students would not be attending college in the fall. Luckily for San Diego State, eight were coming "home" to us. I saw them on campus, mixed in with our other 32,000 students. Their backpacks were full of books and they were smiling. I cannot explain how I will feel at their college graduation. As they continue to learn and mature, I want employers to know how lucky they will be when they are available to have them join their staff. Come to think of it, we were all pretty lucky.

SELF-HELP GROUPS

It is a very nice gift to be able to watch young students grow. The class itself is interesting. We developed a workbook with questions that required students to write and reflect on topics discussed in the previous class. They wrote about discrimination, gay rights, the juvenile justice system, and the causes of poverty. Their papers revealed time and time again how practical and balanced their responses were. Some were surprisingly strict and even traditional. Others were progressive and open. One assignment required them to expand on the methods they would use in juvenile court if they were judges. Some wrote about the importance of intimidation while others stressed fairness and balance.

One of the most interesting assignments pertained to when they were asked to respond to the concept of protective influences. Studies have proven that inner-city youth fare much better in life when they are fortunate enough to find another person, usually an adult, who takes them under their wing and aids in their development. The person can be almost anyone, a family member, member of the church, pastor, or neighbor. The students are asked to describe someone who has been a protective influence for them and whether they have the potential to become a protective influence for someone else. Invariably, students we admitted to class did have a protective influence. For some, it was the very first time they were asked to comment on the person performing this crucial role. Their appreciation poured out with heartfelt emotion in their papers. Just as consistently, they clearly saw themselves returning the help to another person. Many already proudly reported that they had already begun to play that role. This rebuilding and developing of new relationships (social capital) is the glue that is needed to return health to our inner-city communities. This glue is in the "tubes" of these young people. We need to come around and help remove the caps and have this glue applied to other surfaces.

One student wrote about losing a successful, beloved athletic coach to a richer, better-equipped high school. Instead of using it as an excuse that led to a losing, blame-filled season, he spoke instead of his desire to provide leadership as a veteran player and to even provide coaching to the younger players. He felt this was a fitting tribute to his old coach, who had been a protective influence for him. He did not begrudge his coach for moving on. He would, in turn, take more responsibility. Many of these young people understood, wanted, and even craved responsibility. We have to tap this positive desire with real opportunities.

In another class, we explained the concept of self-help groups. This is when a person with a particular problem rounds up others with similar problems and everyone tries to help one another out. The feeling is that those suffering from a problem can be very helpful to others even though they may lack professional credentials. This model is used successfully in organizations such as Alcoholics Anonymous, Gamblers Anonymous, and many others. The students are asked for their opinions about the effectiveness of this approach. They then are asked casually, "Can you see yourself starting a self-help group with others on a common problem you would all want to address?" In our class, we eagerly search the room for a sea of wildly waving hands with excellent suggestions. I saw one hand, at half-mast, weakly held up over a slumping body outfitted with giant pants, a backward-facing baseball cap, and stereo headphones wrapped around his neck. I recognized my star pupil for the semester. He is the kind of kid who is so smart that he tries to cover up his intelligence. He doesn't want anyone to ever suggest he is less than 100 percent cool. So he looks me directly in the eyes, his right eyelid raised a millimeter to reveal a hint of a human eyeball, and into my teacher face, laced with anticipation, he slowly says, "Mas-tur-ba-tion."

Now, you be the teacher. Your first impulse is that this kid has just goofed on you and he is ridiculing you. Your second reaction should be, wait a minute; this kid proved he was listening. He had to be listening to come up with this answer. Didn't it fit the definition of a problem that many suffer from, and each could help the other? Come on, admit it, it fits. Some of you may choose to ignore both potential reactions and instead laugh like you heard this in a bar or bowling alley. You might respond as if you were watching yet another rerun of the movie, *Animal House*.

The other students, of course, are now watching the teacher, like a cat watching a slow-moving mouse. I decided to look him right back in the eye, and in the most authoritarian voice I could come up with, said, "Some people might not call that a problem." So you see, you are allowed to have fun, too. When consensus organizers work, we still have to enjoy people. Of course, there is a seriousness that can sometimes overwhelm us. But if we do not have fun, I'm afraid we will burn a slow death and our effectiveness will be lost in the fire. Enjoy your work and gain for yourself real enjoyment from those around you. This student was a great student. I had to remember that he was all of that and more. I had to enjoy him for who he was. Fun and enjoyment should be your reward. Without reward we fail.

A couple of weeks later I was at a fund-raiser. Across the room, I saw our university president and his wife. I know that you've been in a similar position before. You know when you will only have a few seconds to talk to someone important. You have time to make one point and you better make it stick. You have time for a small sound bite. If it's good, you are still on the person's computer screen. If you are mundane, or worse, boring, you can see him looking for the delete button. I decided to go over. By now, you might have guessed, I'm going with the masturbation vignette. There was a pause after I finished. Then he followed with a giant heartfelt laugh. His wife was laughing, also. Then he said, "Hey, you could have added that some people look at it as an opportunity." All three of us shared in a genuine laugh. Mission accomplished; the president and his wife knew that we were committed to our work. We had proven it. We still had fun, and we had deepened our support.

To grow the number of practitioners using consensus organizing, it makes sense to start finding candidates in their mid-teens. Many students at this age are some of the most practical thinkers you can find. When they are affected by the same problems every day, they seem to see the issues very clearly. They tend to draw conclusions about possible solutions using practical suggestions. They have a great combination—hope and realism. Incorporating consensus organizing into their lives, we can lead them to become more engaged in their families, their communities, and their futures.

Reflection Questions

1. What do you say to someone who feels that young people are too inexperienced to understand community organizing?

2. How typical is Hoover High School and its students in comparison to the inner-city high schools near you?

3. What was sophisticated about Jessica's stress clinic proposal?

4. What famous baseball player graces the "Wall of Fame" in Hoover's gym?

5. What advantages do youth have over adults in developing effective community improvement efforts?

6. Do you believe "Once a Cardinal, always a Cardinal"?

12

USING CONSENSUS ORGANIZING IN OTHER PROFESSIONS

In this chapter, you will learn:

◆ The concept of social marketing.

◆ The six tendencies of human behavior.

◆ Using consensus organizing to increase effectiveness in many different careers.

There are a very, very small number of you who might like the idea of actually becoming a paid community organizer. A much larger number of you will move on to become teachers, nurses, public health workers, social service administrators, city planners, child protective services workers, counselors, and members of other helping professionals.

This chapter is designed to show you how consensus organizing is a skill that you can use to be even more effective in professions other than organizing. In other words, this chapter should be relevant to all of you.

I am always alert when meeting new people to see if they might think like a consensus organizer. I see people who fit the bill everywhere, from a supermarket manager to a school superintendent. The more I look, the more I find. My good friend, writer Shep Barbash, once came up with a great suggestion. He said one of his friends could introduce me to a guy named Bill Novelli. In a previous life, Bill worked for the Centers for Disease Control, and in another previous life, he started the marketing firm Porter Novelli. He had always been interested in the terrible health effects of tobacco on teenagers and approached his interest from different angles. I could understand why he would want to work for the Centers for Disease Control, but I couldn't understand his interest in marketing. I thought only people interested in selling products were marketers. It turned out that Novelli started a division in his company that did something called social marketing. Instead of selling us a product like soap, he was selling teenagers an idea, namely, "Don't smoke." This idea, social marketing, intrigued me. It was a real pleasure meeting Bill and explaining consensus organizing to him. We had a lot of similar ideas and a very similar outlook on how to create positive change. I learned that marketers have studied human behavior and concluded that we have certain tendencies in our daily lives. We tend to respond positively in very patterned ways. These patterns can be summarized in six easily explainable concepts—six tendencies. If we use these tendencies to influence how we interact with others, we become more effective. If we ignore, or fight against, these tendencies, we will become less effective (see Figure 12.1).

- ◆ Reciprocity
- ◆ Commitment
- ◆ Liking
- ◆ Social Validation
- ◆ Authority
- ◆ Scarcity

Figure 12.1   Six Tendencies That Affect Our Daily Lives

WE ALL HAVE TENDENCIES

The six tendencies are reciprocity, commitment, liking, social validation, authority, and scarcity. Right now they might seem like just words to you; but those who try to convince you to buy something understand these words very well. If you studied how to market effectively, you would have learned how the human mind works and how it causes people to respond when they interact with others. Usually people use this skill to sell products to you and me. McDonald's, Coca-Cola, and Home Depot all use this skill successfully. But if, instead, you were like Bill Novelli, you would use the skill to get teenagers to stop smoking. You wouldn't use it to sell cow meat, sugar water, or septic tanks. Social marketers, like Novelli, use these concepts as their bible. Let's look at each tendency, one at a time.

1. *Reciprocity.* Marketers send us a lot of stuff we never asked for when they want something from us. All of us receive mailing labels, greeting cards, and calendars in the mail. Did you every wonder why in heaven's name so many organizations do this? Have you wondered why they waste their time? They do it because they understand how our brains are "wired." Statistics show that a certain percentage of people respond to requests for contributions to charities by mail. The percentage of contributions doubles if they include something for free. Deep, deep down we feel we "owe" them because they gave us something first, even if it's something we don't want. Think about how profound this is. So all that free stuff, which costs money to produce and send, increases the donations by 100 percent. That huge increase makes the cost of the mailing labels, greeting cards, and calendars well worth it. As humans, we are triggered by the concept of reciprocity—I do something for you, you do something for me. See how different a concept this is from mobilizing crowds and making demands. No marketer uses the tactics of confrontation and they seem to get pretty good results.

2. *Commitment.* This is a very simple idea. We tend to follow through much more after we make a statement that we will. For instance, restaurants that take reservations have a hard time filling all of their tables because of so many "no-shows"—people who have not honored their reservations and never called to cancel. Marketers want commitment. They always advise the restaurant employee who took the reservation to say more than just, "Would you please call if you need to cancel the reservation?" They are told to wait and wait until the patron says, "Yes, I will." Once we make a commitment to do something, we tend to follow through. If someone wants you to make a

commitment, but you don't actually make that commitment ("Yes, I will."), then you will tend not to follow through. Many of us in the nonprofit, helping professions fail to ask for a commitment. We refuse to press for a commitment until we get one. In other words, we stop short of getting a commitment and instead explain we would like a commitment. Why? Because we don't want to seem like we are some pushy salesperson.

3. Liking. People prefer to agree with people they like. They say "yes" much more often to people they like as opposed to people they don't like. How many times have you heard a family member or friend say, "I just had to buy it. The salesperson was so nice"? OK, how about the opposite: "I was all set to buy it, but I changed my mind because I couldn't stand the salesperson." Remember all the old police and detective TV shows that had the good cop who wanted to understand the criminal and the bad cop who wanted to beat him up? They played their roles so the criminal would confess to the good cop. Many lobbyists, advocates, and activists believe that pressure is the key to creating change. This flies in the face of the human tendency to respond much better to people we actually like.

4. Social Validation. Before any of us decide what to do in a given situation, we look around to see what other people have done or are doing in a similar situation. We think that behavior is more appropriate if others are doing it as well. Other people can validate our own behavior. This concept is understood by some elements of our society and misunderstood by others. Novelli and his associates noticed that a great deal of antismoking and antidrug advertising talked about how all the young people out there were participating in these undesirable behaviors. What young people remembered from these advertisements was the fact that many young people were doing it, and therefore they wanted to do it, too. The teenagers reacted to the social validation, not to the message of abstinence. Some ads started to change, based on recommendations of the social marketers. One commercial had a handsome young man with a cigarette walking down the street. The camera showed attractive girls running away from him after seeing the cigarette. Every girl ran. That was a much more effective ad.

Many nonprofits and social change organizations make the mistake of trying to gain support by saying no one else is supporting them! This is a complete violation of the concept of social validation. Instead, we should be creating "bandwagons"—making potential supporters feel they are missing something if they don't join with others. We must make them feel that they don't want to miss out on such a great opportunity. That great opportunity is the opportunity to help us.

5. *Authority.* Lots of helping professionals stress the importance of connecting to the people they are trying to help. They want to build trust and respect. One way we try to increase connectedness is to get other people to feel we are just like them. One method of doing this is to dress and look like the people we are trying to help. The human behavioral tendency to respect authority tells us to do just the opposite.

This is based on the human tendency to believe that those in authority have earned their positions and know what they are doing. One measure of authority is appearance. A doctor who looks like a doctor gains respect. A banker who looks like a banker seems more confident and competent. In some helping professions, we put a lot of emphasis on fitting in and relating to others. We sometimes feel we should look like peers and not professionals. We don't want anyone to think we are "better" than they are.

Maybe it helps to analyze how you feel when you see a mother and father in their forties trying to look and act like their teenage children. They are trying hard to relate to them. If we are being honest, I doubt that this strategy has increased respect for the parents. It may, instead, simply decrease the parents' positions of authority. Even though it is controversial, I always advise community organizers to dress professionally when they enter low-income neighborhoods. Often residents tell me they believed in the organizers and participated more because the organizer showed them respect by dressing and behaving the same way they would with wealthy people. Try to keep an open mind about the human tendency to respect authority and honor it rather than dismiss it. Test your own feelings toward doctors, lawyers, financial advisors, and other professionals. Do you respond well to authority?

6. *Scarcity.* Turn on your TV. Watch how many ads say, "For a limited time only" or "Hurry, sale ends Saturday." Quite a few ads adopt this theme. Why? Because as humans, we are wired to believe that the less there is of something, the more valuable it is. Advertisers and marketers have understood this for decades. Cars have limited edition models. Sandwiches are available for only a few weeks. Even artists sell a limited number of their prints. So what do helping professionals do regarding scarcity? Again, we miss the boat. Some client misses an appointment or comes in extremely late. What do we do? We become available again and again. Someone doesn't follow through on a plan we have both agreed to? Start all over again. On the surface, this availability may seem admirable. Marketers will argue that it doesn't work. They say we will be respected less and ignored more by our availability and understanding. This will happen because we are fighting against the human tendency to value scarcity.

Think of it this way. Suppose, God forbid, you needed brain surgery. You had the names of two surgeons. You call the first one. That surgeon can perform the operation in a month. That surgeon is booked solid with other patients needing the same operation. You call the second surgeon. This surgeon says, "Sure, come in tomorrow and if you can't come in tomorrow, how about the next day? Either morning or afternoon will be fine." Which surgeon is preferable? Most of us would choose the first one. We would assume this surgeon is superior because of his or her scarcity. We do not look at the second surgeon and appreciate the availability and willingness to help. Instead, we worry that surgeon is "too" available.

So there you have a little scenario about what marketers believe about us. How many of these human tendencies did you recognize? How many do you find unpalatable? I try to look at people's actions to see how they match up to these human tendencies. The more they conform, the closer they are to practicing consensus organizing. We have talked a lot about how consensus organizers think and strategize. Let's compare consensus organizers to advocates on a chart of human tendency behavior.

Behavior	Advocate	Consensus Organizer
Reciprocity	You "owe" me	We can help each other
Commitment	You do what we want	Everyone plays a crucial role
Liking	"Pushy," in your face	Nice, polite, understanding
Social Validation	We are special people fighting the good fight	Most of us have a lot in common
Authority	Looks, dresses, like those in the community	Looks professional, acts professionally
Scarcity	We will never give up	If you are not interested, we move on

When you look at others, no matter what their job, you begin to see that some people, in all professions, think like consensus organizers. Some are naturals. They are, in effect, self-taught. Others gravitate to the approach and are easily teachable. Others fight against the idea of practicing consensus organizing. They dispute and resist the six human tendencies. They remain unconvinced and have no desire to consider any new approaches to help others.

Let's take a look at you and your career. I think that the methods of consensus organizing could be very helpful in increasing your effectiveness. Some of you may be or may about to be employees of social service agencies. You are going to have some type of client caseload. If you see a pattern in the issues brought up by the clients, you can put yourself in the position of the only one who may have the interest, desire, and ability to help. You can begin to use consensus organizing methods. You can link the clients by introducing them to each other. You can show them that they are in the same boat. Then, most important, you can look for others who may have their own self-interest in becoming involved. By changing your thought processes, you could increase your job satisfaction and your effectiveness.

If you are interested in a career in criminal justice, just look at the potential to use consensus organizing strategy and tactics. You could view those who are incarcerated as potentially helpful to some employers, school districts, and anticrime efforts instead of prisoners who have been a burden to society and a drain on its resources.

If you are interested in public health, you can see families with health problems in an entirely different light. The family members can now become health care educators, researchers, and policy analysts helping philanthropists, legislators, and health care professionals. Once you start thinking about applying the methods of consensus organizing to your professional goals, you may find helpful tools to put in your toolbox.

I thought you might like to hear about some people who are out in the real world practicing consensus organizing. We are going to focus on three people. One is a women's basketball coach. One works for the Ronald McDonald House. The third works for Catholic Charities. For most of their lives, none of them had ever heard of the term *consensus organizer*. The coach was already practicing it and the other two were extremely quick learners. I met the coach at San Diego State University (SDSU) while in the process of becoming an avid Aztec sports fan and the other two took a class I co-taught with the Reverend John Hughes at the University of San Diego (USD). (The University of San Diego's sports team, the Torreros, play the Aztecs each year. Go Aztecs!) I wrote the coach story and the other two students, Annette Eros and Leif Ozier, wrote theirs in their own words. So let's go out into the San Diego community. Put on your shades and wax your board. Take a look at three people who are, whether they know it or not, consensus organizers.

Coach

In the course of a typical day at the university, I make a routine visit to the social work office to check my mailbox. My mailbox is like your mailbox. Most days I wonder why I bother. On one particular day, however, the trip was definitely worthwhile. Tucked into local ads and announcements was a neatly folded sheet with my name on the outside of it. This letter had been sent to every faculty member in the whole school. I opened it and it read, "Dear Professor Eichler, I would like to invite you to a basketball practice. . . ." Now I happen to like basketball, so it caught my interest. But what followed in that letter captured much more than the interest I had in the sport. It captured the excitement of finding another consensus organizer.

The letter was cleverly crafted. It stated: "You already know that our young women excel off the court. Last year, our players had the highest grade point average of any men's or women's sports team at SDSU. Our team performed the most hours of community service. Now, here is your chance to see how successful we will become this year on the basketball court." It then proceeded to invite me to a practice and meet the coaches and the team. I read the letter to some of my staff and they marveled at the strategy contained in it. First of all, think of what the average university professor would expect of a college basketball player: not interested in academics, looking for easy classes, gift grades, and putting a ball through a hoop. Then think of some of the same university professors and what they would think of a college basketball coach: narrow-minded, anti-intellectual, rule breaker, and interested only in players who could put a ball through a hoop. As unfair as this might seem to some of you, the image is believed by many. The letter tore down all these negative stereotypes in one fell swoop.

So, who was this coach and how did she learn to write a letter like that? I went on the information superhighway. The website said that Barb Smith had attended Ohio State University where, as a tiny 5'5" guard she decided to try out for the basketball team. She was not considered good enough to be offered a scholarship. Against all odds, she was kept on the team and was called a "walk on" (non-scholarship player). She ended up starting and leading the team into the NCAA tournament. For non-sports fans, that's like someone who never wrote anything in their life, sitting down and quickly authoring what becomes a bestseller (I don't know, it just seemed like an appropriate example). She went on to attain her MBA, followed by some very successful stints in assistant coaching jobs. She was then hired to her first head coaching responsibility at SDSU.

I attended my first Lady Aztec game. The team was not the most talented team I had ever witnessed, but it only took 5 minutes to see that they played as a team and they played unbelievably hard. They never quit, never coasted, and never hung their heads. They played very intelligently, constantly supported one another, and listened intently to all of their coaches. On this day, however, the Lady Aztecs came out on the short end of the stick. The team lost by 5 points to a clearly superior group of athletes. The players met at half-court after losing and congratulated one another. It was fascinating to watch. I went to a second game. The team played with the same intense style and lost another close game.

I sent Coach Smith a short note and told her what I was doing at SDSU. She told me to come over to the bench and introduce myself before a game. I remember laughing to myself about the chances I would get that kind of offer from the "win-at-all-costs" type of coaches that populate today's sports scene. I enjoyed meeting her. She was genuine and because of this I liked her very much. I invited her to speak to one of my classes at the conclusion of the season. She graciously accepted. The Lady Aztecs lost more games than they won. The enthusiasm of the coaching staff, however, never waned. You could tell the coaches loved the players and the players loved them. The coaches and the players always gave their maximum effort and always supported one another. It was such a feeling of great joy when they actually won. It was almost as if they had gotten a second piece of cake at a birthday party. Just being on the team and learning from their coaches was like their invitation to the party, very satisfying in and of itself.

At the conclusion of the season, all the fans were invited to a reception for the team. There really was a lot of emotion in the room. All the people there felt they were a part of something very significant. They were proud of one another. Each young woman who was graduating and had played her last game of collegiate ball spoke with grace about the school, the community, and the team. I remember feeling that these women had developed as individuals and had developed into people of integrity. They had been educated. The players gave Barb a giant photograph of Cox Arena (our home court) and she was genuinely touched. She was developing a core of supporters who shared her vision of what a basketball team could become. It was a very different vision than would be seen with most coaches; and she was doing it using the exact same methods that I felt I was teaching my students. She was building something from the ground up.

The coach was early the night she was to speak to my class. She wanted to be prepared. I had her explain in detail her head coaching strategy. She talked about a three-pronged strategy of studying, community service, and winning. She talked about how one would lead to the others if given enough time. She talked about how recruiting centered on the athlete and her family believing in this three-pronged strategy. She believed that studying and learning could never be sacrificed in favor of winning. She was not a pushover. If one young woman missed a class, the whole team would run extra laps around the court. She initially forced all of her players to do community service. After being exposed to it, however, they liked it so much that the seniors just led the other players into participating naturally and voluntarily. Then she really got my attention. She engaged my entire class as strategists to try to further help the team. My students had some great ideas. One African American student said, "In my community, athletic programs take our talented kids and chew them up like dog food. They don't care about them as people; they don't care whether they graduate, or whether they get an education. Civil rights and minority rights groups should support what you are doing." It was great to see this analysis going on. The students were learning from and helping, of all people, a basketball coach.

While this process was going on, another burglar was lurking in the bushes in the middle of the night. Barb had a losing record. The athletic director, her boss, wanted a winning record. Rumors started to swirl. Perhaps her contract would not be renewed. A long article hinting at this appeared in the San Diego daily paper, *The San Diego Union Tribune*. I read the story to my students. The Step Up class was the most fatalistic. "She's toast," one of them blurted. I thought this could be a great chance to practice consensus organizing. I asked members of the class if anyone would support a coach with a losing record. High school kids responded with enthusiastic support for Barb. They pointed out that the players seemed loyal to the coach, respected her, and would want her to stay. Another student pointed out that the parents of the players probably appreciated her emphasis on education. Yet another one said, "Wouldn't professors like her because she tells the players to listen to them?" And finally another said, "All the community groups where the players volunteered would support her." They were definitely learning. They composed letters, they lobbied, and they met with the athletic director. The students were using consensus organizing. Barb Smith received a contract extension.

The following season the team record stayed about the same. Team members loved their coach so deeply that they started to try too hard. They felt that if they didn't win, their coach would be fired. Late in the season, in one last-ditch effort, we went to center court and presented Coach Smith with the first annual "Consensus Organizer of the Year Award." I called Tony Gwynn, the future hall of fame baseball player and head coach of the SDSU men's baseball team. He provided us with a signed number 19 baseball jersey for us to present to her. He said he liked her very much as a person and as a coach. The radio announcer said he never saw so many fans on the court to present an award to a coach. He paid tribute to her as well. A few weeks later she was told her services would no longer be needed at SDSU.

She came over to our house for dinner and she still had that same wonderful spirit. I told her that everyone I had ever brought to a game loved to watch her team play. Fans became attached to the players and cared about them. It felt like a growing family. I told her she was just a little ahead of her time. I could identify with someone who was catching flak for questioning some of the premises of a profession that usually does things only one way. We felt that if there were a buy-in to her vision from the higher-ups at the university, the team would have eventually won more games. A much bigger question was, "What was the true function of a college athletic coach?" Maybe people should open up their minds to a whole new definition of success. Maybe a larger, more exciting following would develop around a new definition.

So, what's the lesson here? Don't ever receive a consensus organizing award, because you will be fired? No, rather, think about the consensus organizers around you and how they need your support. Our society and the media, specifically, give attention predominantly to those who divide. People are drawn to the self-promoters, the controversial, and the divisive. Instead, try to look for the motivators who turn the attention elsewhere. Look for those who shine the light on others, just as Barb did for her players. We reward those who garner attention, status, money, people who talk big, the superficial, the controversial, and the ridiculous. We glorify them. Instead, please look under the surface for those who build support for a different vision. Watch those who deflect the attention elsewhere, actually minimizing the recognition of their skills. Support other consensus organizers and nurture their approach. They are in our police departments, schools, athletic teams, hospitals, businesses, and houses of worship. They should no longer be ahead of their time because now is the time we need them most.

Barb Smith was not out of a coaching job for long. She became an assistant coach at a pretty decent school. You may have heard of it: the University of California, Berkeley. She mailed me her new team's media guide with a nice personal note. In the guide, on her page, it mentioned that Barb had developed great community support while in San Diego. To illustrate the point, it proudly stated that she was the recipient of the Consensus Organizer of the Year Award. After Berkeley, she was given one of the most coveted opportunities in all of women's college basketball. She was hired as assistant head coach at the University of Minnesota, one of the top programs in the nation. Sometime, maybe in your lifetime, she will get another job. She will be hired at a university as the athletic director. Then, the whole athletic department will be implementing her vision—every coach, every sport, male and female. Now that's a school we can all root for.

Annette Eros and Leif Ozier are former students of mine. Here, in their own words, they explain learning about and applying the model of consensus organizing. Try to imagine what it would feel like to be working alongside of them as they reveal their strategies.

TAKING A STEP BACK—ANNETTE EROS

As I started the course in consensus organizing, I was a little cynical about how the course material would apply to me. I work for a rather small nonprofit that benefits families under very specific circumstances. Members of this organization didn't recognize the need for community involvement to instigate significant change. As the class was introduced to case studies during lectures, I would try to imagine how I would approach the situation to create improvement or change. I was surprised and frustrated to keep coming up with an ineffective approach. I felt like I just wasn't getting it. As I learned more, I could understand and appreciate the theories, but still had difficulty when strategizing how to apply them. It became clear that to put the theories into practice, I would need to completely change my way of thinking and consider alternative ways to get things done.

Throughout my career, I have always been involved in a top-down approach to management in which executives would decide what needed to be accomplished, built a competent team, and moved forward with the implementation of new strategies or programs. The process usually began with a meeting in which management or formal authority figures decided what needed to change and how the change should take place. The executives determined what resources were available and who should be involved in the process. I learned that the downfall to this approach is that the grassroots community or the constituents are not involved in the process of determining what is really necessary or what would work best. The course stressed that to effect adaptive change, it is important for the community to become engaged in the issue.

To identify mutual self-interest, it is usually necessary to flip or reframe an issue to determine the focus of the assessment correctly, that is, to look at the problem in a new way. Consensus organizing also requires the mutual self-interest approach to be constructive—to consider possibilities as opposed to focusing on a problem (to look at the positives as well as the negatives). This sounds easier than it really is. To assess a situation or relationship correctly often requires identifying approaches that will create discomfort, be counterintuitive, or require someone to give up power. This is where the consensus organizing model became extremely difficult for me. This approach did not feel natural and required me to allow myself to become vulnerable, but in a proactive sense that is critical to developing leadership competence. The course helped me to recognize how vulnerability can help consensus organizers to develop multiple perspectives toward the challenges we face.

For my practical project during the course, I had to accept that I could not be successful on my own, which is how I usually operate. It was necessary to take a step back to identify the needs, strengths, and, most important, the self-interest of others. Another challenge was accepting that the consensus organizing could take longer than the traditional approach with which I was comfortable. Once the strategy was activated, however, results were achieved quickly.

In identifying a focus for my project, I looked at a key relationship between my organization, the Ronald McDonald House Charities of San Diego (RMHC-SD), and a collaborative partner, the Children's Hospital & Health Center. The key link between the hospital and the house is that both deal with sick children and their families. The hospital focuses on the medical treatment and clinical care to help the patients heal. The house, on the other hand, focuses on improving the quality of life for the families while the children receive medical treatment. This is accomplished by operating the Ronald McDonald House, which serves as a home-away-from-home, located on hospital property. Both entities want families to focus on one thing—the health of the children. Any family with a child being treated at the hospital is under an enormous amount of stress. The house and hospital both deal with the multiple layers of disruption that occur in families when a child is undergoing treatment. It is of mutual interest for the hospital and the house to focus on the needs of the patients and families to reduce the amount of hardship and inconvenience families face during a medical crisis.

There are currently 250 Ronald McDonald Houses worldwide, each with the common mission of providing assistance for families whose children are being treated at local hospitals. San Diego's Ronald McDonald House was built in 1980 on the grounds of Children's Hospital & Health Center. The 12-bedroom facility has provided more than 100,000 nights of lodging to more than 10,000 families from San Diego and Imperial counties and to families from other states and countries who come to San Diego for access to some of the best pediatric medical services available.

The existing 9,000-square-foot house has served its purpose well. A number of factors, however, point to the urgent need for a larger Ronald McDonald House. The existing facility is woefully inadequate relative to the demands of families in need of its services. In fact, on average, 20 families are turned away every week, more than 1,000 annually, due to the house's limited capacity.

The RMHC-SD board of trustees considers a new Ronald McDonald House to be a critical and immediate need. The property on which the house is currently located is owned by Children's Hospital and does not provide the opportunity to create additional space for special services or to build the additional bedrooms that are needed. Building a new Ronald McDonald House would create the opportunity to better serve the families and the needs of Children's Hospital and other nearby medical facilities.

Since identifying the need for a new house more than 5 years ago, the RMHC-SD has faced numerous challenges, the biggest being the identification of land within walking distance of Children's Hospital upon which to build the new facility. The ideal location would be part of the Children's Hospital campus; however, the hospital had been in the midst of a crisis and all plans for expansion were put on hold. This disruption caused a breakdown in communications between the two agencies and, despite numerous attempts, RMHC-SD could not get answers from the hospital about its plans for the future. Staff changes at the hospital also resulted in deteriorating relations.

I began my project by interviewing representatives from each organization to help identify mutual self-interests. As I was interviewing a McDonald's owner/operator and a Ronald McDonald House board member, a light bulb went on in my head. We were discussing the possibility of opening a Ronald McDonald Family Room within Children's Hospital. The family room program is a new concept from the global RMHC charity that has taken off in recent years. Family rooms enable local chapters to extend the comfort and support of the Ronald McDonald House into hospital settings by providing a place that offers a comfortable and supportive environment in which families can relax and take a break. Family rooms must have a homelike feel and include general living space, kitchen/dining areas, and bathrooms with showers and/or baths. I was aware of the popular program but always put off the idea of opening a family room in the Children's Hospital because I believed the need for a new Ronald McDonald House was much more urgent. I finally realized, however, that a family room might provide a stepping-stone to getting a new house built as soon as possible.

A common problem in meeting the needs of patients and families is the result of a lack of space at both the house and the hospital. A family room intervention would allow each collaborator help the other enhance services. The hospital currently has a parent center in the facility, which provides a respite for families. The center is centrally located, has a small kitchen, vending machines, bathrooms and showers, a playroom, a quiet room, a TV room, and a few dining tables. The space, however, is uninviting, underutilized, laid out inefficiently, and has a clinical feel, much like the rest of the hospital. Converting the existing parent center into a Ronald McDonald Family Room would enhance services to patients and their families and improve the quality of care offered by both entities. A successful conversion of the space and subsequent operation of the facility would present an opportunity for a mutual response to a mutual need and require resources from both entities. The project would also create an opportunity for both entities to share power and responsibility for the program while ultimately enhancing the relationship on numerous levels. This intervention would enable the hospital and the house to better meet the needs of their clients while providing opportunities for growth and positive visibility and relationship-building opportunities at many levels.

The strength of this strategy is that it builds on the assets of each stakeholder. For the hospital, it improves the quality of care and enhances the experience of the patient and family members so they can focus on the health and well-being of the child. For the house, it extends services to more patients and families and builds on the success and resources of the current program. For the patients and families, it offers a convenient resource that allows them to focus on the strength of their loved ones and support groups by reducing other responsibilities and worries. The strategy presents a capacity-building opportunity that can only become reality as a result of the house and hospital working together.

The execution of the strategy began by building a committee of parents with children who had been treated at the hospital. This committee would help us determine what the needs of the community were and how to meet those needs within the family room facility and through developing activities. The committee would also form a bridge between the house and the hospital to help in communications and building momentum toward the goal of opening a family room.

This strategy, which was based on consensus organizing theories, played out well in real life. I initially approached parent liaisons (parents who worked

to help involve other parents) and staff members at the hospital, to help identify parents that would support the family room concept and serve on the
planning committee. As the parent liaisons and staff members of the hospital
helped to form that committee, they also helped me to set up an appointment
with the director of the hospital's hematology/oncology department to discuss the family room idea. She became excited about the project and then
invited the senior managing director of facilities plant operations and planning at the hospital to a meeting with me. This was the person I needed to see
to make things happen and somebody I had never met. We started discussing
the possibility of converting the parent center into a family room and the
facilities manager's response was that it was a "no brainer." During the course
of the conversation, we also began discussing the overall goals of the RMHC-
SD to expand services by building a new Ronald McDonald House. The facility manager began discussing the opportunity to build a new house on top of
a parking structure, an immediate project of the hospital. His predecessor had
ruled out this option before, but none of us could determine why that would
be. So, I left that meeting excited about the new relationship with a supportive go-to person at the hospital and with two major goals accomplished—
preliminary support for the concept of converting the parent center into a
family room and, more important, the opportunity to build a new house on
Children's Hospital property in the immediate future.

   This consensus organizing exercise is proving to be successful because its
execution is based on the following general strategies:

1. Identifying mutual self-interests that exist between two (or more)
   organizations.

2. Creating and communicating conditions in which members of organizations recognize the need for enhanced partnerships.

3. Realizing success as a result of helping one another.

4. Beginning with small successes to demonstrate the visible value of
   expanded partnership efforts.

5. Starting with bonding relationships of those immediately affected
   and later building bridges to additional positive relationships.

6. Identifying a problem that can only be fixed by working together.

   To ensure buy-in when presenting the family room idea to key stakeholders, I strategically incorporated the six human behavior tendencies I learned

about in class, so the project would appeal to everyone. I talked about the relationship between RMHC-SD and the hospital, framed the issue in a positive light, and presented the issue in a way that everyone could agree upon—to provide a healing environment. Reactions to the intervention strategy were immediate and positive. First, the discussion was a conversation communicating initial buy-in, and then, as the discussion continued, it became more of a brainstorm for continued expansion. I knew that everyone got it when one person present commented, "Wow, we never really looked at the hospital before. By focusing on the hospital, we figured out what can help us." This told me he appreciated the process, approach, and the potential outcome of the consensus organizing method. The family room opened and it has helped the hospital, the families, and the Ronald McDonald House.

Lessons Learned

- I experienced more success by putting a positive spin on what had been perceived as a negative situation regarding the deteriorating relationship with the hospital.
- Stakeholders felt energized, empowered, and effective. The approach allowed all participants to take ownership of the program as they became a part of the process and were ready and excited to move forward.
- Stakeholders saw the value in asking what people needed as opposed to assuming what they needed.
- Stakeholders appreciated the effort that went into the information-gathering process and were impressed (and perhaps a little surprised) by the number of people who wanted to be directly involved in the project.
- The more I interviewed people, the more a solution became clearer and the goals more realistic.
- There was a definite shift in perceived power within RMHC-SD, which will most likely extend as we at the house reach out more to the hospital. The solution requires shared responsibility and power, which represents a shift in power. The process will definitely change the way people at the two institutions relate.
- I now see the value in consensus organizing. At first it felt counterintuitive. The process of reframing helped me to see it differently and value other aspects of the organizing model.

- By going back and forth to the various stakeholders throughout the process, I was able to keep the process on track and it helped me to figure out directions for conducting interviews and refining my thoughts. I was able to take all the steps to gather the appropriate elements to increase the odds for success.

A SUMMER OF CONSENSUS ORGANIZING—LEIF OZIER

The social change course I took in the summer of 2004 at the University of San Diego, taught by Michael Eichler and the Reverend John Hughes, had a powerful and everlasting effect on my life. During that summer, I was introduced to the techniques of consensus organizing and the term *social capital*. Knowledge of these two concepts would change my life forever, especially my understanding of social capital and the value of it. Before that summer, I had never heard of social capital and had no idea how important it was, even though it affected every aspect of my life.

That summer was a typical, very beautiful summer in San Diego—one of those stereotypical Southern California summers you hear about in songs, see in movies, or read about in travel magazines. The last thing I wanted to do was spend more time in a classroom learning about something that I already knew about (or rather, thought I already knew about). Little did I know, it would be an educational summer I would never forget.

When I read the course description and went over the class syllabus, I thought I already knew what the course would be like and what I would be studying. At that point, I had absolutely no desire to reexamine social service delivery models; especially within the organization I worked for, Catholic Charities, Diocese of San Diego. I also had no idea that the course would change my view of education, politics, and life in general; it reshaped my private and professional worlds. I had no idea that I would repeat the term *social capital* hundreds of times at home, at work, at meetings, and even at parties. I have never learned so much from one summer course.

The course provided me with tools that enable me to recognize and fully understand how important and *very* powerful social capital is. It is not only a key component and crucial in consensus organizing, but it is also an essential element in understanding how to create effective community projects and initiate social change—especially in the nonprofit sector, where resources are very limited. My assigned classroom partner and I used the principles of consensus organizing to develop Cathedral Plaza Kitchen

(CPK), a project that would address the problem of homelessness in downtown San Diego.

Focusing on the principles of consensus organizing, my partner and I were able to identify potential partners that could develop relationships based on mutual self-interest. We then used these self-interests to strengthen current relationships and bring other disparate groups into the plan. Once all of the stakeholders were clearly identified, we brought them together to address a problem, and we employed relationship-building strategies and techniques to strengthen new developing relationships and build bridges to a broader constituency. This strengthening of the relationships created what Michael Eichler called social capital. Consensus organizing is a process and not an activity, which is something my partner and I had to learn—and it didn't always come easily. Learning the value of social capital and its importance to consensus organizing was itself a process.

My partner and I began the process by meeting to discuss an organizational issue, opportunity, or inconsistency at Catholic Charities. This was not an easy step because as we understood the assignment, we needed to address an issue, opportunity, or inconsistency that had the potential of building bridges between a variety of potential participants. We knew Catholic Charities had eight departments and many service locations that served various and very different populations. We briefly researched the different departments by looking at their current client statistics (such as total number of clients served), the types of services offered to clients, and the geographical locations of service sites. We then brainstormed on what types of issues, opportunities, and inconsistencies might be present. We examined a number of issues to select one. We wanted an issue that resonated to a high degree among Catholic Charities and the local community.

After comparing the different departments, options, and possibilities, we zeroed in on the Homeless Women Services (HWS) department. We chose to examine the HWS department because of its client base (homeless women), the location of HWS service sites (mostly in downtown San Diego), varying attitudes in the community regarding homelessness, and the urgency of the homeless problem. Almost all service locations and programs for HWS are located in downtown San Diego. This includes a day center, an emergency/short-term shelter, transitional housing, and sober-living apartments. All of these facilities are within a few blocks of the newly built Petco Park (the home of the San Diego Padres), and there is a significant homeless population in the area. There have been many formal and informal conversations at Catholic Charities about the location of Petco Park in downtown San Diego and the impact it is having on the local homeless community. Thus, we thought this would be a good place to start our search to identify an organizational issue, opportunity, or inconsistency at Catholic Charities.

The most recent conversation regarding Petco Park's impact on the local homeless population occurred at a Catholic Charities Health and Wellness Committee meeting. The committee, which consists of staff from each of Catholic Charities' eight departments, was discussing the possibility of organizing an agency event at the new park, when objections arose from HWS department representatives. Members of that department were unhappy with the park's impact on the homeless in the area. This provided us a good opportunity to probe Catholic Charities for issues, opportunities, and inconsistencies involving Petco Park and the local homeless population. It allowed us to examine which issues resonated the most among staff and ask many questions about the new ballpark, its location, staff interest in attending games at the park, the number of homeless around the park, the number of clients utilizing HWS facilities near the ballpark, client attitudes toward the ballpark, HWS department staff attitudes toward the park, types of services offered by HWS near the park, and the types of additional services needed.

The collection of these data helped us to identify many organizational issues, opportunities, and inconsistencies at Catholic Charities; now we had to select one to focus on. We looked for an issue, opportunity, or inconsistency that had the potential to build bridges between a mix of participants and not just one to the homeless population in the downtown area. Because we identified multiple issues, we had to examine all of them to find one that resonated more than the others. After a careful review of the data, we decided to focus on whether or not the placement of Petco Park in the downtown area was positive or negative for Catholic Charities. We had a lot more work to do!

After input and redirection from our instructors, we conducted an assessment that helped us to clearly define the issue. We began our assessment by evaluating the social capital of the potential partners. The roles and self-interests greatly varied among the potential partners and each would need to play important roles in any successful initiative. Petco Park (the San Diego Padres) and the Centre City Development Corporation (CCDC) were key players and would loom large because they had built the park and they held most of the monetary resources. Their two main self-interests were future profits and maintaining a positive image of the downtown area. The strength of their relationship became very clear to us at a regular meeting of the Centre City Development Corporation. The CCDC presented the San Diego Padres owner,

John Moores, with the CCDC Directors Award. Representatives of CCDC spoke about all the wonderful things he was doing in the community and thanked him for agreeing to build Petco Park in the downtown area. He, in turn, thanked the CCDC for helping him to build the new ballpark and asked for the group's continued support on future projects in the area. This was a very interesting meeting because, after the presentation, the first comment from the audience was from a resident. She made her way to the microphone and started by saying, "I'm glad I made it to *this* meeting because I've got a lot to say. I think we need a new stadium like we need a hole in our heads. How can we build a new stadium when there are people sleeping on the streets? Is baseball more important than people?" This clearly showed the disconnection between the Padres, the CCDC, the homeless, and some of the local residents.

The homeless men and women of San Diego, also stakeholders, could be viewed somewhat like pawns in a chess game, meaning that they may not have much voice in area decisions, but their moves were no less important than any of the other players. They generated the homeless issue and all the players were watching their moves. Their self-interests were the quality of services (direct and indirect), the amount of services available (food, shelter, clothing, etc.), and the future of service providers in the surrounding area. Some of the comments collected from the homeless included, "In San Diego, people only listen to you if you have money, and isn't it time for the homeless people to stand up for themselves?" The homeless population and those who advocate for them have serious concerns regarding Petco Park and feel as if they are not being heard. The homeless depend on their relationship with social service providers (including Catholic Charities), residents, and even some local businesses.

Small businesses could also play important roles. Like Petco Park and the San Diego Padres, they brought valued resources to the table such as money (tax dollars), current and future site locations, customers, influential partnerships, and networking (making valuable contacts); but not all the businesses welcomed the new park. One business owner that we interviewed had operated out of downtown since he had founded the business in 1958 and the operation was seen as a downtown institution. Unfortunately, this business owner did not own the building (on 7th street, half a block from Petco Park). In 2003, the building was sold and the building was turned into a parking lot to serve Petco Park. Another business owner that we interviewed had operated in downtown San Diego since 1978. That business is now in the process of relocating due to what its owner called *adverse conditions*, such as increased traffic that makes it difficult for clients to access the office, increased parking rates, and a substantial increase in the monthly rent. Both of these businesses had lived side by side with the homeless population for years and considered the homeless population a better neighbor than Petco Park. Leslie Wade, a spokeswoman for the business-oriented East Village Association, stated that the reason there were so many homeless people in the downtown area was that it was one of the only places where services had been allowed. She added that more services were needed for the many different types of people who are homeless in locations throughout the San Diego region. The self-interests of the East Village Association, which borders downtown, included increased revenues, maintaining a positive area image, creating and maintaining a healthy economy, and new networking opportunities. Our research indicated that the area's business operators' attitudes were divided. Some welcomed the new ballpark and others saw it as a bad neighbor.

San Diego social service providers also played and would continue to play an important role. The roles and self-interests of this group were determined by an evaluation of Catholic Charities' self-interests. Like Catholic Charities, they brought valued resources such as a sense of duty, a sense of community, a support network, multiple services, and public attention to the table.

The roles of the residents of the area would largely depend on their self-interests. Self-interests included property values, and factions that were pro-development, antidevelopment, pro- and antibusiness, and so on.

The assessment helped us to address key questions raised during the issue identification process. We now knew why some potential partners did not acknowledge the issue, why some wanted to steer us away from the issue, and why others considered it too controversial to discuss. There was a huge disconnect between them, so we had to start a conversation about homelessness and developing a community response. We wanted to increase social capital.

We shifted our focus to increasing social capital among Catholic Charities, the local community, and other potential partners. The placement of Petco Park near agency facilities in the downtown area created a unique partnership opportunity for Catholic Charities with the potential of building bridges to a broader constituency. The data indicated that a successful strategy to employ would be one that adjusted the perception of power in the community. During the intervention phase of this action plan, we designed and recommended interventions that built stronger relationships (increased social capital), encouraged shared decision making (power), and created a positive image of the area and all potential partners (mutual self-interest).

A crucial part of the process was to frame the issue in a way that all potential partners saw how a solution would serve their self-interests. So before we could frame the issue, we needed to identify, analyze, and evaluate internal and external self-interests and resources of the potential partners. Identifying mutual self-interests among the community resources was a challenge because the potential partners were very different. They consisted of those who were directly or indirectly affected by the placement of Petco Park, such as the Padres, the homeless, local businesses, social service providers, and residents (owners and renters). These many groups made up a very diverse community with varying self-interests. After a careful analysis of each potential partner, we came up with the following mutual self-interests of the ballpark community: an increase in public safety, an increase in the quality of life, an improvement in the overall image of the area, and an increase in residential demand. Our hope was that all the potential partners would view these as benefits.

The Padres would view an increase in public safety, an increase in the quality of life, an improvement in the overall image of the area, and an increase in residential demand as benefits because they would directly affect ticket sales. People would feel more comfortable and attend more games if they felt safer and lived closer to the ballpark. This, in turn, would increase the Padres' profits and their image as a good neighbor. People throughout San Diego would begin to appreciate the placement of Petco Park instead of questioning it, which would lead to growth in the team's fan base.

The homeless in downtown would benefit from increased public safety and quality of life in the area by focusing the public's attention on the homeless issue. This increased focus might lead to long-term homeless concerns being addressed and an increase in the homeless population's three basic needs of food, shelter, and clothing for survival. If the intervention plan was successful, the homeless community might be viewed as more of an asset, which would create momentum toward positive change. A successful intervention plan *had* to include their presence.

Local businesses would benefit from an increase in public safety, an increase in the quality of life, an improvement in the overall image of the area, and an increase in residential demand because it would increase the number of potential customers and clients in the area. Similar to the Padres, such an intervention would increase their profits and their image as good neighbors.

Local social service providers (including Catholic Charities) would also benefit from an increase in public safety, an increase in the quality of life, an improvement in the overall image of the area, and an increase in residential demand. They would be able to increase their pool of local volunteers, help a needy target population, and advertise their success in addressing the issue. Their success in addressing a difficult issue like the homeless situation in their local or service areas could ultimately lead to an increase in funding (awards, donations, grants, and other income). An increase in funding would give them financial capability to support their programs, expand their services, and reach more clients.

Residents who owned their homes or condominiums in the area (owners) would benefit greatly from an increase in public safety, an increase in the quality of life, an improvement in the overall image of the area, and an increase in residential demand. They would not only feel safer in their homes, safer at local schools, and have more access to local businesses, but they would also see an increase in their property values. Residents who rented their homes or apartments in the area (renters) would also see some benefits. They too would feel safer in their homes, safer in local schools, and have access to more local businesses.

It was also very important that the mutual self-interests we identified for our internal community resources also worked for external community resources.

After we completed identifying the mutual self-interests of the potential partners (internal and external), we evaluated the available resources. The potential partners that existed in the ballpark area provided many different types of assets to the local community. These various assets were valuable resources that needed to be utilized. They included but were not limited to financial support, diversified funding, political authority, decision-making power, political relationships, business relationships, general community support, a larger fan/client base, a diversified fan/client base, and jobs.

The San Diego Padres (Petco Park) brought many assets to the community. The franchise provided financial support through tax revenues, generous donations, and political and business relationships. The team had a large and diverse fan base, which included the gathering of approximately 41,000 fans on a game night, an excellent physical presence and location in the community, some media coverage and influence, and many other networking contacts.

Although not obvious to all the potential partners, the homeless could also be viewed as a group with assets. These assets included diversified funding from sources that addressed the homeless issue, some community support from advocates, their availability as immediate laborers or trainees, their physical presence in the area (they were there in San Diego neighborhoods and must live somewhere), and their ability to attract media attention.

Local businesses supplied the community with financial support (tax revenues), a political voice, and some decision-making power from business owners who were active in the community. They also generated general community support from members that used their services or products, labor opportunities (employees, staff, etc.), and networking capabilities through chambers of commerce and other associations.

Local social service providers provided the community and its members with many diverse assets. These assets ranged from financial support through grants, awards, and scholarships to political authority based on business, religious, and casual relationships. The fact that most social service providers were funded through diversified funding sources with different agendas and guidelines made collaboration among them a must. No single social service provider could address the needs of the entire community. Some had political authority and decision-making power but not general support from the local community. Some had a large fan or client base but lacked the necessary business relationships. Social service agencies also provided jobs, many diverse services, media influences, and networking capabilities.

Community residents (both owners and renters) provided very valuable assets. In terms of diversity, they supplied the most assets. They provided financial support to the community through taxes (property, sales, schools, homeowner associations, donations, etc.). They were a political force, with decision-making power, nurtured political relationships (the power of the vote), established business relationships, and could gather community support for or against an issue. Business owners that lived in the community had a large client base, a good location, supplied jobs (paid or volunteers), showed a dominant presence at community events, provided diverse services to other community members, and numerous networking connections.

We framed the issue so that potential partners viewed an intervention as benefiting each of them. Our proposed community action plan had to encompass the development of a community-based response to the homeless situation—a situation *magnified* by the placement of Petco Park and a solution that focused on relationship building among the potential partners.

An internal and external analysis of the neighborhood helped us to see that there was a strong need to develop a productive relationship between the homeless and the community. It seemed as if the disconnect among the potential partners was caused by different groups within the community responding to the homeless situation in different ways, based on their own self-interests. Once again, the lack of social capital was a major factor. Based on the mutual self-interests, available community resources, and how the issue was framed, we wanted to develop a community-based response to homelessness that had the possibility of starting change within the community. We started the intervention process by looking at the six human behavior tendencies as explained to us in class. We knew we wanted to expand on an idea introduced to us by the deputy director of Catholic Charities and incorporate these key tendencies of social marketing (reciprocity, commitment, liking, social validation, authority, and scarcity) during the process.

First, we developed a way to approach potential partners. The approach was designed as a dialogue that would get potential partners' attention by focusing on their self-interests. We focused the dialogue around these initial questions:

1. Wouldn't you like to be part of a community in which the homeless situation was not a problem?

2. Wouldn't you like to be part of a community in which public safety, the quality of life, and the overall image created an overwhelming demand for residential and commercial space?

3. Can you imagine the property values, the profits, the growth, and the quantity of clients/customers generated by such a community?

4. Can you imagine the media attention the community would draw from others in the county, the state, and even the nation!

5. Wouldn't you or your agency (or company) like to be part of such a movement?

Finally, we would tell potential partners, this could now happen in *your* community and that place is San Diego, *your* neighborhood, and we want you to be a part of it! The success of the plan is dependent on maximum community support and participation.

Conversations were conducted and input gathered from all the potential community partners. We would invite them to meet to discuss the mutual self-interests and benefits of addressing the homeless situation in their community. Then we would invite key community partners to share in the development of a project built to highlight the community's response to homelessness. The project, we told them, would attempt to utilize the homeless in creating a solution for their current situation. We expanded on an idea that originated from the deputy director of Catholic Charities. During a meeting, he had mentioned that Catholic Charities recently had acquired a full commercial kitchen that was not being used. The kitchen was equipped with commercial equipment and Catholic Charities had no immediate plans for the kitchen. Based on this information, we envisioned establishing a facility that would offer training services. We then went one step further and thought about all the other unused facilities we might be able to locate and use as training facilities. We fine-tuned a number of options and came up with Cathedral Plaza Kitchen.

This community action plan would take an unutilized kitchen facility and turn it into a revenue-earning culinary training program for homeless, low-income, and recent arrival (immigrants and refugees) women. It would provide them with an opportunity to obtain specialized culinary training from industry experts and then provide job placement services to graduates who successfully completed the training. The 18-month program would cover culinary areas such as basic skills for culinary arts, quality food preparation, sanitation for food service, soup and sauce preparation, catering, baking, and pastry making. Women in need would not only gain practical vocational training and a great educational experience, but would also be provided a chance to become productive, contributing members of our community. It would offer women in need in San Diego the chance to obtain dignity, respect, and hope through education. The ultimate goal was to provide each woman with suitable means to escape the homeless cycle and poverty that many young homeless women before them had faced but were unable to escape. If successful, the outcome would be the development of a community-based response to homelessness, an increase in social capital among the community members, and a solid bridge created between internal and external resources.

As I mentioned earlier, it is important to understand that the process of developing a community-based response to an issue is essential, and in some ways more important than the outcome of the classroom project. Introducing the community to the process of community-based solutions, establishing key partnerships along the way, maintaining these relationships, and constantly nurturing social capital is essential. These elements are what initiate progress and social change.

Consensus organizing is a unique approach to community organizing that can be much more effective than the standard conflict approach to community organizing. Consensus organizing addresses an issue by utilizing already-present community resources and empowering potential community partners. The partners normally buy in because of the focus on building strong relationships based on self-interests, which means the conflicting groups see their involvement as a win-win situation. So, they readily agree to come together to achieve a common goal. New and existing relationships are built and strengthened and become bridges to a broader constituency, which increases social capital.

Being able to recognize and utilize social capital to address an issue becomes a tool and a valuable skill. It is a skill that I do not take lightly, which is why, whenever the opportunity arises, I try to build as much social capital as possible. Social capital is powerful and plays an important role in the local and national nonprofit sector. That summer of learning consensus organizing had a powerful and everlasting effect and it affected every aspect of my life, both personally and professionally. So don't be surprised if I bump into you at a party and the conversation develops into a passionate spill regarding the value of social capital.

YOUR STORY

Well, there you have the stories of three people who used consensus organizing to achieve their goals. I hope their stories begin to show you that you could be writing about how you have applied the method and how you have achieved some success as well. Think about doing something differently. Think of some issue you are struggling with and search for a new opportunity. Begin engaging some new people and building some new relationships. It does not require you to be a genius. The people you have read about are not geniuses. They are hardworking, caring people. Try to look at what you are doing with a fresh set of eyes and remember the work of these three people. You could be next.

Reflection Questions

1. Name two people in your life who practice consensus organizing. What do they do and how do they do it?

2. Can you think of any profession or job where consensus organizing would not work? Why not?

3. Which of the six human behavior tendencies is the toughest for you to accept? Why?

4. Why are many of the youth-directed ad campaigns ineffective at curbing dangerous behavior?

5. Is it a natural human behavior to be lazy?

6. Is it a basic French tendency to like Jerry Lewis and a basic Hawaiian tendency to eat spam?

13

THE FUTURE OF CONSENSUS ORGANIZING

In this chapter, you will learn:

◆ The importance of doing something that "works."

◆ External resources need to have a real participatory role.

◆ The four walls that can prevent you from practicing consensus organizing.

There are many different efforts underway to help those in need throughout the United States. People with noble purpose, dedication, immense effort, and personal resolve initiate most of these efforts; but you need to look at the motivation behind these efforts. Is a particular effort lasting and strategic or more of a flash-in-the-pan emotional reaction to a crisis? You need to look and judge every effort based on actual results, not on purity of purpose.

You need to look at and judge every effort based
on actual results.

Long term, intensive, strategic efforts with real results are not only
needed, they will also be more and more often demanded. If the next generation is not appreciably better off than the previous one (and all economic
indicators say they won't be), we will want much more from our charitable
dollars and much more from our tax dollars. We will be expecting efforts to
be measurably successful.

I have always been a big believer in having others look at what I am
doing, listening to their observations, and then becoming better and more
effective in the future. Avis Vidal and Ross Gittell played the roles of partic-
ipant observers during a 3-year demonstration program utilizing consensus
organizing. Their experiences led to a book, *Community Organizing: Building
Social Capital as a Development Strategy* (1998). The authors attended community meetings, training workshops, and strategy sessions. They talked
about strengths and shortcomings they encountered over the 3 years. This
type of detailed analysis can assist all of us as evidence-based practice
becomes more operationalized.

Throughout my travels, it is not unusual for me to hear, "I'd like to help,
but I feel it would be like throwing money down a rat hole." Rat hole is an
interesting phrase. Such statements, and others with similar themes, follow
a pattern and an ever-popular trend: If you can prove something works, or
give people a real sense of optimism that it will work, they will be glad to
help support it. Plus, if you show people the benefits they will receive in
supporting your effort, you greatly increase the chances that they will see
value in participation. If you instead rely only on altruism (help "out of the
kindness of their heart"), you will find short-term, inadequate support.
Projections about the future show fewer resources available. That's true if we
rely on altruism. It will not be true if we rely on mutual self-interest.

Most of us want to see a lot of effort exerted by those who need help
before we are asked to help. If we see no self-help efforts, and instead feel
our help is demanded or even expected, we do not respond positively in the
long term. This negative response cuts across all racial and ethnic lines. It
seems pretty universal. In terms of those who need help, we tend to say to
ourselves, "What are they doing to help themselves? If they are doing all they
can, then maybe I can consider helping." This should tell you that there is a
tremendous need to get into communities and help the people start to do
something for themselves. If you can just get something started, just a

flicker or a spark, others from the outside will join in. Inside many communities, the problems are so entrenched that the people will feel fatalistic, pessimistic, and will lack the confidence or the ability to even know where to begin. The future will cry out for people like you to help others find their starting points. There will be great demand for the person who can play the role of bringing people together, building confidence, and starting the consensus organizing process.

The second pattern I see developing is that external resources (those from outside the community) want to have a real role and gain real benefit from participation. This means you will be needed to make sure that all efforts are reciprocal—help from one party leads to returning the help to the helper. I cannot stress how important reciprocal relationships will become. In a society that sees limits to its resources, there will need to be "something in it" for everyone. This is where you come in again. As social workers, teachers, health care workers, clergy, planners, public administrators, and so on, you will be in a perfect position to broker these reciprocal relationships. You become the matchmaker and the ignition that starts the engine.

This one-two punch of a local effort enhanced by reciprocal relationships is an idea whose time has come. We are all tired of people talking only about themselves. Everyone is yearning for something that gets us past empty rhetoric. We all suffer when we become polarized—rich/poor, young/old, black/white, yellow/brown. We are tired of the rhetoric—all it seems to do is divide us. We are tired of television pundits—all they do is divide us. We are tired of most politicians—all they do is pass the buck, take no responsibility, and further divide us. In each category, there will be exceptions to the rule. Barack Obama delivered one of the most talked about speeches at the Democratic Convention of 2004. His theme was that the nation needs to unify for everyone's benefit.

Consensus organizing is a technique that you can learn and practice and will put you on the cutting edge of a national desire to unify. People are fed up with listening to "leaders" saying, "It's not my fault" and instead want to hear "Here's what I can do to help." There will be a growing mandate to reject efforts that divide us and nurture efforts that bring us together. Many times our interests are much more similar than anyone previously imagined. Let's just focus on three issues that consensus organizers can address in the years ahead.

1. The environment. Of course we need to be changing our outlook and behavior to stop destroying our environment before it is irreparably damaged. We cannot make lasting change if we continue to polarize this issue into two "sides." Environmental issues need to be reframed in ways that allow new partnerships to be formed. Everyone needs better communication. We have to take a long, hard look at the self-interest of all the parties involved in shaping our environment. A consensus organizing strategy would require taking a fresh look at all those who have been doing battle over the years. We need to see value in industries making a profit in light of environmentalists' calls for preservation. If this is an issue of importance to you, your skills will be needed.

2. Poverty. No matter how healthy our economy appears, we always have an unconscionably large percentage of our population that remains desperately poor. We blame the victim. We blame the rich. We have to stop blaming and instead begin to look for points of mutual self-interest. There are many small, significant efforts in housing, job training, and health care that are making a positive difference; but no one knows why they work and how they can be implemented on a larger scale. What relationships were built to make these efforts succeed? How were partners recruited and utilized? Consensus organizers look for patterns that lead to both failure and success. Americans will give resources to antipoverty efforts if they believe they will work. That's why consensus organizing needs you.

3. Education. Talk about finger pointing! Some say if it weren't for the teachers, if it weren't for the parents, if it weren't for the school board, if it weren't for the students—the schools would be fine. All of us, setting policies aside, know that our educational system can't have real improvement without meaningful involvement from everyone. How can you even consider a strategy that starts out with blame and ridicule? Gradually, everyone is beginning to see the need to find small points of agreement among the wide variety of participants that can build new, positive relationships.

At the same time that domestic issues cry out for attention, our shared world grows smaller and smaller, forcing us, no matter what our job or profession, to deal more and more with people internationally. This means that those of us who understand more than one culture and speak more than one language will be in demand. There will be a time when those of us who don't will become almost unemployable. If we understand and communicate with people only like ourselves, we may find little demand for our services. The days of "keeping to yourself" and prospering are numbered. We need to find commonalities of interest throughout the United States and the rest of the world. Skills of multiculturalism and multilingualism will be required, not preferred. Gradually, we will lose tolerance for people who are ethnocentric and racist and homophobic because these attitudes will become barriers to effectiveness in both the for-profit and nonprofit worlds. We will refuse to deal with people and organizations that divide us. We will support talented individuals who can bring us together. With problems that are worldwide (pollution, poverty, access to health care), we will need worldwide solutions. Consensus organizing will be a skill that will be in demand.

Some people's reaction to consensus organizing is "That's it?" They can't believe anything that simple can possibly work. Well, the practice of consensus organizing is a series of steps that are quite simple. What is not simple is the decision you must make to practice it in the first place. Many barriers stand between you and your decision. Most of the barriers are self-imposed. There are a number of reasons why an idea so simple can be so scorned. I have been accused of all kinds of things for believing in it and for practicing it. Ironically, most of the scorn comes from people who are trying to help the same types of people I try to help. We are all trying to improve their lives.

I have come to look at these barriers as the four walls; four walls that will prevent you from even attempting to practice consensus organizing. Most community organizers and community activists do not tear down these walls; rather, they reinforce and fortify these walls (see Figure 13.1).

The first wall is a reluctance to see value in all people. Instead, some see value primarily in powerful, successful people, feeling that position determines the level of respect. Others value only the underdog, the downtrodden, and the oppressed. Such people assume all those in power are corrupt. Consensus organizers, on the other hand, have to search for the positives in everyone. Our culture, especially as portrayed in the media, focuses on negatives and conflict. We are acculturated to believe that it is conflict that is significant, newsworthy, and worthy of attention. Conversely, focusing on positives and consensus is portrayed as weak, oversimplistic, and naïve. This first wall is very tough to demolish. You have to be prepared for philosophical quotes about power from, for example, the black political activist Frederick Douglass. You will be constantly reminded that power must be

---

1. Reluctance to see value in all people.

2. You are right, others are wrong.

3. Aversion to work and long-term effort.

4. The need to be noticed and get credit.

Figure 13.1   The Four Walls to Practicing Consensus Organizing

taken from those who have it. You will be accused of not living in the real world. I would like to tell you that you will be rewarded for your outlook, but you will not. You will frequently be blamed.

The second wall is people's strong desire to feel that they are right and others are wrong. We see constant attention placed on arguing. An ever-increasing percentage of our entertainment revolves around in-your-face screaming. We contend that we have the superior point, whereas "they" do not. We exhaust ourselves defending our superiority. This superiority can be acquired through accumulated wealth and power and just as vehemently through a moral position and a sense of righteousness. Everyone is expecting deference. Most people prefer to be in the position of dispensing knowledge rather than to be in the position of needing or receiving it.

The third wall is an aversion to work and long-term effort. We are all conditioned to look for the quick fix, the diet without sacrifice, and the pill to make it all go away. For every person that tells us we have to work to succeed, we have a hundred more trying to sell us magic elixirs. Rarely do leaders tell us that real progress will take years, and most improvements do not appear to work immediately. We want to fix everything with one meeting. Modern wars are declared under the illusion that they will be over quickly, with a lasting, swift, complete victory. Many of us believe that we should be rewarded for just pointing out a problem. We feel no obligation to either propose or implement a solution. We feel absolved of responsibility once we are done pointing out a problem. We prefer the simple step of problem identification rather than the complicated steps of problem resolution. If someone finally musters up the courage to tell the complicated truth about what efforts are required to fix a problem, society reacts by turning a deaf ear.

The fourth wall is the desire to be up front, to get noticed, and to get credit. It is sobering to see our scramble to be recognized and to be given attention. Very little recognition or appreciation is bestowed on those doing the hard work behind the scenes. If we don't get credit for it, we don't want to do it. We have a complete undervaluing of the role of confidence building, the setting up of relationships, and the subtle diplomacy of getting everyone to pull in the same direction. We like the press conference, the grand opening, and the big announcement. We seldom pay attention to those working behind the scenes. They are uninteresting and boring. There is no indication that recognition will ever come to people doing consensus organizing.

You have to be willing to push down all four of these walls. If you want to push past these barriers, you can begin the surprisingly simple steps that constitute consensus organizing. I had the pleasure of being mentored by the late John Gardner, founder of Common Cause, presidential adviser, and cabinet member. He had tremendous influence throughout his career even though he never had to be the center of attention. In the end, after all the positioning on controversial issues, he said it was the moderate worker, working behind the scenes, who actually produced the strategy that would ultimately provide help to people. He said without the moderates, no progress would ever be achieved. Consensus organizers are the moderates.

In our society, this moderate approach is considered radical, even revolutionary. In community organizing, the idea that power does not have to be taken away but instead can be grown and shared *is* a radical idea.

The idea that power does not have to be taken away but instead can be grown and shared is a radical idea.

It is only people willing to approach situations as moderates who can practice and implement this "radical" idea. So if you want to begin, and your walls finally have tumbled, what do you do next? First, find a real issue that affects you and that people care about. Look at the situation in the broadest way possible. Look at everyone who is affected by the issue, whether they realize it or not, or whether you agree with them or not. Make a list of all those people, organizations, and institutions, and determine their self-interests. Work simultaneously inside the community that accepts you, along with those outside the community who can help to create change. Second, quietly build relationships. Build relationships in the most surprising ways possible. You can link up people who will cause others to take notice. Enjoy the process. Take great internal satisfaction in how you are underappreciated. Try thinking of it as sneaking downstairs on Christmas Eve to put your kid's presents under the tree. You purchased and assembled the toys, but Santa Claus gets all the credit. Remember, there is no Santa Claus, and there are no kids, without you. Amaze yourself with your creativity; but take the greatest joy from the relationships you build. Third, after trust and common self-interests have been built, bring everyone together in different settings. See the power grown rather than stolen or taken. Keep doing it over and over and over. Finally, teach others everything you have learned and enjoyed.

There you have it. Our trip is ending and the car is pulling up back at your door. I hope my beginning promise has been kept and you have enjoyed yourself. I hope your appetite has been wetted. So remember all these stories and please know that I have fully enjoyed the "curse" I stumbled upon. Nothing would make me happier than to feel that this trip has taken you to the point of stopping to talk to someone about his or her feelings and ideas about an issue. After talking, tell that someone that another person has said the exact same thing to you. The two people you talked with may both be surprised that the other person had the same opinion. You then say that you would like the two of them to meet. They meet, they relate, and their power and your power grow. You are now a consensus organizer.

So what kind of momentum is out there in the community? Are there any practicing consensus organizers? Are they being nurtured and developed? I thought it would be good to take a look at two young people who are in the process of studying and learning about consensus organizing. Rubi Aguilar was among the first group of high school students in the Consensus Organizing Center's Step Up Program. Raquel Ramirez took the same class a few years later. What did Rubi learn? What did she do with her knowledge?

The Rubi Aguilar Award

The first 17 students from Hoover High School who took our first consensus organizing class were filling out college application forms. I was granted permission from their high school teachers to remove them from one of their classes, set up 17 desks in the hallway, and help them to fill out the forms. I looked over at two of my students who were speaking quietly but intensely in Spanish and English. Something was wrong. One student had a blank space where she was asked to fill in her Social Security number. I had no idea at the time about the enormous significance of that little blank space.

Eventually, I realized that because of the way the student's family had entered the country, she was unable to obtain a Social Security number. This meant that for university purposes the student was not considered an "in-state" student. Her application had to be processed as if she were a foreign student. Sound fair? Just picture a typical student from Brazil or France. Perhaps her father or mother holds a key government job back home. She speaks three languages fluently. Her parents have traveled extensively. She is now temporarily in the United States to study and broaden her educational experience. There is nothing wrong with students like that. But in return for their "broadening," they pay out-of-state tuition, more than 100 percent more than the in-state students. Now, picture the typical child of undocumented parents—dirt poor, from a family in which no one attended high school, let alone college, living in overcrowded housing. Such students are here permanently, not broadening their education and then going home.

These kids are already home. So, in the wisdom of the California State Legislature and the Board of Trustees of the California State University system, my student was foreign.

Rubi Aguilar was 16 years old when we first met. She knew the rules. The only way she could attend college was to raise more than twice as much money as her fellow classmates. Of course, she didn't think it was fair. She was still determined to play a poor hand well. She never acted like a victim and she never used discriminatory policy as an excuse to fail. She was a solid student; she always showed up, she paid attention, she learned, and then she worked. In her senior year of high school, she spent night after night researching and applying for scholarships and financial aid. She made presentations to service clubs. On the side, when she wasn't trying to raise scholarship money, she helped blind people and joined a church. By the time May came around, she had secured the funds to enter SDSU as a foreign student. She had been accepted to SDSU on merit. Her test scores and academic achievement had surpassed the normal admission standards of the university.

She did not stop there. She began speaking to politicians. She wrote letters. In her freshman year of college, the state legislature, with the signature of the governor, changed the law. In the future, Rubi, and thousands of others in similar circumstances, would now be considered Californians. They were now "in state."

Every year since then, I tell the new high school students about Rubi. Sure, it is important that students learn about civil rights and labor leaders such as Rosa Parks and Cesar Chavez; but it is equally important that they learn about Rubi Aguilar. At each subsequent graduation, the Consensus Organizing Center has honored a student who most epitomizes her spirit and determination. The center has created an atmosphere in which the students want to be recognized for these qualities. They consider this award a great honor, and it is. One recipient of the award was so happy that she couldn't stop jumping up and down. The award is just a piece of paper; but this is the type of strength you have to find in your community. This is the type of effort and desire you have to amplify. You can start these new traditions by recognizing exemplary people in the present day.

A couple of years later, I was scanning the metro section of *The San Diego Union Tribune* over breakfast. I saw a title that grabbed my attention, "Bill to Grant Legal Immigration Status Backed." The national bill aimed to help immigrants who were brought to the United States by their parents when they were young. These immigrants attended school and wanted to go to college, but couldn't work legally in the country because of their illegal status. Josh Bernstein, spokesperson for the National Immigration Law Center, was quoted, "Their parents brought them here illegally, but they themselves have done nothing wrong. They have done nothing to be ashamed of. They've done everything they have been asked to do. They have stayed in school. They have worked hard." Then, there was one other person quoted. Only her first name was given, but I recognized the name. It was the same unusual first name of a student from our second class. I anticipated the quote and hoped that she did not come off sounding like a victim. I hoped she had learned what a good consensus organizer would try to say when given a chance. The article continued, "An 18-year-old San Diego City College student who is undocumented said paying in-state tuition has allowed her to continue with her studies but without U.S. residency and a work permit, her dream of becoming a nurse will not come true (we have a crisis level nursing shortage in Southern California). [She said,] 'I want my work permit so I can earn money for my education.'" I was extremely proud of that very effective response. God bless all the Rubi Aguilars.

Several years later, another student in a situation similar to Rubi's (Raquel Ramirez) took the same class and did very well. In the beginning, she was hesitant about speaking up in class. It was not because she didn't have anything to say. It was because of her unfamiliarity with English. She improved her speaking and writing skills weekly. Her community service was outstanding. She had that desire that makes a learner successful. She was the type of student who made you glad you became a teacher. She wanted to learn so badly that you could almost feel her determination while she sat attentively at her desk. She was selected to receive the Rubi Aguilar Award. She was asked to give a short speech to all the other students and their families. What follows here is her speech.

Good Evening!

Thank you for giving me the opportunity to speak with you at this special event. Thank you dear parents, relatives, and friends for being here. Congratulations for completing the Step Up's Social Work 120 class. Keep up the hard work!

My fellow students and peers, feel proud of yourselves because in the long run not everyone gets to the finish line. And your being here tonight shows you did it, you finished your race. However, this does not mean that you are all done, because this is just the beginning of a whole new experience—your senior year and soon COLLEGE. Yes

COLLEGE! Because this is the place where your goals for the future should be heading.

For the ones who think college is unreachable, let me share with you a story.

There was a girl who never, ever, thought of, dreamed of, furthering her education for many reasons. One reason was money and the others were discouraging comments such as, "Don't even think about going to college because you are not going to get there. You are just not good enough, and you are not smart enough. Your education and goals will stop once you graduate from high school."

However, she thought that this was worth a try, so she left her lovely parents, her lovely homeland, in order to come to America in search of new opportunities. Once being in the United States she never imagined all the obstacles she had to overcome, such as adapting to the way people live in the multicultural nation, overcoming the language barrier, and learning to survive and succeed without the support of her family. She would get frustrated translating English into Spanish and vice versa. Sometimes people would laugh at her mispronunciation of words and her broken English, but her desire to learn the language was so great that she overcame her fear. Now she is bilingual. Entering her senior year she was offered a Home Depot shack as a home in the backyard by her own blood. It was either that or go back to Mexico. She was at risk of homelessness, but luckily someone offered her a place to live and with the help of all of the ones that loved her and supported her, she stayed to accomplish her goal of going to COLLEGE. This girl is me and I am proud to say that I will be coming to San Diego State University in the fall of 2005. That is going to be you in the fall of 2006, because it can be done. You can go to college, too.

Don't let anyone stop you from achieving your goals.

Don't let anyone tell you that you set your goals too high.

Keep working hard because you will get your reward in the future.

Keep focused, keep trying, and keep dreaming.

Reach high, you will get there. And remember, never give up.

Once again, thank you to the Consensus Organizing Center's Step Up Program.

Thank you Antonio and Liliana Espejo for being my role models.

Thank you Rubi Aguilar for believing in me and for giving me all of your support.

Thank you.

There is talent, determination, and heart in people all around you. You just have to open your eyes and arms and nurture it. You have an opportunity to find some Rubis and Raquels and have them go out and find even more. That is the future of consensus organizing.

Reflection Questions

1. If our society is more splintered and divided than ever, why shouldn't the trend continue?

2. How many of the four walls or barriers to consensus organizing have you knocked down?

3. What other issues besides education, poverty, and the environment can be addressed using consensus organizing?

4. What kinds of jobs could Rubi and Raquel do in your town?

5. Can power really be grown? If yes, give an example.

6. Which is the least likely to happen in the future?

   a. The Cubs win the World Series.
   b. Ben Affleck is in a good movie.
   c. Professor Eichler teaches a course in clinical practice.
   d. Vanilla Ice makes a comeback.

Reference

Vidal, A., & Gittell, R. (1998). *Community organizing: Building social capital as a development strategy.* Thousand Oaks, CA: Sage.

"ANSWERS" TO REFLECTION QUESTIONS

1. Members of many organizations still actually wonder, "What would Saul do?" Near the end of his life, he started to organize the middle class hoping to get those people to use their power in the stock market to effect social change. It's anybody's guess whether today's realities would make him become interested in a concept like consensus organizing or whether it would make him even more radical and confrontational. I do think he would have held onto his principle of starting local with important local issues that resonate in each particular neighborhood. He would still exhibit his irreverence and sense of humor and still care deeply about "the little guy" and our democratic society.

2. Of course if you had the power to choose the speakers, I couldn't influence your choices. You could choose authors, politicians, musicians, actors, anybody. But I still get to tell you who I would choose if I had the power. Here are my top five choices:

    a. Dennis Kucinich. The congressman from Ohio and former candidate for president may be the most interesting of all elected public officials over the last 20 years. He grew up poor and for a while, he and his family lived in a car. He became the youngest mayor in the history of Cleveland, Ohio. He has a very unusual, thoughtful perspective that shows insight into what makes our country great and what needs to be improved.

b. Melinda Gates. She and her husband have given away more money than anyone else in the history of the world. She really seems to believe that no one life on this planet is more important than another. Many believe there may have been no Gates Foundation without her urging.

c. Don Rickles. The comedian represents the end of an era—totally, absolutely, politically incorrect racial and ethnic humor. Offstage, by all accounts, he is reported to be a really nice person, charitable and kind.

d. Gerry Adams. Northern Ireland's leader of Sinn Fein came out of the terrible violence of the 1970s and 1980s, but since then he has chosen the democratic, political path to social change.

e. Bill Clinton. He wouldn't run out of things to say, and love him or hate him, no one could say he would be boring. Getting his perspective on current issues would be fascinating.

So how does my list compare with yours?

3. This is a very important question. Many people go through their entire lives and never really develop much of a desire to help others. You, however, have the desire. Where did it come from? Your family? A particular experience in your life? A person who inspired you to help others? Your motivation will tell you a lot about yourself. It will also tell you a lot about your reaction to consensus organizing. Discipline yourself and look into this question deeply. Get past a simple "knee-jerk" answer.

4. Your personality is unique and an important indicator of how you look at creating change. What kind of personality do you have? Outgoing people don't become quiet and withdrawn in community work and introverts seldom become spellbinding speechmakers. Do not think that you will be ineffective as an organizer because you may not be riveting, dynamic, and mesmerizing. Remember, the most important skill of a consensus organizer is the ability to listen.

5. Our childhood neighborhood may have an important impact on our lives. Much of what shapes us comes, of course, from our families. Almost as influential, however, are the experiences you remember in your neighborhood. What was it like for you? Did you move a lot? Did you stay in one place? What was your neighborhood like? Was it close-knit? Was it poor, working class, middle class, or wealthy? Was it diverse? Was it safe or

dangerous? How do you think your neighborhood experiences affect how you look at other neighborhoods? I think you will see more links between your neighborhood and your current outlook than you ever imagined.

6. The answer should be yes! All of you who live in warm climates should visit in January. I'm serious. It will show you how frigid temperatures and howling winds can increase the neighborliness and helpfulness of the people around you. There are plans in the works to turn my childhood home into a national historic site, like the homes of John F. Kennedy and Elvis Presley. So that should be a "must see" on your trip. OK, I was kidding about the last part.

CHAPTER 2

1. You can't believe in both myths because they are too contradictory. Many people in the helping professions subscribe to the anti-myth theory. Be honest and think through both concepts. Ideally, a consensus organizer eventually bursts past both myths and looks at issues in a less ideological way. It will not happen overnight.

2. This may seem like a silly question to you, but it really is not. Lots of people in the helping professions propose suggestions that basically call for the redistribution of America's wealth. The trick for a consensus organizer is to get help from those same wealthy sources in a way that produces mutual benefit—to the wealthy and the poor. This will be an impossible task if you picture yourself as a "Robin Hood."

3. I would hope that you are not in the group that answered yes to this one. Quite a bit of the rhetoric from the right-wing portion of our media constantly blames the victim. That is, they place all the blame on the poor for every problem they have. This, of course, is a nice little theory that just happens to absolve those subscribers from all sense of responsibility. Wouldn't it be nice to lead your life by blaming everyone but yourself for absolutely everything? This attitude may be easy for you to spot. Do not confuse it with the idea of people taking personal responsibility for their actions. Taking responsibility is a good thing. Absolving everyone else from helping is not a good thing. For the most part, consensus organizing requires personal responsibility and community effort along with

partnerships from outside the community. Consensus organizers need all of these ingredients in their recipes.

4. Yes, blockbusting still occurs. The real estate industry is a major player in our economy. Because enormous amounts of money are made in the buying and selling of property, we will always have a sizable number of people who will cross whatever ethical and even legal lines necessary to enhance their profits. To be fair, many in the real estate profession try to demand an end to blockbusting and racial steering. But always remember a profession that polices its own will never have perfect results. Just look at the police! There are still some communities in the United States that have people using ethnic and racial fears to make huge profits. There are laws in place at all levels of government that call for the elimination of this practice. But we still need a vigilant, educated, and well organized public to blow the whistle and lead efforts to prevent these illegal tactics from destroying neighborhoods.

5. Community organizers are not alone in fighting for justice and equality. We have partners all over the place. What did you come up with? No profession will get a score of 100 percent on this test, but some obvious professions include teachers, social workers, counselors, public health workers, nurses, rehabilitation specialists, hospice workers, and public defenders. I hope you have composed a long, long list because the point of this question is to show that whereas no profession scores 100 percent, no profession scores 0 percent either. Look for kindred spirits everywhere. Remember the people who surprise us with their help may be the most effective. Their impact may be even larger than the "usual suspects," where help is expected.

6. You may have lost some sleep trying to look for the answer to this one. You would have had to live in two cities to even know what the heck I was talking about. These sandwiches are exclusive to the cities in which they were born. A beef-on-weck originated in Buffalo, New York. It is a roast beef sandwich made very special because of the crusty, flaky roll known as a kimmel-weck roll. The roast beef and the roll form a marriage as united and inseparable as a couple celebrating their golden wedding anniversary. In Pittsburgh, Pennsylvania, everyone at one time in their life has either eaten or watched someone eat a chipped-chopped ham sandwich. Created at Islays, a local chain of delis, it's a paper-thin cut of ham that almost floats from the slicer to the bread. It has a very distinctive taste—almost nothing like "regular" ham. The correct answer is—a tie. You have to eat both and you will see there is just no way to decide. Tony Bennett or Frank Sinatra? Take both.

CHAPTER 3

1. Now this is an interesting question. Both have a lot of similarities, if done the right way. You should be talking about the person's strengths. You should be talking about their options. You should be making sure they are in charge of their effort to change. I would argue, however, that there is one very important difference as well. In an organizer's one-on-one meeting, we talk about the need for collective action and point out that the same barriers and problems are affecting many others as well. We will point out that there are political and economic factors at play that must be analyzed and then changed through the actions of many people. We would seldom turn the problem inward.

2. Poor and working-class people have very few connections to people in other circumstances. They don't know the people who are doing fine while they continue to suffer. As they suffer, it is not felt by others, not shared by others, and frequently not even noticed by others. Without connections, it is very hard for poor and working-class people to create change. Since many problems caused by poverty seem to affect only the poor, the rest of society appears to be uncaring. Wealthy people have much more social capital. They contact their contacts. Their agendas are understood. Others help carry out their agendas. Consensus organizers believe that there would be more help for the poor if more of us knew poor people. The more there are personal connections, the greater the chances to develop genuine concern. Genuine concern can lead to serious efforts to create positive change.

3. Let's start with what you wouldn't say. I wouldn't recommend, "I hate you and everything about you. I am disgusted with this shallow suburban lifestyle and this is my way to reject everything and get back at you." Instead, how about something like "You always taught me to care about others and that we are all our brother's keeper. I finally have found a career in which I feel I can make a difference." Community organizing should not be seen as a choice representing rebellion, angst, or disgust. It should be a genuine, optimistic, strategic, and positive decision. Consensus organizers are positive people who look for positive qualities in others.

4. While still at the pinnacle of a spectacular baseball career in Pittsburgh, Pennsylvania, Clemente, a native Puerto Rican, was saddened by a hurricane that devastated Nicaragua in 1972. He became even more distraught by reports that relief supplies were not reaching those in need but were being commandeered instead by criminals and thieves. Hearing this,

he gathered supplies and made large personal contributions. To make sure that the supplies got to where he intended, he decided to ride along with the cargo on the next plane. Overloaded, the plane crashed upon takeoff into the sea. He perished, leaving a widow and three young boys. His body was never found. Because of this, and the exemplary life he led, the National Baseball Hall of Fame waived the rule that players must wait at least 5 years after retirement to be considered for admission. Clemente stands in stark contrast to many of today's professional athletes who are too often caught up in greed, illegal drugs, and self-promotion.

5. There are a lot of professional people who are skilled and trained to show all of us the seriousness of a problem. They can point out the need for the problem to be addressed. What they don't do is make a personal or organizational commitment to help solve the problem. Beware of those in our society who point the finger at the need for "the other guy" to do the actual work. Try instead to find a smaller number of people who make a commitment of their own time, skills, and resources. The consensus organizer must find people who are willing to work. That is a much different task than finding people who point things out.

Chapter 4

1. You can build a great deal of respect when you commit to doing something, plan well, implement, and eventually succeed. The respect that others give to you for saying you are going to do something and then successfully following through is significant. If, instead, you play the role of lobbyist, or advocate, or pain in the butt, tangible results may still be achieved but the depth of respect will be shallow. Depth of respect leads to others supporting your future endeavors. You will get even more help and participation the next time around.

2. People are good at some things and are terrible at others. Think of yourself, for example. Some tasks are easier and more fun than others. To achieve success, someone must perform effectively at each required function. You can't operate a circus with everyone selling tickets and no one taming the lion. Your job as a consensus organizer is to understand the tasks at hand and the work that lies ahead. You must understand the talents and skills of your participants. Most people will respond very well when they are told they are indispensable. You need to steer people into their roles. It won't happen on its own.

3. Consensus organizers want everyone to benefit through their participation. We think that benefits are not only acceptable, but they are also necessary. The only problem is that sometimes people want hidden, secret benefits at the expense of others. For instance, if a homeowner wants his or her property values to rise, we are fine with that. On the other hand, if there's a man who owns a company that makes signs that people put in their windows to show they are block club members and he wants to recoup the expenditure of his funds for making the signs, we are fine with that. If, however, he is in charge of the signs and withholds the fact that he owns the sign company and charges the neighbors double, we are not fine with that. Simply put, benefit must be gained openly, honestly, and in clear sight. People must be comfortable and articulate about their expected benefits. Everyone else must be aware and comfortable as well. If so, you will be fine.

4. Bill Maher and you both like to be complimented. Oh, you may not want to admit it, but you love it. Deep down, even June enjoyed Wally's friend Eddie on *Leave It To Beaver* every single time he said, "You look lovely today, Mrs. Cleaver." The reason I am stressing this is that sometimes in our desire to be professional we forget the common sense and importance of showing our appreciation. Never worry about "laying it on too thick." You have the ability to absorb all the compliments anyone wants to give you. Bring it on.

5. The consensus organizer is the person who shows people their options. Your job is to discuss all the possible different directions, the choices, and the different avenues. You can have a personal favorite, but you can't just present one way of doing things. There will be no group "buy-in" if people have no choice. The entire group must decide among all the choices. You just lay them all out.

Chapter 5

1. Cultural competency is much more than an academic term, but it is up to you to make sure of this. If you think of it only as something you are forced to memorize, then that's all it will become. Try instead to make sure it means something to *you*. Don't see it as something relevant to only your professor or your employer. See it as a living, breathing idea that resonates with you everyday.

2. Our society is not unified on much of anything. The writer Mark Gerzon (1996) refers to our country as the "Divided States of America." Not

only do we have divisions, we sometimes see the ability to divide as a skill. We even elevate and admire some of those who divide us. Talk show hosts have celebrity status. We repeat their outrageous comments to our friends, neighbors, and family members. This question probes whether you play a role in this division. In your personal life have you pitted one group of friends against another? Have you done the same thing with a brother and sister? You must discipline yourself to stop this behavior or you will find it spilling over to your professional life as well. Try instead to look for things that could unify your friends and family. Get in the habit of developing commonalities. Don't let societal trends move you into a corner. Similarities among people are right in front of your eyes. Start to see them now.

3. This answer will surprise you unless you are a Texan. "Don't mess with Texas" was a slogan coined by the state highway department to try to influence people to refrain from littering. It was put on a lot of garbage cans, trash barrels, and refuse trucks. It was everywhere. It was a brilliant slogan, intended to tap into the immense love and pride people in Texas have for their state. Its impact was felt in such a profound way that it zoomed past its original intent and merged with the state's macho swagger as well. It unified the citizens more effectively than others states that tried stuff like "Land of Enchantment."

4. I think you have to understand yourself first. We use ourselves as a benchmark to form our opinions of others. How are other people different from you? Are they as dedicated, hardworking, committed, and caring as you are? Or are they lazier, shiftier, more deceiving, and aloof than you are? Spend a good amount of time analyzing yourself in an honest, straightforward manner. Don't skip over your self-analysis and move on to someone else. Think of Bill Clinton's definition of humility or Mother Teresa's definition of commitment or Bruce Springsteen's definition of a concert. See how it would affect their analyses of others?

5. What's your opinion? There are efforts sprouting in different parts of our society pushing the idea that we are now becoming "all one." Some demand we become color-blind. Some eschew the use of race and ethnicity on job and college application forms. There are those who say the idea of cultural differences in America is an idea that is passé and no longer significant. This debate will not be going away anytime soon. If we concentrate on our differences, will we miss out on our similarities? On the other hand, what will be lost if we ignore our differences? Does cultural competency hold us back or move us forward? Try to be specific in your thinking. Back up your opinion with real examples.

CHAPTER 6

1. People can do a lot more than they think they can, but most constantly stress their limits and not their potential. We set the bar too low. As a result, people start to believe what we tell them. People who are told they have limits self-impose the limits, and those who predicted those limits look like geniuses. We are "proven" to be right. As we become professionals, we see nonprofessionals as severely limited. We want the nonprofessionals to depend on professionals. I want you to take a really hard look at this. What if a teacher said to a student, "I have more knowledge than you do. You don't understand the topic. You are limited. I will do it for you rather than show you that you have the capacity to learn how to do it yourself." Wouldn't you think this was a terrible teacher? Well, you should become a great teacher. No matter what your profession, break down what you have learned and teach others what you know. Judge yourself by your ability to have nonprofessionals gain confidence and ability. That is not setting up your "partners" for failure. That is helping them succeed.

2. No. He just threatened to do it. He was trying to prove that the threat of disruption and embarrassment could be a powerful motivator. He got what he wanted and did not have to carry out the action. Suppose he did have to follow through. Imagine all of the bad jokes and puns. I'm tempted to start, but if I do I'll never stop.

3. Strategy needs to constantly evolve. Our plans are not devised in a vacuum. We have lots of other people reacting, changing opinions, adjusting their tactics, and so on, so we have to do the same. Do not be intimidated by the idea of constant change. Change is what keeps you from becoming bored. Change makes the situation more interesting. Watch out for those who dig in their heels and keep repeating something over and over, expecting everyone to do what they want. If you are into baseball, think of it as a nine-inning game. If you play chess, think of it as a match. If you like mystery novels, unfold your plot with twists and turns. Strategy needs to fit into particular situations and situations constantly change.

4. If you chose, you lose. Suppose you make the strategy choice and it is ineffective. Well, then, it was your fault. Suppose you make the choice and it works. No one will feel much satisfaction and no one's confidence will be built. That is, no one but you. It's not about you. It's about the people you are working with. They need to build their self-esteem, confidence, and social capital. This can only happen when they, as a group, make decisions and

benefit or suffer the consequences. That does not mean that you can't frame the discussion. It just means that you don't get to choose.

5. Yes, as long as you don't just remember the word "manipulative" and forget the word "honest." When I finished a meeting once, a financial supporter said, "You seemed to set up everybody to say just what you wanted them to say. It just seemed so manipulative to me." I said, "That wasn't manipulation. That was planning." As a consensus organizer, you need to bring together people who have never been together before. There won't be a lot of comfort and trust as you attempt to do this. It will not happen on its own. You can never lie to people to make it happen. You can, however, certainly help orchestrate the process.

Chapter 7

1. When you make people feel guilty, they do not respond well. Oftentimes they become defensive or negative and overreact. If you want help but make people feel guilty, they either will refuse to help you or not help you for very long. On the other hand, people tend to respond positively to people who are trying to help themselves. It's a very consistent pattern. People respect others who work hard. So you would be wise to encourage people to do what they can on their own first. This will be respected. Help and partnership will be easier to find.

2. There are very few people out there who will respond well when they receive nothing in return. Most of us prefer reciprocity. It may not be money. It may not be public praise. It might be a simple matter of feeling better about yourself or getting a letter from the kid who received the scholarship or knowing that the help led to more people being helped. Never forget the crucial concept of reciprocity—give when you receive and receive when you give.

3. You should be able to talk all day about this one. The whole model of consensus organizing is built on the idea that people respond more effectively and productively when they know you than when they don't. Problems in low-income communities require long-term strategies for improvement. Think of your deepest friendships. Think of people who stand by you through thick and thin. Those are the kinds of relationships that isolated people in isolated communities need.

4. This may seem a little superficial to be included here, but it isn't. There are many significant reasons why your best friend is your best friend. Best

friends are trustworthy. They can be counted on, always, no matter what. They are a pleasure to be around (usually). They reinforce your value as a person. They cheer you up when you are feeling down. They build your confidence. Maybe, most important of all, they understand you. We need connections to the haves and have-nots. These connections need to include all those factors included in friendships. It cuts two ways, with everyone benefiting. It's as simple as that.

5. I know people who refused to go out with their real friends on Thursday nights because they couldn't bear to miss one episode. I mean, what is so compelling about the comment, "Oh Ross!"? They were all annoying and I always thought we tried to get rid of annoying friends. Contact me. I need an explanation.

6. Buffalo. Yeah, that's right. If you picked Chicago, you lose. When I went back to visit my family in Buffalo, after being away for years, I took the newspaper and walked outside intending to read it on the front porch. My father saw me and chuckled. He said, "You've been gone for quite a while." I didn't know why he said that. I mean, why the chuckle and the comment? I'm just going to read the paper on the porch. I went back inside in about 20 seconds. I had the classified section plastered onto my face. It seemed like it was glued there from the constant blasts of wind.

CHAPTER 8

1. It is very hard to create partnerships when the primary, initial purpose of getting together is to secure funds. Whenever I am asked to work with an existing partnership, I always ask how the parties got together in the first place. The more lasting, productive working relationships are developed through a mutual desire to accomplish something. The partnership may have needed money at some point to help reach certain goals, but it was the participants' need to get to the same end that brought them together. Rarely do partnerships last when they are formed to chase money.

2. The Mon Valley people were flattered when they were told that they had knowledge and expertise that was appreciated and needed. They were especially flattered that people from such a large city so far away would invite them to share their expertise. This desire to be appreciated and needed created a reciprocal desire to help in any way possible.

3. Technically, partnerships could last, but only if self-interests evolve in tandem. This would be quite a long shot. Instead, what almost always happens is that partners' interests go in different directions, making it very hard to stay together. Once self-interest diverges, you no longer have a real working partnership. Instead, you have a shell that continues to exist, but has no real, tangible benefit.

4. Think about it—Bonnie and Clyde died in a shootout. Siegfried and Roy—one watched the other being mauled by a tiger. Ben and Jerry remain socially responsible businessmen. You have to go with Ben and Jerry.

5. Raphael had to think about the person he was talking to and analyze that person's self-interest (even his own mother). Once he understood the person's self-interest, he tried to take his own agenda and link it to the other person. It was a lot of work and a lot of thinking. It sometimes made his head hurt. When he found himself drifting back to simpler times, when he just bullied or ignored others, he called consensus organizing a curse. Not that you would ever do such a thing. Right? Right?

CHAPTER 9

1. In the beginning of a relationship, it is much more important to show the other person you are interested in them rather than vice versa. Don't ever make the mistake of trying to prove your value to a person before you show them what a value they are to you. People are uncomfortable around someone who keeps harping on why you need them. Think of it this way— most people would rather spend 30 minutes being complimented than 30 minutes hearing about you.

2. Some people don't notice the differences that are caused by differences in class. People are constantly surprised by others who don't see things from the same perspective. We are frequently oblivious to class issues. Thus, we are exasperated when others see the same thing we see and draw an opposite conclusion. Try thinking about the richest person you know and the poorest person you know. Compare yourself to both of them. You should begin to see the differences. Much of this is a class matter.

3. No. Never. Ever. Not even if someone offers you hard cash. As a rule, try to avoid all phrases that are overused. They sound hollow and almost without meaning. Instead, prove how important others are to you through your

actions, not catchy sayings. Sound bites do not prove that you are a caring person. Your actions will.

4. Listening is the key to consensus organizing. We are certainly not a society of listeners. We "listen" to someone while we drive, eat, use the computer, shower, and read, and sometimes we doze off. Try listening not as if it were a little something extra to do while doing something else. Instead, listen as if your life depends on it. Stop cutting other people off in the middle of their sentences while you say what you think is more important. It is crucial to stop planning your next comment while you should be listening. Learning to be a community organizer is not learning how to herd sheep. You have to know each person you are working with to begin to understand his or her self-interest. You can't do that by talking. You do that by listening.

5. Go ahead, tell me, I'm listening. Hey, want to hear about my fascinating family history? Sure you do. My great-grandfather came from the small, but historically significant German town of Überallis. It was the fall of 1901, it was snowing, blah, blah, blah (please see the answer to question 4).

6. For a consensus organizer, every person is important. Each person is a potential match to another person. The match can lead to helping more people. Each person is an important part of a puzzle and you have all the puzzle pieces in front of you. You should be in the process of improving your listening and your open-mindedness, allowing you to find more resources than ever. Try to answer this question in as much detail as possible.

7. OK, if you don't know all three songs you have to fake it and just take a guess. All three sing about pieces of the kinds of relationships that occur in consensus organizing. Stephen sings about relating to new people, not just the ones you already know; Bruce about staying close to those you grew up with; and Mariah about reliability and dependability. All three answers, in any combination, can be considered correct. If only the SAT and GRE exams were like this!

CHAPTER 10

1. Most of the time lobbying is done on a series of one-way streets. *We* want *you* to do this for *us*. Lobbying, however, can be done on much more of a two-way street. *We* will do this for *you* and then *you* will do this for *us*.

Lobbying on a one-way street will have only one dimension and will not lead to an institutional relationship. The person or group you are lobbying will be more of a target and will resent your lack of reciprocity. Institutional relationships must be built around mutual benefits and will evolve over a period of time.

2. You have to start somewhere. In any institutional relationship you begin by contacting a person within the institution who sees benefit in knowing you. The first contact needs to keep expanding your contacts within their institution. Never stop after knowing one "inside" person. Make sure you constantly expand your contacts through their help. It's not that important where you start. It is very important where you end up.

3. Families traditionally do laundry on Mondays. While washing and drying their clothes, they begin to soak and cook the beans. Both the washing and cooking take all day, so it's a perfect partnership. This makes Louisiana the home of the multi-taskers.

4. It is funny to watch as people who once worked well together are amazed when their partner is no longer their partner. People are shocked because they just worked so perfectly together in the past. Consensus organizers believe that partnerships only continue to exist when all the partners continue to benefit. As issues evolve, there may no longer be the mutual benefit that there once was. The deeper and older the partnership, the more rough waters it can withstand; but if there is no longer mutual benefit, partners start voting with their feet. They walk away. You should see this as a natural process. There is no one to blame for this. Fluidity is a factor in all partnerships.

5. Remember the analysis we did on both sectors. You should have a strong preference here. The key for you is to analyze why you have your preference. What is it that makes government or business more difficult to work with? It should tell you a lot about yourself.

CHAPTER 11

1. All you have to do to prove your point is to have an example of young people doing community organizing successfully. Most people are impressed with success. Try to avoid philosophical arguments regarding young people (e.g., they are part of the community too, they deserve a voice, we have refused to listen to them for so long, or no wonder they feel

so alienated). Instead, just show some real proof of their value. Show others what they have achieved.

2. This question is designed to see if you have any knowledge of real inner-city schools. Do not let the media, friends, or families influence your outlook on kids from inner-city schools. Form your own opinions. Go to some schools. Look around. Sit in on some classes. Talk to the administrators, teachers, and students. Contrast your own experience to what others have told you. Then compare what you have seen to Hoover High in San Diego. If you have gone to a school like this yourself, go back and see if anything has changed since you graduated. Has it gotten better or worse?

3. Jessica's strategy avoided a big trap that many of us fall into. We feel justified in our cause and blame others for their lack of sincerity and concern. While we continue to place justifiable blame, nothing improves. She felt that advocating directly for sex education with an ultra-conservative school board would not be practical. She refused to get stuck in the mud. Instead, she came up with an innovative strategy to help get what her classmates needed. You have to admire her ability to work around the problem while she simultaneously addressed it. You can't get stuck when you find opposition and are unable to "win." She showed a great deal of sophistication to work around the roadblock while adhering to her goal.

4. OK, so this might be impossible to answer. I didn't give you a single hint. In the gym, there is one whole wall with pictures of past Hoover athletes. The biggest picture belongs to a baseball player. He went on to become a great hitter for the Boston Red Sox. He interrupted his career twice to defend his country in World War II and Korea. He was nicknamed the "splendid splinter." His name was Ted Williams. I have a picture of him at Hoover High with his teammates.

5. Kids have some advantages. They can be creative. They can look at an issue you have been struggling with for a long time and come up with a different angle on a different starting point. They can have an impact. When others see their determination and effort, they can attract additional supporters. They have fun. No matter how serious their cause, they are still kids and kids like to enjoy themselves. They can be honest and blunt. They can push past the waltzing around and pontificating and get to the heart of the matter. Now what reasons did you come up with?

6. Even though a school might look forlorn, worn out, and totally "ghetto" (their term—used by many high school students), there still can be real pride and caring within the school. A slogan can help unify a school or

neighborhood if the people in the school or neighborhood really mean it. The Hoover school students use the phrase "Once a Cardinal, Always a Cardinal" to show their feelings. Some even sign it below their name on their class assignments. Get a slogan that means something to you about your life or career goals. It helps.

Chapter 12

1. If you think about this for a while, it should be easy to do. The people you choose should have a track record of getting others to work together while they themselves don't become the center of attention. I would hope you came up with people who are good at finding common interests and bringing people together rather than dividing them. They should be hardworking and dedicated but also lead a balanced life with a good sense of humor and have other interests outside of their job.

2. This is an interesting task. Some people think that all lawyers are too adversarial to be consensus organizers. Some pick union activists and antiunion activists. Some choose public officials. My hope is that you have a short list.

3. You should go over the six tendencies carefully. Sort out the six into three piles. The first pile should contain those tendencies that you found easy to practice and seemed natural and logical. The second pile should contain one or more tendencies that seemed odd to you at first but as you thought about them, they gradually made more sense. The third pile should contain any that were such a struggle for you that you are still fighting against them. Many people have trouble with the concept of authority. Was that true for you?

4. Many advertising campaigns for youth are ineffective because they portray inappropriate behavior as both dangerous and popular. Young people are so anxious to fit in and gain acceptance among their peers that they fixate only on the "popular" part of the message and don't even notice the "dangerous" part. Their desire to be popular vastly outweighs their desire to avoid danger.

5. This question is debated. Consensus organizers are optimists at heart regarding the human spirit and realists at heart regarding human behavior. People will not become lazy if there is a spirit of hope and possibility in their

everyday lives. If instead, they are surrounded by despair, pessimism, and lack of opportunity they may, after a period of time, behave as if they are lazy. They do this as a protection from failure. Simply put, they start to believe they can't fail if they don't try. Please don't misinterpret this. Your job should be to help find or create new opportunities for achieving success. Most people will then rise to the occasion.

6. Many have tried but no one can quite explain it. Jerry Lewis is still very popular in France. If you can figure out why, you have unlocked one of life's greatest mysteries. As for the mystery meat in the blue can, spam, we have more amazing facts. The belief is that the vast majority of it is purchased, prepared, and actually eaten by Hawaiians. The most popular theory for this bizarre truth is that the large military presence makes Hawaiians either nostalgic, patriotic, or both. It's even on the menu in some casual restaurants.

CHAPTER 13

1. Author and social commentator Robert Putnam says that when our society saw huge declines of social capital as people left their livelihoods as southern sharecroppers for factory jobs in the northern cities, we created new organizations to help people connect to their new communities. In other words, in the past when we felt severely disconnected, we devised new ways to reconnect. You may be entering another rebirth of community creation. It will take new forms, but we will be coming up with new ways to stay close to our families and our neighbors.

2. These four barriers need to come down for you to practice consensus organizing. If all four are still standing, do not despair. They can come down, if you concentrate and want them to topple. If you only have one or two remaining barriers, good. Just start to imagine all the things you can begin to do when they finally tumble. If all the barriers have been removed, great. What are you waiting for?

3. I hope you came up with some other issues. I'd like to think that the list is almost endless. We are so polarized that we tend to create divisions on every new issue that pops up. See if there is one item on your list that motivates you. Focus on that issue and start to imagine doing something about it.

4. Rubi and Raquel and others like them should be valuable to you. They should be able to help you reach your goals of creating change. They should be in high demand, like free agents in sports, available to be signed up by your team. We need people like them throughout the entire nonprofit world. They can understand the agendas of the community and their potential employer and be able to help both, simultaneously.

5. Consensus organizers believe that power can grow without being taken away from someone. This is a radical idea in the community organizing field. Many other organizing approaches say that power is limited and must be redistributed to create a fair and just society. Are you open to the idea that power can grow for an entire group of partners without having anyone's power decreased? What examples did you come up with?

6. Because this chapter focused on how positive the future can be, I thought we should push the envelope and propose that even those things that seem the most impossible may still have a slight glimmer of hope and a tiny chance of success.
   a. Cubs. Holy cow, it is possible. Look at the Boston Red Sox.
   b. Ben Affleck. A long shot, I'll admit, but what if he had a really, really small part?
   c. Clinical practice course. I did it once. I think all the other professors had complex scheduling problems. I seem to remember I did OK. So, of course I believe it is possible I may be asked to do it again someday. After all, I am experienced.
   d. Vanilla Ice. In popular music, for a while, even the "Macarena" was huge. Why not a comeback for Ice, Ice Baby? He was pretty bad the first time. How hard would it be to improve?

REFERENCE

Gerzon, M. (1996). *A house divided.* New York: Putnam.

EPILOGUE

I remember turning on the weather channel and watching the storm's path. I said a prayer. My prayer appeared answered as Hurricane Katrina veered slightly to the east but then unanswered when the levees gave way. The "Big One" had finally come and it came under the cruelest circumstances. It came in such a way that mothers, fathers, children, and grandparents went to bed feeling safe, only to awaken with rising water spilling over their mattresses. People gathered their families and ran to their attics and then to their roofs. My beloved city—the one I tried to show you in its wonderful, quirky uniqueness—was entangled in a nightmare. People I had worked alongside of were dead. I started to think of all the other communities I had worked in that were at the mercy of the water. Always, the poorest neighborhoods were the most at risk. It was not a coincidence that the disaster plan contained no provisions for the poor people who did not own a car. Thousands waited for help to come that for many came too late. It showed all of us a great deal about who we really are. We do not treat people equally. We hide behind bureaucracy. We do not take responsibility. We often avoid the golden rule.

It also spoke to how isolated we are from one another. Some chose to focus on looters and avoided thinking about the help that thousands of law-abiding citizens so desperately needed. We saw problems that somebody else needed to address. Those who did help did so because of a feeling of connectedness, a feeling of "There but for the grace of God go I." But most, instead, pointed fingers. Much of the food we eat, the coffee we drink, the gasoline we guzzle, and the music we enjoy came from New Orleans. It helped make us who we are. We are all connected to the city of New Orleans and the Gulf Coast region even if we have never been there.

When the city was still dangerous, toxic, and flooded, I remembered a bunch of New Orleans musicians, and how much the city meant to them. I remembered Harry Connick, Jr., going on his own to the convention center in the first hours of the flooding and trying to help. I remember Fats Domino still living in the lower Ninth Ward, the poor neighborhood where he grew up. I fondly remembered Reggie Harley driving me over to his house years earlier. It was a very modest dwelling, nondescript except for the wrought iron on the front porch that spelled out F-A-T-S. That's the house he had to be rescued from after Katrina hit. I remembered the Neville Brothers playing in my neighborhood with T-shirts that declared they were the "uptown rulers." Despite being international recording stars, they were most proud that they were the best band in their uptown neighborhood! I remember, in particular, Art and Aaron Neville. One time, before the flood, "Mr. Art" was supposed to be on tour in Europe with his brothers, but a few weeks earlier he had seen a burglar stealing a TV from my friend Rhonda's apartment. He missed some of the European tour dates to stay behind and testify at the thief's trial. The judge sent the burglar to the slammer thanks to Mr. Art. Aaron once heard about a pastor in the Tremé neighborhood that had no one show up for his church service. He felt so bad for the pastor that he offered to sing at the church's next Christmas Eve service. I walked over and heard him sing "Ave Maria" by a rickety upright piano in front of a packed house.

I remembered how all these New Orleans musicians loved their city and gave back to it in countless ways. They were connected to the people. The people of New Orleans were not consumers that they profited from. They were their friends and their families. Harry Connick, Jr., spoke for all his fellow musicians when he said, "It is hard to sit in silence, to watch one's youth wash away. New Orleans is my essence, my soul, my music, and I can only dream that one day she will recapture her glory. I will do everything in my power to make that happen and to help in any way I can to ease the suffering of my city, my people!"

I started to remember my apartment and hoped it was still there and the current tenant was safe. I remembered the smell of crawfish boiling and people playing accordions down the street. I remembered dancing to a Cajun waltz sung in French by Zachary Richard and hoping it would never end. I remember the boats on the Mississippi and how comforting it was to hear their horns blowing as the fog settled in at 2:00 in the morning. I remembered the little boy walking down the middle of Camp Street every morning playing his trombone on his way to school.

We need to bring back the sense of community in our great country. We need to treasure the sense of community we are still lucky enough to have. A popular radio talk show host, when asked about helping New Orleans after the disaster said, "Who told those people to live there in the first place?" Shame on all of us who tolerate comments like this.

Consensus organizing can be a way to build relationships so people can see the value of connectedness. We need to connect more and more people until we spin a web so tight nothing can destroy it. No disasters, natural or manmade, can rip us apart. We need to stop saying, "It's not my responsibility" and start saying, "How can I help?"

Our "leaders" need to stop hiring political advisers to make them look good. They need to stop hiring spin doctors to make them sound good. Instead, all of us, every one of us, should start actually *doing* good. We need to do good because our friends need us. Our real and extended families need us. We need one another.

INDEX

ABOUT THE AUTHOR

Mike Eichler is a faculty member of the School of Social Work at San Diego State University and the director of the school's Consensus Organizing Center. He has more than 20 years of experience in community organizing and is the creator of the method of consensus organizing. He has worked with unemployed steelworkers, casino owners, welfare recipients, bankers, corporate executives, and the homeless, bringing them together around common self-interest. He began his organizing career in Pittsburgh, Pennsylvania, where he helped a neighborhood battle the illegal practices of racial steering and blockbusting by joining forces with a for-profit real estate firm. When hired by Pittsburgh executives to help address economic problems caused by the closing of the steel mills, he brought the unemployed and the business leaders together to begin revitalization of the region. He was asked by the Local Initiatives Support Corporation (LISC) to expand his work throughout the country and organized new grassroots efforts in such diverse cities as West Palm Beach, Florida; New Orleans, Louisiana; Las Vegas, Nevada; and Houston, Texas. He also started his own national nonprofit, the Consensus Organizing Institute, which trains organizers in the consensus organizing method. In 1999, he joined academia, where he said he "would never be heard from again." He has been recognized for his contributions by receiving the Mon Valley Initiative's coveted John Heinz Award and has been selected by San Diego State students as Professor of the Year in 2001, 2004, and 2005.